UNFORTUNATE

UNFORTUNATE

BOOK 1 IN THE UN SERIES

KAILEY BRIGHT

NEW DEGREE PRESS

COPYRIGHT © 2021 KAILEY BRIGHT

UNFORTUNATE

Book 1 in the UN Series

ISBN   978-1-63730-704-5 *Paperback*

        978-1-63730-795-3 *Kindle Ebook*

        979-8-88504-011-2 *Ebook*

To my nanny for reading my endless and often bizarre imaginations

To my tireless mother, my sister's desktop, and my grandfather for giving me the time to flourish

To Joel Seymour, Michel Way, and David Rolon for indulging me in this story for the past five years

Contents

Author's Note

Dear Readers,

How do you feel about the rain? Do you prefer the whitish-grey winter fog? Or the rolling charcoal clouds on a summer day? Does rumbling thunder sooth you into slumber? Or does a lightning strike paralyze you in place?

I ask because *UNFORTUNATE* poured out of my mind on a rainy day. Looking out through a trembling school bus, I started imagining a young woman (who would become Nora) working out in the rain. Curiously, I wondered why she would be out there, and her world unfolded around me. As a self-proclaimed "radical feminist" myself, my lens focused on feminist and classist themes.

Growing up, I've always been hyper aware of our status teetering on poverty's edge. My mother tried keeping the details close to her chest, taking odd and often back-breaking jobs left and right so my sister and I wouldn't go without. But poverty would linger like the half-empty coin jar tucked in the corner of our living room; it would bleed out in our fantasy conversations about winning the lottery; and it would cling onto my subconscious whenever I desired something deemed nonessential. But I didn't truly know the scope until my mother and I were going through old photographs, and we came across one that struck me as odd. My sister and I wore pretty dresses in the forefront of a bare background, much barer than I remembered as a child.

I lifted the photograph up with a confused look and asked my mother about it.

And for once, my mother did not sugarcoat her words. Instead, she laughed and said, "Oh, that was when we were exceedingly poor."

Her need to add *exceedingly* widened my eyes. She explained that she needed to save funds for several months for us to go out to a nice restaurant—a restaurant I could walk into today and be reasonably comfortable in accepting the charges.

Living like that set my sights on breaking free from my situation, to use my ambition and intelligence as a weapon against the poverty death spiral. I will never defend poverty. Anyone who tries to convince you that poverty "builds character" or "betters your life" or something as nonsensical is someone who wants you to remain content while constantly on fire so they can continue hoarding life's splendors. Poverty is not beautiful or poetic or in any sense relieving or calming. Trying to free ourselves from an established hierarchy that solidified well before our lifetime is all the more horrifically draining. But it's what we need to do to better our quality of life.

In *UNFORTUNATE*, Nora must navigate a similar segregated class system on her journey breaking free from servitude.

In our world, women are often forced into restrictive roles of servitude—whether as a servant to a child, to a husband, or to something greater like a religion, an ideal, or a desire. It's an expectation we find ourselves confined in. Even when we break free from the typical mold, women are often still held to servitude within the professional world. We feel obligated to stay later to demonstrate our productivity; we ask if others want coffee to demonstrate our care; we smile and nod our heads at meetings to demonstrate our unwavering attention.

In the Kingdom of Iridion, I highlight that real-world invisible expectation as a tangible requirement. In our world, women share similar traumas of misogyny. In the Kingdom of Iridion, every Unfortunate servant shares a similar trauma of their Choosing Ceremony. For Nora, the rain floods her senses with the memory and forces her into a frozen state. She shudders with each grumble of thunder; her body quivers as the rain soaks into her skin. But she works in silence...

If I tried to capture every instance when men branded me with their idea of what I should be as a woman, this letter would become an entirely new novel in itself. Instead, I will only give you one of the most recent examples that truly encapsulates why I wrote *UNFORTUNATE* in the first place.

Over the COVID-rampid summer, I worked at a local grocery store. It was later in the day, the type of later when cashiers have nothing interesting to do and sparse customers grab our desperate attention. A woman came in, her stomach swollen like a beach ball, accentuated by her bright yellow maxi dress. I noticed easily, bored and closest to the entrance. I looked back to the magazine I was reading. As if on cue, the two eldest men at the grocery store approached either side of my register, shaking their heads and leaning forward to whisper.

"Did you see that pregnant woman?" the custodian asked.

Raising an eyebrow, I nodded.

"Would you ever wear something like that?" his cashier counterpart chimed in.

The inclination in his voice indicated that his question was rhetorical. The two didn't approve of her choice of clothing. And now I was suddenly the spokesperson for all women, the mouthpiece they were hoping to use as a justification for their disproval.

I refused to give them a comfortability they constantly denied me.

"I would never be pregnant," I replied, effectively targeting me on a different subject altogether.

This book is ultimately for anyone who has ever felt "other," for anyone who cannot fit inside the mold formed carefully by outside hands. *UNFORTUNATE* is for anyone who is trying to determine their own identity and their own destiny.

I hope to inspire you and empower you as you take your first step into this fantasy setting not too far off from our own. The road to a better, more freeing life is not an easy path by any means; I will not deceive you with sugarcoated pleasantries. But the bravest step of all is your first.

Stay ambitious.

From one Unfortunate to another,
Kailey Bright

Mixed population
Mati
Lux
Auras
Makans
Imitations
Unfortunates
Feras
Avlis
Mares
Norburn
Ironcrest
Cherryville
ThunderBay
Stone Creek

Caliel
Osthall
ldor
Northbrook
vater

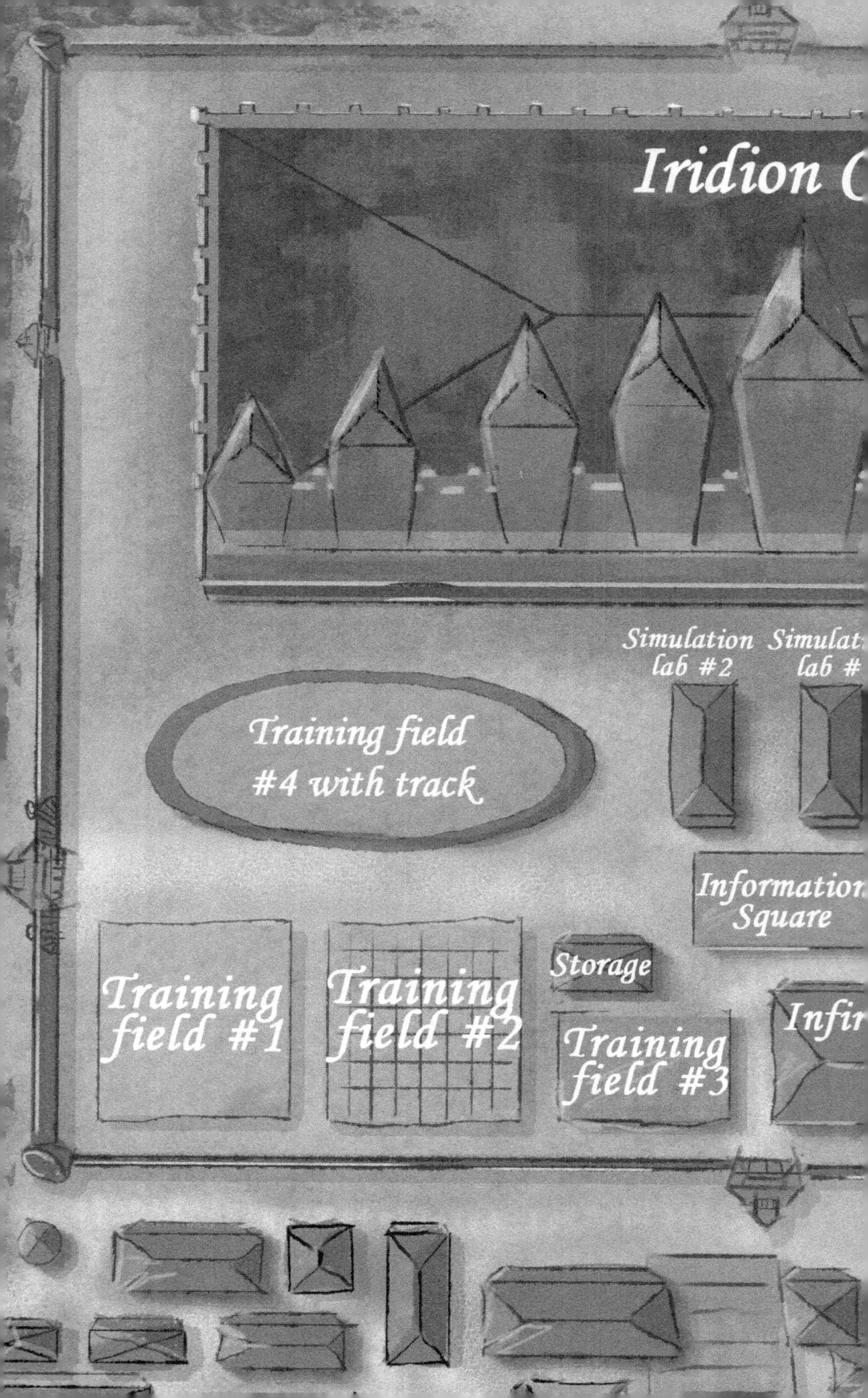

Iridion C
Simulation
lab #2
Simulat
lab #
Training field
#4 with track
Information
Square
Storage
Training
field #1
Training
field #2
Training
field #3
Infir

Student living #1
SL #2
SL #3
Student Canteen
SL #4
SL #5
SL #6
Servant canteen
Servant quarters

CHAPTER ONE

Property of Montgomery House

Rain splattered against the Montgomery mansion. Each drop the same as the last, no different from eight years prior.

Like all other servants of Iridion, I could recall my Choosing Ceremony within an instant from a seemingly random trigger. I saw it in other servants' eyes when their House came over; how their eyes widened, expanded, and darkened; how their bodies stiffened in odd postures as the recollection began; and how their bodies loosened back to normality as the recollection ended and numbed. I'd seen it when a bird chirped, when a particular Gifted yelled too loudly, when someone laughed or cried a certain way, or even on clear days when nothing could possibly go wrong.

For me, the rain commanded the memory to flourish from its dark corners, flashing in fragments every now and then as the wind grew stronger, as thunder and lightning shattered the sky.

I could hardly look out the window without becoming completely immobile. There used to be another servant who comforted me during these rainy episodes, but you're gone now.

Instead, I distracted myself with the routine morning chores around the house before the Montgomerys arose from their beds—polishing all open surfaces of the house, polishing them again for good measure, and kindling a fire in the living and foyer areas on opposite sides of the manor.

The fire crackled to life. Satisfied, I left it to grow, consume, and brighten. Entering the kitchen, a breakfast menu formed in my mind. Someone cleared his throat from above.

I craned my neck upward. Mr. Montgomery, Head of the Montgomery House, stood at the staircase, peering down at me with his distinct yellow eyes. Even with cane in hand, he kept his posture straightened and professional. I did the same.

"Good morning, Mr. Montgomery," I greeted, bowing to him. "Any requests for breakfast, sir?"

"The gutters were not cleaned yesterday before the storm."

Had I not cleaned them yesterday? No, that was a task originally set for this upcoming Monday.

"Right away, sir?"

Mr. Montgomery's already narrowed eyes squinted dangerously thinner. "Is that a problem?"

"N-No!" I waved my arms violently in front of me, my voice elevated. "It'll be done before breakfast, sir."

"Good," asserted Mr. Montgomery. "Remember Mr. Harris and Mr. Walton will be here today. The house must look perfect for their arrival."

I nodded, no longer trusting my voice. If I woke Melanie now and moved the first laundry duties immediately afterward, maybe the storm would pass before I ever had to step foot outside.

But Mr. Montgomery didn't leave. Waiting. Watching.

I took a trash bag from under the sink and begrudgingly walked toward the manor entrance, placing one foot shakingly in front of the other. Closer now, I could no longer ignore the sound that came with rain. Harsh winds whistled through the door hinges. I halted as a memory flashed.

My mother placed a decorative pin behind my ear.

I jolted, patting my hair for a piece that was no longer there. Taking in a deep breath, I opened the door.

My eyes caught sight of the dark blue coloring of the world. I inhaled sharply, the muscles along my spine instinctively tightening.

A pale pink dress. Huddled, crammed together. With other dresses. Other Unfortunate girls.

I blinked, and the outside yard came back into focus. I left the safety of the manor.

Droplets drilled into my skin, drenching the pink dress my mother had bought for this special occasion. Gingerly moving through the stone walkway became futile. I slipped, fumbling on the cobblestone road in hopes of reaching the town square in time for the ceremony.

I looped around to the side of the manor. The front-yard garden stretched out before me. Remembering when the flowers automatically sprouted there—the work of an Avlis contractor—I wondered how the lilies were holding up in such dark weather, desperate to cling onto a distraction. But the flowers were intact, unlike me, swaying in the wind to the beat of every droplet.

I moved on, stopping dead in my tracks as I caught sight of a ladder amidst the grey haze. Reaching forward, my feet sank into the garden mulch. Panic spread through my body with every heartbeat.

If I was going to be picked, I could not appear dirty.
We were divided by age.
Forcibly aligned with other ten-year-old Unfortunate girls, a City Guard scoffed at my muddy shoes. We wore tacky lavish outfits dampened by the rain.
Eyes glanced about nervously.

I shook the memory away, turning my attention back to the task at hand. Thunder crackled above; I gripped the ladder for dear life. My chest tightened and didn't ease as the rumble faded in the distance.

After several shaky breaths, I silently screamed at my left hand to move. It did, followed hesitantly by the other as I advanced upward toward the roof of the Montgomery manor.

Rain pelted downward in harsher waves. A loud booming noise erupted from above, followed by a strike of bright light that illuminated the roof. I screamed, hunching down and covering my ears. My fingers felt icy against my wet face. A silence enveloped the sky once more as the thunder dissipated. Every nerve in my body spiked, telling me to leave, get off the roof, and go back inside—where you would be waiting for me. You would rub my shoulder, laugh off the situation, and tell me you'd brave the rain in my place.

But you were gone.

And the thought of leaving now was laughable. I didn't have that luxury. My body betrayed my desires, rising and walking toward the roof's edge.

A thick buildup of dead, wet leaves greeted me.

I reached in, my hand sinking into the mass, as I made a mental note to clean the gutters earlier next summer. Transferring the mulch from the gutter to the trash bag, I ignored the dirt and grime as it crawled up my arms.

One side complete.

Hauling the trash bag to the back of the house, I began the process again.

The gutters cleared, I cautiously moved down the ladder and toward the front of the house.

"What about this one?" the mother asked, gesturing to a girl only two children away.

The father frowned, but before he could respond, a Gifted child stood directly in front of me with an excited grin on her face. "Mother!" she called. "Look at this one!" The Gifted child pointed straight at my Unfortunate heart. I held back a flinch.

The parents turned their attention to me, their eyes blank and noses raised. "What is it, sweetie?" the mother asked.

"Molly sees something she likes," commented the father as the Gifted child came closer and pushed me down. I hit the concrete hard.

I stepped out to the roadside without injury, placing the filled trash bag in a bin. A large vehicle would come through sometime later this week for pickup.

Light began to pull through the clouds, the rain dulling to less droplets. My breath steadied, the Choosing Ceremony receding back into the dark corners of my mind. But it would come back, as it always did when the sky broke out into tears.

Stepping back into the foyer, a chill ran inside my bones and rattled my body in sudden and long shakes. I ran into the servant bathroom down the left hall, drying myself off with a worn towel instead of waiting for the fire to warm me.

Within the reflection of the mirror, I could clearly see the words that inscribed my life. A plaque resided in every Gifted House and in every public space where servants spent a considerable amount of time in. Here, a plaque resided in the foyer and this very bathroom. The sign read off the six Unfortunate Laws of Servitude I had to abide by:

- An Unfortunate servant must carry out any and all orders given by their Gifted House and those their Gifted House permits.
- An Unfortunate, once selected from an annual Choosing Ceremony, becomes a faithful servant to the selected Gifted House. An Unfortunate cannot leave their current Gifted House unless dismissed or released to another designated Gifted House by a leading member of the current Gifted House.
- All unchosen Unfortunate girls and women are required to attend the annual Choosing Ceremony from the time they turn ten years of age to the year of their twentieth birthday.
- An Unfortunate can be punished in any extremity their Gifted House deems necessary and by those their Gifted House permits.
- An Unfortunate servant is permitted one Sunday off each month unless specified differently by their Gifted House.
- An Unfortunate cannot harm any Gifted under any jurisdiction beneath Divine power.

Underneath the rules was a string of bold capitalized letters declaring,

**FAILURE TO UPHOLD ANY AND ALL LAWS IS
PUNISHABLE BY IMPRISONMENT AND/OR DEATH.**

"You know what is required of you, yes?" the mother inquired.

*I nodded, knowing the Unfortunate Laws of Servitude
like a brand on the back of my hand. Studying the six rules
for almost a year now, my mother prepared me for my first
Choosing Ceremony in the hopes of being chosen.*

"I do, ma'am."

I glanced away from the plaque, shaking my head as
though that would stop the memory from crawling its way
to the forefront of my mind.

The Montgomery manor was easy to memorize. A large
gourmet kitchen sat to the right of the house where I cooked
for the Montgomery family. The dining room where the
Montgomerys ate connected to the kitchen at the back of
the first floor. The table was long, with more seats than family
members, perfect for any Gifted guests. An entertainment
area and living space lay straight ahead from the foyer at
the back of the house. A guest bathroom and bedroom were
down the hall on the left before the living room, and to the
left of the entrance was a short hallway that went to a small
bedroom and bathroom where I resided.

I raced back to the foyer, relishing in my fluid movements
now that the rain had stopped.

A large staircase spiraled upward to the second floor,
where several minutes prior Mr. Montgomery was looking down into the kitchen. Running a little behind in my

duties, I almost tripped on the slick wood as punishment as I ascended upward.

Molly was the elder child of the Montgomerys, so her room was the door promptly ahead of mine while two other doors resided on the left.

I caught my breath before lightly knocking, hoping Molly wouldn't notice how damp I still was from the rain. I recognized a faint noise as, "Come in," and I turned the knob.

Molly was a year older than me, merely eleven when we had met, and even though we grew in the same timeframe, we had not grown together.

Though Molly was shaped like a human, her Imitation Gift meant she took on the traits of an animal—that of an albino snake. Her bright red hair moved down in soft waves without much effort, contrasting sharply with the lack of pigmentation in her skin.

I did my best to avoid eye contact with any Gifted as I was trained to, but I always made an extra effort to avoid Molly's gaze.

Molly sat idly on her bed with her legs intertwined at the ankles. A simple blue dress hung loosely on her fit body and rested on her knees. Her hair fell smoothly from her face the way it was when the house wasn't hosting some sort of party, and a book rested in her lap.

Her flat nose scrunched as I stepped into the doorframe, but she didn't comment.

"You've been awake long, Miss Molly?" I asked, standing in the doorway.

Molly's jaw twitched, but she did not look up from her story, turning a page instead. If I wasn't so keen on assisting her, I would wonder what it was like to read outside what was necessary for my duties.

"Yes."

"You must have been, seeing as you've dressed yourself already," I intentionally spoke. Saying anything with a hint of sarcasm struck a nerve in Molly, and the faster Molly wanted me out of her room, the shorter time I had to endure her.

Molly looked up from her pages now, but she couldn't catch my eyes in time. I darted away, becoming suddenly interested in the floor. Molly stepped off the bed and slinked forward, her eyes burning into my Unfortunate soul. One hand gripped my chin. I forced my eyes up at the ceiling.

"You're late on the most important day of my life, and you dare talk back to me?"

"I apologize, Miss Molly. Would you like me to start with your outfit or your hair?"

Molly lingered, releasing her hold. "The outfit."

I nodded, lowering my gaze to the floor again and moving toward the drawers in one quick motion. I pulled out the sparring gear Molly wore to practice for this day—a skin-tight suit that kept the Gifted's movements streamlined.

"Here you are, miss." Gently laying the garment down on the bed, I turned my body away as Molly's shadow snuck forward. "I will look away for your privacy."

Once Molly was dressed, I brushed her hair. I ignored the reflection in the mirror for as long as I could, attentively watching my hand movements instead. As I tied her hair, Molly hissed, and I finally looked up with a flinch.

Black slits for pupils narrowed and focused on its prey. I couldn't look away now, anticipating a strike. Molly opened her mouth, a black opening.

"I need my hair in a bun today," the Gifted ordered. "I can't be humiliated."

I swallowed hard, my shoulders trembling. "Understood, ma'am."

I fiddled with her bright red hair again, this time with pins.

The Gifted moved her head methodically, searching for any mistake. "You look beautiful, Miss Molly," I assured.

"Yes." Molly's voice was calm but lathered in venom. "It's adequate. It will have to do with the time. Now, leave." She shooed me out.

I tilted my head in a small bow. On to Melanie Montgomery's room.

As I opened the door, a four-year-old ran past me, giggling in a high-pitched squeal. I sidestepped, scooping Melanie up in my arms. She laughed, pushing my face away.

"No catching, Mora!" she whined, pronouncing my name with an M instead of an N.

"I got you!" All worry washed away from my face.

"No!" Melanie squealed in my hold; her voice was too loud this early.

I bounced her on my side. "Shh," I hushed her. "We want to use our inside voices."

"What's for breakfast?" Melanie ignored my suggestion.

I walked with her downstairs. "I have a few ideas. Do you have any requests, miss?"

"Pancakes!" She waved her arms in the air.

"Pancakes?" I encouraged with a gasp. "If you insist, Miss Melanie."

She giggled as we entered the kitchen. I set her down on the counter. Melanie swung her legs as I rummaged through the cabinet for the pancake mix.

"I will make sure you get a pancake or two," I assured, walking over to one of the various stoves. Bending down to the lower cupboards, I retrieved several pans in different sizes.

I turned on the heat, removing Melanie's hand from the stove's edge. "Careful, miss," I warned. "We don't want to burn ourselves. This will get hot soon."

"Yes, miss!" Melanie chimed.

I jolted as the Gifted child spoke with formality. "No, sweetie," I corrected her softly. "You don't call me 'miss.' Alright? I call *you* 'miss.'"

"But whhhhhyyyy?" Melanie dragged out her confusion.

Before I could explain further, a woman cleared her throat behind us. I turned.

"Good morning, Mrs. Montgomery." I tilted my head in a polite gesture.

"Breakfast this morning needs to be large enough for the entire family, plenty of carbohydrates and protein." The wife of the household wasted no time.

"Yes, Mrs. Montgomery," I replied without missing a beat. "I will get on that right away, ma'am."

"Yes, ma'am!" Melanie yelled at her mom.

My eyes widened, freezing in place.

Mrs. Montgomery gestured Melanie forward, her expression unfazed. "Come along, Melanie. The servant has work to do."

"Oh, she's not a bother, ma'am. Would you like me to dress her now? I can prep breakfast after." I picked up Melanie, ready to run up the stairs.

"Not right now," Mrs. Montgomery gestured forward again. "Everything needs to look perfect for Mr. Harris and Mr. Walton, so I'll put Melanie back into her room."

I tried handing Melanie over, but she struggled, clinging onto me, "I don't want to go anywhere! I want pancakes!"

"You'll get them, miss," I assured. "They'll be ready when you get back."

"Promise?"

I held back a flinch, my eyes staring at her pouting face for too long.

You have to make me a promise first. No. I couldn't think about Valerie right now. Too much already weighed on me today. Too much needed to be perfect for Mr. Harris's and Mr. Walton's arrival.

"Yes, miss," I forced the words out, extending in a bow as Mrs. Montgomery and her daughter left the kitchen.

I turned back to the stove, distracting myself by going down the list of things I needed to do once the eggs were perfectly sunny side up and breakfast could be laid out cleanly on the dining room table.

***

The rest of the Montgomerys walked downstairs as I placed the last knife perfectly aligned with other utensils in the dining room.

"Mora! Mora!" Melanie called out from the stairs.

I smiled to the sound of my almost name.

Melanie raced in with her arms outstretched in a gesture to hug.

"Mora! Mora!" she chanted again, laughing hysterically as I lifted her from the ground.

I shushed her again to no avail. Mrs. Montgomery entered next.

"Breakfast is prepared, ma'am." I nodded to her, putting Melanie in her favorite chair and walking back to the safety of the kitchen, away from Gifted eyes.

Silently, I munched on my plate of leftovers, staring blankly at the wall that resided across the room.

The Montgomerys' voices bled through the closed door separating the kitchen from the dining hall.

"Before Mr. Harris and Mr. Walton are here, you are training in order to give them a good show." Mr. Montgomery's voice was clear. "I want no holding back for this interview. Go for the kill every time."

Silence filled the air as his words sank in. I chewed on my toast cautiously, waiting.

Molly laughed with a nonchalant air to her words, "That won't be a problem."

"Good. And don't forget to address Mr. Harris first. He's the highest ranking official at Galdor, so you show respect."

Mrs. Montgomery tapped her long fingers on the table. "I can't wait to see you in a Royal Crest uniform!"

"She has to get into Galdor Academy first," replied Mr. Montgomery.

My stomach squeezed. I couldn't imagine what Molly was feeling at the moment.

Galdor Academy was a simple name for such a prestigious military school, where all the Gifted mastered their Gift, and the best of the best would move on to higher and wealthier rankings. Merely attending Galdor Academy would secure a prestigious future. A Gifted not placed into the academy would still be respected purely for what Gift they had, but their lives wouldn't be as lavish.

"I want to go to the academy!" Melanie announced, her voice muddled as she stumbled over the word "academy."

I scoffed underneath my breath, already knowing what Mr. and Mrs. Montgomery were going to say to that statement.

"No, sweetie, you are too young for that," Mrs. Montgomery assured her.

Melanie didn't protest. "Okay," she responded softly.

They continued to eat and talk. I zoned in and out of the conversation as it was about what they were going to train for today and what to expect for this afternoon. I had no reason to listen in on the minor details. I knew my place, and I knew my place well.

Once I finish cleaning up the kitchen, I'll quietly draw a bath for Melanie and be back downstairs to put the laundry into the dryer.

As I cleaned off the dining table, Mr. Montgomery drilled Molly in the backyard. I encouraged Melanie up the stairs like clockwork.

Melanie splashed in her bath. I strained to look through the small window pane next to the bathtub, slightly ajar to alleviate the hot steam. I watched as Molly sparred against her father. Molly bared her fangs, hunching over and preparing for an attack. Seconds passed.

Molly lunged forward, snapping her jaws and narrowly missing her father. Mr. Montgomery sprang away without his cane, more spry than I expected.

"Anticipate your opponent!" her father yelled.

Melanie's voice broke my concentration. "Am I going to the... to the... to the," she struggled to get the word out again, "the big girl school, Mora?"

"Maybe one day, sweetie."

"Are *you* going to the big girl school, Mora?"

My lips stretched into a line. I pushed a loose piece of hair out of Melanie's face. "You have to stop calling me that, sweetie."

"Well, *are* you?"

Mrs. Montgomery did not knock when she entered the bathroom. "Mr. Harris and Mr. Walton should be arriving any minute now. Why is Melanie still undressed?"

"I'll get Melanie into her pretty yellow dress right away, ma'am."

Mrs. Montgomery shook her head, "No, I'll get her dressed myself. Clean yourself and put on the *presentable* outfit. Now."

My jaw tightened, but I nodded, my voice rehearsed. "Yes, ma'am."

***

A quick knock at the front door alarmed me. I straightened the extra fabric that hung loosely over my chest, ruffling the skirt of the beige dress Mrs. Montgomery considered presentable. Delicate red flowers on green vines embroidered the dress with color.

I swung the door open and leaned forward in a bow. In a rehearsed and chirped voice, and with a convincing smile, I said "Sirs. Welcome to the Montgomery House!"

CHAPTER TWO

Mr. Harris and Mr. Walton's Arrival

I remembered Mr. Walton from previous visits, but his wrinkles hung lower on his face today in a deep, unimpressed frown. His mud-colored eyes did not meet mine, obscured by a long, pointed nose. Mr. Walton wore a dark blue suit with white markings today, the stark colors denoting his elite status as a House wealthy enough to merit a color palette.

Mr. Harris stood a fraction in front of his colleague, at about the same height with wrinkles of his own, though they appeared to be a part of him rather than formed over time. He wore the distinct peacetime Royal Crest Knight uniform—a white collared shirt underneath a black blazer securely fashioned and accompanied by a black tie and black pants. No House color to associate with the Harris House.

Among the glimmer of medals on his uniform, a purple and gold pin stood out by itself over his heart—the royal colors that denoted him as a Senior Royal Crest Knight. Mr. Walton held the same pin over his heart too. But unlike Mr.

Walton, Mr. Harris made a cautious effort to look directly at me with a smile upon his face.

I gestured for Mr. Harris and Mr. Walton to hand me their blazers. Neither did, much to my surprise. I recovered quickly, smiling again instead and pointing straight through the corridor. "The Montgomerys are waiting in the entertainment room, sirs. If you will follow me."

Mr. Walton's face remained stoic, but Mr. Harris nodded.

Leading the two Gifteds down the small corridor into the living room, I pulled open the double doors for the sirs with a smooth gesture.

Molly stood rigidly, facing the door that led into the entertainment room from the hall. She still wore the same skin-tight suit that reminded me of what divers in my hometown would wear when they went out into the ocean. Melanie sat next to her mother on the couch, also facing the entrance way. The younger Montgomery child kicked her legs in the air, wearing the promised cute yellow dress that matched her blonde hair.

I took my place in the background corner of the room, folding my hands behind my back—ready to assist at any moment.

Mr. Montgomery stepped forward, his cane noticeably vacant from his side. Though he sometimes fumbled through the manor, he walked over to the two men with an almost fluid stride as though he didn't need the cane at all. An unusually bright smile lightened his face as his fangs made an appearance.

"Mr. Harris, a pleasure to have you here." He shook Mr. Harris's hand, his voice inviting but solemn.

"A pleasure to meet you, Mr. Montgomery."

"The pleasure is all mine, Mr. Harris," assured Mr. Montgomery, staring at Mr. Harris's purple and gold pin with greedy eyes. "I've heard nothing short of greatness about you. It's an honor to have the First Senior Royal Crest Knight in our home. You're a Fera, correct? Suppose you're a feline or reptilian one?"

Mr. Harris's lips twitched before turning into a smile. "Unfortunately not, Mr. Montgomery."

"Hm. Mr. Walton." Mr. Montgomery shook hands with the second man. "Always a pleasure to see you, too."

Mr. Montgomery gestured to Molly. "Let me introduce you to my oldest," he suggested. "Molly Montgomery, a snake Imitation."

Mr. Walton took out a clipboard. As he wrote with intense purpose, Mr. Harris spoke.

"You are an Imitation too, Mr. Montgomery?"

Mr. Montgomery nodded, "I am indeed, sir. Panther."

"And how old is Melanie now, Mr. Montgomery?"

Mrs. Montgomery replied this time. "She's four, sir. A Lux like yours truly."

"Right. How is she doing?" Mr. Harris asked.

Mrs. Montgomery pulled her daughter closer, "We've been practicing object identification in the dark since she could talk."

Mr. Walton scribbled unseen notes.

Mr. Harris opened his mouth to say something else when Melanie's high-pitched squeal called out from the couch. "Don't forget Mora!"

My blood ran cold, but I forced my expression to stay neutral.

"Mora?" Mr. Harris raised an eyebrow, glancing my way before looking to the younger with curious eyes.

Mr. Walton stopped writing and glanced to Mr. Montgomery with a confused expression. "I don't have any information on a Mora Montgomery."

The Gifteds stared at each other for several seconds.

I inhaled sharply, compelled to dismiss Melanie's behavior, but I knew that would only make matters worse.

"*Nora,*" Mrs. Montgomery strained, "is our servant. *Not* a part of this family. Melanie is still too young to understand that yet. Please excuse her."

Mr. Harris's stare burned; my eyes fixated on the floor.

"Gentlemen." Mr. Montgomery clapped his hands together. "May we continue on with the proceedings?"

The two men nodded. I tried my best to nonchalantly walk over to the other end of the entertainment room, opening the door for the Gifteds and following them outside.

While it was no longer raining, the late summer air left a dripping humidity that clung to my presentable dress. I forced a neutral expression as though unaware of the heat.

"Are you going to fight against Molly yourself for the interview, Mr. Montgomery?" Mr. Walton asked as they walked along the grass.

Mr. Montgomery nodded, turning toward his elder daughter. I was exactly where I needed to be to collect his coat. Underneath, he wore a plain white T-shirt, exposing the vitiligo along his arms.

The two Imitations straightened their postures, shifting into their respectable stances and fixating their attention on each other.

Mr. Harris raised his hand, "Commence round one."

Molly lunged first, fangs exposed.

Mr. Montgomery maintained a concentrated expression, using the loose grass as a way to fluidly dodge the attack.

Molly fell hands first into the mud. Mr. Montgomery sank his claws into his daughter's side and threw her to the left. Red droplets dripped from his clawed finger tips.

Molly flailed and hissed, her stomach exposed. Mr. Montgomery stalked methodically forward. As he leaned down, Molly hissed, throwing mud in his eyes. She lunged forward at him again.

The two Gifteds tumbled. Mr. Montgomery landed on top, using one hand to press Molly's head into the ground. An inhuman growl surfaced from Mr. Montgomery's throat as he opened his mouth and revealed the full length of his canine teeth. He leaned down to his child's exposed neck as she struggled beneath him.

Molly wiggled her hand free, grabbing under her father's weak knee. He recoiled, allowing Molly to slip out and successfully pin him to the ground. Mr. Montgomery's forearm acted as a shield as Molly's fangs clenched down into his flesh. Mr. Montgomery winced through gritted teeth, the only indication of his pain.

I flinched, my heart pounding as I remembered when Molly sank her fangs into Valerie's arm—the last straw before we decided to leave.

Mr. Harris stared in my direction. I forced my body to remain calm, oblivious.

Mr. Walton's high-pitched whistle struck the air. Molly detached as she pushed away from her father, blood spilling from her mouth.

Mr. Walton scribbled on his clipboard, exchanging unknown whispers to Mr. Harris.

"When you're bandaged, Mr. Montgomery, we can proceed to the second round," said Mr. Walton.

"No need." Mr. Montgomery waved off any concern. "I'm ready now."

Mrs. Montgomery squinted at him, her jaw clenching.

"Very well." Mr. Harris nodded.

The two Imitations locked eyes, taking their stances against each other again.

"Nora," Mrs. Montgomery called my name but kept her gaze on her husband. "Get the emergency bag prepared but stay inside until I call you. Last thing we need is another dead Unfortunate if you're caught in the crossfire."

Holding back my recoil, I nodded, distancing myself from the Gifteds as Molly's hiss sent chills down my back.

***

I sat alone with the medical equipment at the dining room table, observing the spar from the window.

Molly squared off against her father for the third time now. It felt too surreal—watching the two lunge at each other with animalistic and brutal intent.

Though Gifts were common among the citizens of Iridion, I couldn't help but be fearfully awestruck by their abilities. As an Unfortunate, with no Gift at all, it was difficult to be otherwise.

I allowed my mind to wander too long. A voice perked up from my left, "Interesting, isn't it?"

Turning around, I was startled to see Mr. Harris standing in the doorway. I stood up abruptly, caught between the couch and window.

"Mr. Harris!" I cleared my throat, my heart beating in my ears as my neck dropped. "Did Mrs. Montgomery send you?"

Mr. Harris shook his head. "She did not."

We stared at each other. "Are you looking for something, sir?" I prompted, straining to keep my voice steady. "The bathroom is right down the hall. I can show you."

I stepped forward, but Mr. Harris held his hand out to stop me. "No, thank you." The man cleared his throat, waving his hand dismissively.

A thank you? Strange. "Well could I interest you in something to drink then? Eat perhaps?" I tried again.

Mr. Harris scoffed slightly to himself and smiled as though I had said something funny. "No, thank you. I'm fine," he replied.

Another thank you. Two in a row. My shoulders relaxed until I caught sight of the purple and gold pin over his heart that denoted the royal family colors again. I ruffled my dress skirt once more to distract myself.

Mr. Harris stepped toward the window as he changed the subject. "No, I'm simply admiring from afar. Sometimes students will do something different if they think you're not watching."

I didn't respond, following his gaze toward the fight.

Molly was out for blood, using her Gift to its full extent—a prime candidate for Galdor Academy. Mr. Montgomery dodged again, cautious ever since his first defeat.

Molly ran after him. Closer in range now, the two engaged in hand-to-hand combat. Mr. Montgomery held on, but between his bitten arm and his weak knee, he collapsed easily as his daughter kicked his legs out from under him. Molly's mouth opened; a gasp escaped my lips this time.

Before anything could escalate though, Mr. Walton said something unknown, and Molly withdrew.

Mr. Harris glanced in my direction, observing my rigid posture. "Did you think Miss Montgomery was going to kill him?"

I forced my eyes to look in his direction. "Molly is as ruthless as Mr. Montgomery. She *will* kill him if that means getting into Galdor." Realizing my words, I quickly covered my mouth as though that would take them back. I hadn't meant to convey my thoughts so bluntly, but Mr. Harris didn't appear fazed.

"You would know the Montgomerys better than I. Other Gifteds too, I'm sure. How long have you been working for them?" Mr. Harris asked.

The question hung in the air. No one asked me personal questions, and his casual tone put me on edge.

"Eight years and counting. The Montgomerys bought me at my first Choosing Ceremony."

Mr. Harris made a tsk sound, his lips twitching like he had a bad taste in his mouth.

I glanced at him but didn't inquire.

"So, you basically grew up with the Montgomerys?" he questioned.

What was he trying to get out of me? Surely, he wanted something but wasn't being straightforward. I held back my irritation. "In a sense."

"So, you know how to handle Gifteds?"

"I don't understand your question, sir. I've served plenty of Gifteds from different Houses under the Montgomerys if that is what you're asking."

Mr. Harris's stare burned into my skin. I looked downward.

There was a heartbeat of silence in the air. *Calm down,* I urged myself desperately, but I couldn't read this man. What did he want?

Mr. Harris never moved his eyes away from me, managing to appear both confused and curious. "You're an Unfortunate. Correct?" the man asked.

Like that was a question at all. "Of course, sir," I confirmed. *I would probably be trying to impress you right now if I was anything different.*

Another momentary silence.

I expected him to leave then, to go back to the yard and do whatever instructors of Galdor did. But he stayed, concentrating on the floor like he'd been given a hard question and needed a moment to form the best response.

I began planning out the lunch menu in my head. "Are you staying for lunch, Mr. Harris?" I asked. "Any dietary restrictions I should be aware of?" I already knew the answer, but the silence was awkward, and the echoing of my own words was comforting.

"Mr. Walton and I are staying until Saturday evening actually."

That was certainly news. I should have been notified that the two were staying over for the night. Cleaning the guest bedrooms was not on the itinerary. That very thought spiked alarm, but I made sure my thoughts weren't displayed across my face.

"Oh, of course, sir."

My lips twisted into a convincing smile, changing the subject. "If you don't mind Mr. Harris, I must get started on lunch then." It was a lie. Lunch preparation started later, but he couldn't know that. "I'm sure you need to evaluate Miss Montgomery."

Mr. Harris began pacing, showing no indication of leaving.

"What is it, Mr. Harris?" I finally questioned, no longer caring to go in circles. "Do the Montgomerys disinterest you so much you're spending your time with their servant?"

My teeth clenched together, my mouth wired shut and eyes wide. What was wrong with me today? How could I let my true thoughts spill out like that?

I waited for a strike that never came. Mr. Harris continued, waving his hand carelessly as if brushing off my insubordination. "No. Miss Montgomery is guaranteed a place at Galdor. I'm simply a curious man is all. One more day will satisfy that curiosity."

Curiosity?

I folded shaky hands out in front of me, my mind silently screaming to leave the room. "Please excuse me, sir."

Mr. Harris held his hand out again. I stopped to his command. "You were doing so well just now."

"Sir?"

"Ask me to clarify."

I rubbed my hand along my forearm. "What, sir?"

"Ask me your daunting question. You want to know what that curiosity is. I'll let you leave if you ask me."

Was this a trick? Some sick way of getting me into trouble? He blocked me. I could run through the entertainment room door to my right, but that would be running away from a Gifted and worse, refusing his demand. I couldn't do that no matter what. But did I even want the answer?

I forced the words out, "What are you curious about, sir?"

Mr. Harris smiled the same way he had when he arrived, side-stepping with his arm extended as he cleared a path for me. "Why, I'm curious to learn more about you."

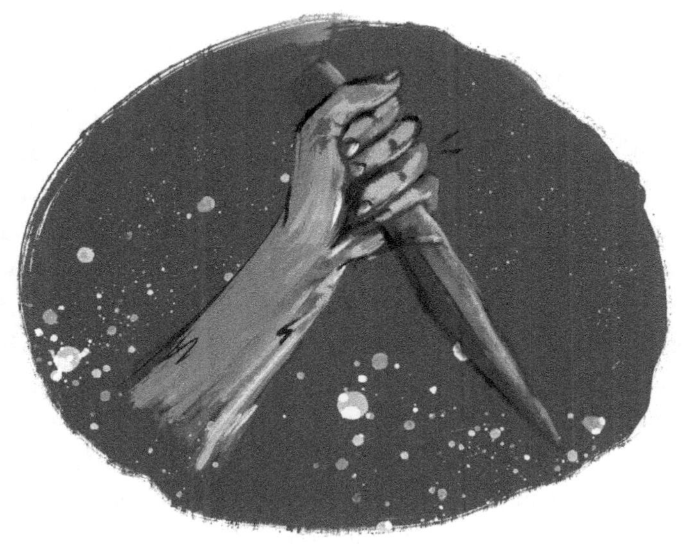

A Knife Plunges Downward

Sunday shone brightly through the rickety train car. Crammed in with other Unfortunate women, I sat squished between one sitting at the window sill and several others clumped together in the aisle. But I was lucky enough to hold any seat at all as I watched the blur of bright green plains float by with the time.

Though I swayed to the train's jagged movements, my shoulders relaxed; my back sank into the warmed seat. This particular Sunday was precious—my one free day each month permitted under the Unfortunate Laws of Servitude.

After Mr. Harris left on Saturday and it was announced that Molly Montgomery was accepted into Galdor Academy, I fully expected Mrs. Montgomery's zealous reaction to forfeit my day off so I could prepare for the party. But perhaps that pride and excitement beat a sliver of compassion in her heart because I was here. She simply ordered that I be back before they awoke tomorrow morning.

Unfortunates trickled in and out at each stop—gleaming at seemingly nothing, exchanging trivial topics, and bristling with excitement rather than apprehension.

"THUNDER BAY" read on the overhead destination marker.

My hometown. Your resting place.

As I exited, the marketplace greeted me, and a wind of sea spray brushed through my hair.

I waved away a persistent merchant selling fish and another who was yelling how fine and inexpensive his silverware was as I made my way through the open bazaar.

Among the Unfortunate shopkeepers and buyers, I tried finding differences, changes from the past month. My eyes still searched for your passing face.

I tugged the side of my dress.

"Fresh fish! Caught in the depths of Stone Creek!" an Unfortunate shopkeeper called.

"Fruit! Lemons and limes!"

"Beads! Beads and accessories!" *Beads?* Turning to my left, a plump man held a turquoise pendant in a teardrop shape tangled in cheap silver wire.

I fiddled with the mila in the small pocket of my dress. Not enough. And even if I did, silver glistening nearby denoted a city guard, standing next to the vendor. The guard's burly hand planted methodically on the merchandise table, his arm obscuring some of the more expensive jewels. Unfortunates skipped the stall. The vendor fiddled with his fingers. His mouth twitched, whispering an unheard comment, perhaps to himself.

I continued onward.

An outraged shout echoed through the air; Unfortunates separated from the epicenter toward my left. The city guard's large stature now stood firmly in front of the jewelry shopkeeper. My muscles instinctively tensed.

Spikes jutted upward from the rocky ground and pointed straight at the Unfortunate shopkeeper's head. *An Avlis.*

My breath hitched, a jolt running through my body.

"Would you like to repeat your words?" asked the city guard.

The Unfortunate shook his head quickly, a wheezing sound his only response.

"I didn't think so." The city guard's hands snatched the necklace in a loud, deliberate motion. He dangled the jewel in front of the Unfortunate shopkeeper. "I think I'll keep this as an apology."

We watched in silence. I knew you wouldn't have.

My body stepped forward as if guided by you, as if unencumbered by the consequences. "Hey, give that back." My words tried to imitate authority, but they came out more like a whisper, a plea.

The city guard turned toward me with a disgruntled look like I was an annoying gnat he needed to squash. I flinched but managed to stay in place.

"Move aside, Unfortunate." He stepped forward, leering down at me. "Don't want to ruin that pretty dress on what? Your one day?"

My skin burned at the comment. Was this what you felt before you died? A poisoning dread?

I didn't respond fast enough. The ground tilted below me with an upward flick of the guard's wrist, shifting upward at an angle. Losing balance, I collapsed to the dirt. The city guard's shadow loomed above. I covered my head, anticipating an attack.

But he walked by without incident, my cower satisfying enough.

I stood up slowly, the crowd already dissipating and walking around me. Looking to the Unfortunate jewelry shopkeeper, I wanted to ask if he was alright, but he kept his gaze downward, his shaky hands reorganizing a display case.

Huffing and regaining my breath, I wiped the dirt off my dress and continued walking through the crowded bazaar.

When I arrived to the small apartment complex, an anxious pit weighed down in my chest as I stared at the door. I hesitated, but my options were limited.

One knock, and the door opened.

My mother ushered me in without actually looking at my form, "Get inside. Your father and brother should be back any minute. You hungry?"

I did as she asked, greeted by the smell of cooking meat to the left where the kitchen resided.

The house looked exactly like it did a month ago.

"No. I won't be here long." I handed her the remaining ten mila in my pocket.

Living inside the manor meant I was paid less than servants who had their own smaller building on the property.

Gifteds considered it a privilege to exist so close to their world, even when I still had the bare minimum like all other servants. But the money I earned was efficiently added to the family pool. If I wasn't chosen at all, I'd just be another mouth to feed. Maybe I'd work as a fisherman like my father, but that idea washed away. I would be stuck in this house instead, serving the men alongside my unchosen mother.

"Yes, thank you." I watched as she counted the balance, a concerned expression crossing her face. "Is this all you have for the month?"

"I bought Neo a new book," I tried defending myself as I watched her turn to the kitchen. "I should get more soon."

My mother didn't respond, her focus on breakfast, but I could see the bitter line stretch across her mouth.

Her hand waved me off, "Go say hi to your brother. I'm sure he'd appreciate a new book."

I took the opportunity to end the conversation there, walking down the short hallway to Neo's room. Opening the door, I discovered him hunched over, reading a book at the edge of his bed.

The younger of the family intensely read as though his life depended on it. I noticed this gesture of his every time the pages were growing thinner. He read to himself out loud.

"...the private would not surrender. No, the very thought of his family crying over his defeat sparked enough energy and determination from the young man that he struggled forward and—"

Neo looked up from his book with curious eyes as the door opened.

"Nora!" he called happily, placing the novel down on the bed and running over to hug me. I held him longer than he wanted.

Neo let go, bouncing slightly like he was a toddler instead of a new teenager. "I just got to the epic battle at the end of the story!" he shouted, his voice cracking slightly. "Would you like to join and see how the private fights *death* itself?"

Death appeared to be a largely popular topic in the stories he read. "Sure," I complied, revealing the book behind my back. "As long as you read this after you're done with that one."

Neo gasped, grabbing the worn cover gently, and turning the book over to read its contents. "Deal!" he agreed.

Sitting at the edge of the bed alongside him, I listened as he read the story with obvious relish. He had a way of making the dramatic even more so, and it almost made me laugh a couple of times.

The front door clicked. My attention shot in that direction as Neo adjusted on the bed and stood. "They must be home," he commented, rushing down the hallway. I made my way back to the living room at a slower pace.

Catching sight of my older brother standing in front of our father, I halted at the doorway's edge. I couldn't hear what my brothers were saying, but I wasn't interested in finding out either.

"Neo?" my mother prompted. "Where's Nora? Get her out of your room to say hi."

Let's get this over with.

Taking a deep breath, I revealed myself.

"Nora." My father half-hugged me, the smell of salt and fish on his shirt. "Your mother was saying that you only had ten mila."

My shoulders adjusted inward. "I'll have more next time."

"You're not throwing it all away on crap. Are you?" Noah spat.

I glared at my older brother. "No."

Plates began to organize on the dining table by our mother's hand. "Nora, go help your mother," ordered Noah.

She's your mother, too. "I'm not staying," I said instead, walking toward the door.

Noah caught my arm with a firm grip. "Do you behave like this at the Montgomerys?" he demanded.

I jerked away. "Do you behave like this at the dock?"

My hand reached the door's knob, but Noah cornered me there. "Your sass only serves to damn this family. You'll do good to stay in the Montgomerys' good graces."

"I always have," I huffed, successfully opening and closing the door as quickly as I could.

***

Picking a flower from the ground, I removed it from life as Gifteds had done to you. Its light-red petals shared the same color as your lips. I watched the flower gently shake with the breeze between my fingers.

I walked the six blocks over to a cookie-cutter apartment building. The entrance steps lay dormant, cleaned. A burn formed within my chest as I laid the flower down in your place.

We were supposed to run away together. What a silly thought now.

"I said *move*, Unfortunate!"

I jolted, searching for the city guard in question. He wasn't in front of me. Standing, I slowly peered into the alley that separated the building to the next one.

The city guard, the *same* guard from the bazaar earlier, stood above an Unfortunate woman wearing a heavy all-black outfit that obscured her form. A hood covered her hair.

"I'm trying to get through as well, sir," the Unfortunate woman politely replied. "Why should I move for you but you not for me?"

Her tone registered as logical, but her words were sharpened. Remarks you would have been brave enough to say. My heart thumped louder in my chest. Remarks that killed, too.

I couldn't watch this. Couldn't let this happen again.

The hairs on my arm raised as I exposed myself to the confrontation. "Leave her alone," I said, even daring to narrow my eyes.

Both looked at me. "*You* again?" asked the city guard. "Just don't know when to quit, huh?"

A smile gleamed under the Unfortunate woman's hood. She made a *hmm* sound before raising a slender hand. "Don't worry, my dear. This Gifted will move out of my way."

With a snap of her fingers, four masked figures jumped down from the rafters in synchronized movements.

Aside from the all-black attire, each wore cloth wrapped around their left arm. I had only seen soldiers wear a badge and certainly none of such a bright red.

They wrapped a bag over the guard's head. He yelled; the concrete rumbled beneath our feet. The hooded Unfortunate woman gasped as she backflipped out of the way, repositioning herself closer to me as the earth crumbled the concrete into a twisted mess.

The masked figures worked with quick, precise fingers to tie the Avlis' hands before he could use his Gift again. The ground stopped shaking as the city guard strained. One masked figure kicked him down.

Small rocks flew in the air but held no direction.

"Keep him steady," the hooded Unfortunate woman ordered.

One masked figure stood on top of the city guard as the other three kept his limbs downward.

I remained frozen, my body pointed away, ready to flee; but I watched, entranced as the Gifted flailed on the ground in front of me. Below me.

The hooded Unfortunate woman brandished a knife, its long point reflecting in the sunlight. Her face remained neutral as I stepped back, my arms close to my chest. "What are you doing?" I blurted.

She gave me a warm smile that didn't match her eyes, placing her index finger along her lips in a hushed gesture.

Clinging onto the brick wall for support, I focused on the city guard's neck as the Unfortunate woman plunged the knife downward.

My hands instinctively pressed against my mouth, muffling the scream. The Unfortunate woman wiped the blood from her knife in one quick motion. She glanced my way; I couldn't find remorse in her glare. She extended into a small, rehearsed bow.

"From one Unfortunate to another."

With a snap of her fingers, she and the others took off, leaving me with a dead Gifted.

A harsh gasp escaped my lungs. "Hey, wait!" I reached outward to the closest assailant.

To my surprise, my fingers gripped onto the hooded woman's cloak before she could run away. The hold was short lived. She swung her leg into a roundhouse kick, knocking me down.

"Wait!" I called again, standing and lunging forward.

The attackers ran away from the scene, zigzagging through alleyways. I found myself doing the same, halting when the assailants abruptly stopped.

"Who are you?" I wheezed.

They didn't answer. The hooded Unfortunate woman waved her hand to signal the others. The masked figures all sprang into the air, scrambling to the rooftops.

"Well, this is certainly new," the Unfortunate woman commented. "I wasn't expecting to be challenged by a servant. It's Sunday for you. Yes?"

Her casual tone didn't match her words. Tugging on my dress, I wished for better fighting attire.

Well, *that* was certainly a strange thought. The idea was laughable, but my desire remained.

"Listen, sweetie, I don't want to fight one of us."

"One of us?"

"We're on the same side after all. That guard had it coming to him. Yeah?"

I wasn't sure how to respond. The woman stood upright, turning to leave when a shadow cast above.

The woman moved out of the way, but she wasn't fast enough. Her attacker grabbed her arms in a quick and fluid motion before turning her around and slamming her into the nearby brick wall. She grunted and fought, but her position remained the same.

"You don't know when to quit. Do you, Ms. Douglas?" the man asked, pressing her face inward.

"Mr. Harris?"

It was indeed him. His Royal Crest Knight uniform appeared more dangerous in an Unfortunate city. I caught sight of the purple and gold insignia that indicated his status as a Senior member.

A force to be reckoned with. What was he doing here?

The woman's hood clasped on her shoulder, exposing wiry black strands twisted in a low bun. She chuckled, "Ah, Mr. Peter Harris. All sources said you were in Cherryville recruiting. Guess you wanted to visit me?"

"It's only happy coincidence to run into you today, Ms. Douglas," he replied with little humor in his voice.

Ms. Douglas? Unfortunates didn't have House names. Could he be referring to her Gifted House?

"Oh?" the Unfortunate woman managed to smirk while pressed against the wall. She stared directly at me with swirling brown eyes. "You don't think the Divine brought us together?"

Mr. Harris scoffed. "No. I don't." He threw her into the wall again, trying to restrain her wrists. "I'm here for the servant you're trying to recruit."

Servant? Was he talking about me? *I'm curious to learn more about you.*

My heartbeat quickened, prepared to flee. Was this a sick fascination? A way for a Gifted to learn about his prey before striking?

"What?" Ms. Douglas snorted as Mr. Harris successfully tied her hands behind her back. She sat down on the curb and laughed at him. "You know this one?"

Mr. Harris stepped toward me. A lump formed in my throat.

Looking down, Mr. Harris pulled a small device from his pant pocket. "That doesn't concern you, Ms. Douglas."

"I agree." The Unfortunate woman sprang up from behind him, separating her palms from the binds, freshly cut by the knife in her hand. She vanished around the corner. Mr. Harris watched her go and sighed, putting the phone up to his ear.

He gave her description to the city guards on the other line and then requested an Emergency Response Service (ERS) team for the guard she killed.

"Well, this works out perfectly," Mr. Harris commented. "Now we can chat without any more interference."

An icy feeling crawled along my back, rooting me in place.

"Because you're an Unfortunate, your life is very… limited." He tried to find the right word.

My eyebrow arched. Very rarely did anyone of his status dare say anything about Unfortunates with a euphemism.

"So?"

I side-glanced toward where Ms. Douglas had been. *From one Unfortunate to another.* "Who were those people then?" I asked.

Mr. Harris smiled as though ecstatic for my curiosity. "They're just a small branch of the Anti-Gifteds Movement. I'm sure you've heard of them."

A sting of embarrassment ran through my body. "I have not." The Montgomerys were my main source of information.

"The Anti-Gifteds Movement is small and scattered, but the longer we wait, the more extreme they become…" Mr. Harris trailed off, looking away in thought. "Ms. Douglas is the most consistent AGM member I've witnessed so far."

The Gifted turned his attention back to me, changing the subject. "Regardless, I'm sorry for startling you. I was curious to see how you behaved outside of the Montgomery House."

That was certainly weird. I bit my lip. "May I ask why, sir?"

Mr. Harris leaned against the wall. "I'm simply exploring my options for a pilot program of sorts. You've become a contender. This trip has been very enlightening."

A contender? Pilot program? What was this madman going on about? My shoulders tensed, knowing I was pushing the envelope. "And may I ask what you're referring to, sir?"

Mr. Harris shrugged nonchalantly like he was sharing a laugh with another Gifted. "I'll see you at Miss Montgomery's acceptance party tomorrow, yes?"

A scoff escaped my throat. *Like that's even a question.* I quickly regretted the action though, expecting Mr. Harris's face to darken and twist into an unwavering rage. But he stared straight through me instead with a gentle expression I hardly saw in Gifteds.

I faltered, "Forgive me, sir. Yes, I will be in attendance catering to House needs."

"Very good." His grin still didn't set well with me. "I shall see you there."

CHAPTER FOUR

An Unbreakable Promise

Every Gifted the Montgomerys knew was invited to Molly's acceptance party: the Crawfords next door, Mrs. Montgomery's side of the family, Mr. Holt and Mr. Pike who had served in the Iridion military with Mr. Montgomery and their respected families, every Montgomery alive, most Waltons, and some instructors from Galdor including Mr. Harris.

To hold such an event, the guests brought some of their own servants out of courtesy.

As the designated head servant, I had almost every House servant who could cook food, make drinks, and clean the marble counters assigned to the kitchen staff. All others moved in and out of the kitchen, catering to the party. Most servants stuck to their own House, which made the guests content.

"Ms. Nora, we're almost out of orange slices!" one of the younger servant girls informed me, a high-pitched concern in her voice.

I sighed. Was I like this when I first started?

"You don't have to keep calling me Ms. Nora. We're all the same here," I reminded her. "And if orange slices are the only thing we run out of, that is fine by me. There's no need to be panicked."

The young girl sighed in relief. "Okay, that's good. I don't want trouble with the guests," she breathed, placing her empty tray on an open counter space. "What should I bring out next, Ms..." The girl stopped herself. "Erg. Nora."

I sighed again, turning to the busy kitchen for a moment. "Who's on seafood duty? I want those fried shrimp bites on a tray and out in two minutes!"

No one responded, but I didn't have time for a reply anyhow, turning back to the young servant. Grabbing a tray, I balanced some prepared drinks. "Take a break. Cut the rest of the oranges before I get back. I'll cater for the moment."

Swinging the kitchen doors open, I weaved through the crowd, waving my tray around for everyone to partake as they continued talking about themselves.

Most Gifteds were congregated in the entertainment room where Mr. and Mrs. Montgomery were chatting away about their children like trophies.

I made my way through the crowd, trying hard to avoid Mr. Montgomery's words. His voice was elevated and unlike himself.

Mr. Harris stood near the far wall. He did not notice my stare as he listened intently to Mr. Montgomery. The man acted mechanically, simply doing what the rest of the Houses were doing—applauding with the crowd, laughing when he needed to laugh, smiling every time Mrs. Montgomery chimed in with a lovely anecdote.

Moving through the entertainment room, my shoulder carelessly collided with a Gifted man. He turned to me with slit eyes. "I'm sorry, sir," I apologized, bowing slightly in hopes of forgiveness.

The man did not speak, staring down at me for several heartbeats. I kept my gaze lowered.

A hand landed securely on my shoulder. I jumped back; the tray wobbled.

Coming face to face with Mr. Harris, I balanced the tray.

"Mr. Harris," I breathed pleasantly.

The Galdor instructor turned to the guest who was still looking down at me with disapproval. "Will you excuse us, Mr. Pike?"

Mr. Harris gestured and I followed him down the hallway, near the entrance of the mansion where Gifted ears couldn't hear.

"Enjoying yourself?" Mr. Harris asked, a warm smile plastered on his face.

I failed to drain the stress from my cheeks. "Thank you, Mr. Harris." I bowed, my voice still shaken.

"He's not an honorable man to begin with. The plea-sure is all mine," Mr. Harris confessed. "I needed to talk to you tonight."

My skin crawled with unease. I looked up at him expectantly.

"I would like you to come to Galdor Academy."

We stared at each other. My face instinctively scrunched in surprise and confusion when Mr. Harris's statement finally registered in my mind.

"I don't understand, sir."

"I would like you to attend Galdor Academy with Molly Montgomery," Mr. Harris repeated the same jarring proposal.

I thrashed my head in a shake. "I don't wish to be her personal servant, sir."

"No, no," Mr. Harris quickly dismissed that idea only to clarify something worse.

"I'd like you to attend Galdor as a student."

I gripped the tray in my hands to keep steady. Anything to stay tethered. I leaned forward, my voice modulating between a whisper and a scream.

"I don't understand, sir. *Me?* At Galdor?" I shook my head at the absurdity. "Have you somehow forgotten, sir? I'm an Unfortunate. Certainly not anything different."

If I wasn't convinced Mr. Harris was a madman before, I was now.

"I've been in search of the right candidate for the pilot pro-gram I mentioned before. I want that person to be you, Nora."

"*Why?*" I asked. "Are you trying to get me killed?"

He leaned closer, his stare serious and words firm. "You saw what the AGM is capable of. It's only a matter of time before they become a larger, more viable threat. If I can make an Unfortunate a student for Iridion, their anger and support will dwindle. They can see a chance for something greater than their current lives."

A chance? Something greater?

Ms. Douglas stabbed and killed a city guard in front of me. I had never seen Unfortunates triumph over Gifteds with the same brutality Gifteds triumphed over us. Nor had I encountered an Unfortunate with a last name.

"Why try and recruit me then?" I asked. "I assume Ms. Douglas declined?"

Mr. Harris scoffed at the suggestion like I was the one being ridiculous. "She's too far gone for me to convince her of anything. No, a member of the AGM will not do. It has to be someone who protects others in a different way."

I shook my head. "But that's where you're wrong, Mr. Harris. I don't protect anyone. I haven't."

He gave me a disappointed look. "Nora, we both know you're lying."

Valerie lay dead on the stairs.

Tears welled in my eyes. No. I couldn't think about her right now.

"What do you say?"

I stared at the floor. Mr. Harris was nothing like any Gifted I had encountered before. How could he smile while asking me to do the impossible? An Unfortunate at a school for Gifteds was the craziest and most ridiculous idea I had ever heard, yet… why was my heart pounding?

"Mr. Harris, do not waste my time with fantasy," I finally replied, daring to stick my nose upward.

"I do not seek to waste your time. Tomorrow morning, after this grand celebratory party. That is when we will leave. Give me an answer before then."

I walked off first, keeping my head down as to not bring unnecessary attention to myself. But my mind was split, a mechanical constant ringing sound in my mind. As I handed the tray over to another Unfortunate, the floor began to sway underneath my feet.

Flashes of Valerie—alive and dead and alive again—all crashed and meshed together at the forefront of my subconscious. *"We can finally be free!" she squealed too loudly in the kitchen. I covered her mouth but could feel the excitement bubble in my chest as it did that day we decided to run away.*

No. Not here. Not tonight. I beelined in the direction of the servant restroom as a sanctuary from this madness.

"I'll go if you promise me something."

"What might that be, Valerie?"

Her face became grave, serious. "Promise—"

I slammed the restroom door shut, huffing. The night sky was clear the last time I checked. No rain had fallen onto my ears. Where was this coming from?

"Nora." Her voice whispered next to me. I jumped although I was alone.

"Promise me you'll escape at any chance you get. No matter what happens. Whatever it costs."

I waited for her—at the midpoint between our dwellings. She hadn't arrived yet.

Five minutes went by.

Ten minutes went by.

Then twelve minutes. Twelve minutes and eight seconds....

My hands cupped my ears, shaking my head, but the image of her body lying on the steps of her apartment stained the corners of my brain. A Mare Gifted killed her. There was no denying her wet and matted hair across her horror-stricken face, mouth agape and looking upward at the sky as if looking up to the Divine in anguish. Her lips were already blued when I found her; her body cold and limp in my wailing embrace.

Countless scenarios ended all the same. She drowned in the middle of town, submerged in water by the merciless hands of a Mare.

"Promise me, Nora."

A flash of what could have been formed in the far reaches of my imagination. Soft grass swayed gently in the wind. We resided far away from others, far away from Gifteds. The sun shined brightly into the kitchen where you and I shared meals we cooked for each other, shared stories that meant nothing and everything until the sky sank into a deep navy color, lined with stars.

"I promise."

Staring at the mirror, the Unfortunate Laws of Servitude stared back. I screamed, stumbling and falling backward. My wrists slammed into the tile, and my breath hitched. I wheezed, bringing my hand to my chest.

Calm down. Calm down. Calm down!

Why were these suppressed thoughts flooding out now? I had promised her. I promised her I would break free from this life of servitude. Any chance. No matter the danger, the risk.

The ringing sound faded into the background of my mind.

I slowly stood up, looking in the mirror again. The plaque reflected back, but the words were far away. Could this be the chance?

Clenching my jaw, fear dwelled inside my heart. But I made a promise. No matter the cost.

I exited the bathroom, my feet shaking with adrenaline, but I forced my pace to remain steady, nimble, servant-like.

I began walking toward the entrance again, staring at Mr. Harris until he noticed.

He broke away from the crowd to meet me away from the other Gifteds.

"I would like to talk about your offer, sir."

Mr. Harris raised an eyebrow. "I'm listening."

The plaque detailing the Unfortunate Laws of Servitude glared on the wall in front of me. My throat clenched.

"Would I be given to the Harris House?"

I didn't like the scrunched and hesitant face Mr. Harris made. "That's too complicated. You'd continue to belong to the Montgomerys, even at Galdor, but only in title. You'll be at the academy as a student instead of a servant."

My eyes trained on the plaque. "But what about the Unfortunate laws? What would I even do as a student?"

"You'd train like any other Gifted student," Mr. Harris replied. "You'd learn how to serve your country rather than splinter it apart."

"Do you really expect Gifteds to be okay with this? To work *alongside* an Unfortunate?" I pressed. "The ULS—"

Mr. Harris waved off the concern with a scoff. "You have nothing to fear from those laws."

"How can you be so sure?" The bold letters at the bottom darkened, "PUNISHABLE BY DEATH" becoming more prominent.

"As the First Senior Royal Crest Knight, I have leeway with those laws. You remember the sixth one?"

An Unfortunate cannot harm any Gifted under any jurisdiction beneath Divine power. Plain as day. The one I'd break the most if I had to do anything like Molly did during her interview. If I even survived a real fight with a Gifted, that is.

I nodded.

"I have permission under Divine power to take you under my wing at Galdor," he explained. "Only the king holds Divine jurisdiction, and he approved of my pilot program long before I met you. You have nothing to worry about."

I finally looked at the Gifted man in front of me. His relaxed posture and casual words ignited my core. Could I ever reach that feeling? Of complete certainty and autonomy? This was my chance. My promise could not be hidden away any longer.

"If you can guarantee safe passage, Mr. Harris, I would like to go to Galdor with you tomorrow."

He beamed the largest smile I had ever seen on a Gifted before, but the expression shifted into a serious one as he looked over to the gleaming Montgomery family.

"They're not going to like it," I said, though I had a feeling Mr. Harris already knew that.

He scoffed. "No. They will not indeed. But you understand what you're committing to?"

I nodded.

"Okay." Mr. Harris's voice lowered even more. "I will announce your leave after the party is over. For the time being, keep your head low and don't talk to anyone else about this."

The party moved closer now, their laughter louder and beating to my irregular heartbeat. Were any of the guests staring at us? Any of the Montgomerys noticing our conversation? I placed more distance between us.

Do not betray me, my eyes begged Mr. Harris, no longer trusting my voice.

Weaving through the party once more, I reached the kitchen safely. "Are those orange slices ready?"

***

Only two guests stayed after the party was over. Mr. Walton chatted away with Mr. Montgomery and the rest of the family in the entertainment room. Laughter echoed through the mansion as the men exaggerated old military stories. Mr. Harris was with them as promised, though I did wish he could reassure me again that everything would be fine, that I was making the correct choice. *Is this what you meant, Valerie?*

The other Unfortunates had left long ago with their Gifted Houses, so I sat alone at the kitchen table, my mind poisoned by the idea of another servant sitting where I was now. *This is ridiculous,* I told myself. Why did I even care? The Montgomerys were nothing more than my employers, my House. Why should I be concerned with the next Montgomery servant?

Mrs. Montgomery chimed the small bell she carried alongside her.

I jumped up from my chair at the calling. Snapping my attention to the dining room, I barged through the doorway more forcibly than intended.

"Yes, Mrs. Montgomery?" I asked, keeping my voice as calm as possible, my head bowed to her.

"Go refill my glass."

"Of course." I gingerly accepted the cup from Mrs. Montgomery's polished fingers.

Just as I turned to leave, a new voice sprang up. "Enjoy the water while you can, Mrs. Montgomery."

Hostile words never sounded calmer coming from Mr. Harris's mouth. I flinched, gripping the glass tighter.

"Excuse me?" Mrs. Montgomery inquired, her voice daring him to repeat his words.

Mr. Harris's smile didn't falter, power swelling in his expression, "You heard me, Martha. Enjoy the water while you can because Nora isn't going to be here for you much longer."

I had never wanted a Gift more in my life to simply turn invisible to the conversation.

Mrs. Montgomery turned toward me. "Go get my water."

I nodded, twisting my body away again when Mr. Harris spoke out, "No, Nora. Stay." I halted at the contradiction. The two Gifteds held the other's gazes.

Mrs. Montgomery raised an eyebrow at Mr. Harris. "What do you think you're doing?"

"As of tonight, Nora will no longer be working as your servant but rather my student. At Galdor Academy."

"Student?" Mrs. Montgomery laughed darkly. "Don't be ridiculous."

"Harris, you are completely out of line here," Mr. Walton chimed in.

"Are you trying to buy her?" Molly asked. "He's doing a poor job of asking."

"Mora is a what?"

Everyone began speaking all at once, their shouting colliding with each other.

Glancing to Mr. Harris, I found his calm stare through the chaos, his expression evident. I had to be the one to stop the commotion. A test of my conviction. My willingness to break eight years of servitude.

But what would you do, Valerie? What could I possibly do?

My eyes drifted toward the empty glass in my hand. Without another moment to overthink the consequences, I threw the glass to the hard, wooden ground and silenced a room of Gifteds with the booming crash that followed.

CHAPTER FIVE

Welcome to Galdor Academy

We had our own train car with Mr. Harris and Mr. Walton. For the First Senior Royal Crest Knight, most of the seats were carved out for more open space. The instructors forced us to sit along the back row. Molly sat to the left window and I sat on the right with Mr. Harris and Mr. Walton facing us.

Mr. Harris slouched enough in his seat for the action to be noticeable, relaxed with a glass of water in his hand. I was sure he had done this on purpose, watching as he rotated his wrist, the water swirling around in its confinements. I was silently grateful that the man did not ask me if I wanted my own glass.

Mr. Walton stood in an instructing posture, relaxed but not in the same way as his colleague, talking about Galdor Academy. I tried to pay attention, but Mr. Walton's attention fixated on Molly as he spoke. Water slid down the side of Mr. Harris's glass like rain.

"...meet your classmates, you will commence your first-year combat exam." Mr. Walton's words came back into focus.

"A combat exam?"

Mr. Walton finally turned to me, his expression a cross of surprise and disdain. A heat flash brushed over my face. I accidentally asked my thoughts out loud.

Mr. Walton composed himself.

"Yes. Galdor tests offensive and defensive combat as I've already stated. Each year, you're placed into an initial ranking within your class after going head-to-head with each other in a bracket. The rankings fluctuate throughout the year as you and your classmates progress. Your combat exam will be this Friday."

At the end of this week. Anxiety bubbled in my chest.

Molly fought her *father* to be on this train. Could I even have a chance against Molly? These Gifteds classmates?

"Any more questions?" Mr. Walton hesitated to ask.

Before I could formulate one, Molly raised her hand and started speaking for me. "Oh, I have a question Nora is dying to know! What happens if you're constantly at the *bottom* of the rankings?"

She slammed her palm into the next seat near my thigh; I flinched and kept my eyes downward.

Mr. Harris answered, "Continued failure will prevent you from moving forward in the academy, and you'd be returned home." His eyes burned into me. "But if you show enough tenacity and keep good scores among the other disciplines, your total overall ranking should not suffer."

Mr. Harris drilled into Molly's glare. "Does that answer your question?"

The Montgomery daughter squinted her eyes and looked away with a small hiss.

"Right," Mr. Walton cleared his throat before continuing his lecture. I kept listening until the train conductor interrupted him.

"Passengers, welcome to Galdor! We're about to enter the city limits, so please be advised to hold on to your seat and belongings until the train has come to a complete stop."

"Ah, we're here." Mr. Walton clapped his hands together with fake enthusiasm.

Molly pressed her face against the glass to get a better view.

Void of any orders or commands, I remained motionless.

Mr. Harris broke the silence. "Nora, come see the city."

Slowly, I moved closer to the left side of the train car, standing a small distance away from the Gifteds.

The train snaked its way through the capital, tall sculptures blocking out the sun. As our position elevated and sank, the train car protested, shaking in an attempt to throw its passengers. I held tighter to the bar along the wall. Pressing my face against the glass, I looked down to see small images of blurred citizens, there, frozen in place, and gone in an instant from the train's speed.

The tracks lowered again, and the buildings vanished without warning, sunlight filling the train car. As I squinted my eyes, a large open space with a dense population of vendors and shoppers caught my attention. It must have been Galdor Square, much larger than the marketplace in Thunder Bay. I had never seen so many Gifteds in one place before, laughing and showing off their Gifts to each other for entertainment.

Farther away, on the outskirts of the city limits, a large circular structure stuck out behind modern buildings. "What's that over there?" I asked, pointing before it could disappear.

"Oh, the Determination Arena," Mr. Harris said. "Mr. Walton, would you like to give your notes on the arena?"

Mr. Walton stared blankly at his colleague. He grumbled a quick response, "It's traditionally where royal members hold Determination challenges when there's a dispute regarding the rightful heir. But it commonly holds large holy events, giant royal celebrations, funerals, and other important gatherings that the whole world must see."

The train did not hold in its position for long, though, turning a sharp left to avoid a skyscraper and traveling outside the dense city center. The Iridion Castle came into view, a pure white structure towering above the city in regal excellence. As the train chugged forward for several heartbeats, the sun disappeared as the triangular points of the castle's design cast me in shadow. The train continued to weave and descend until it finally halted to a sharp stop at a station. I could no longer see the Iridion Castle from my view, but the shadow remained.

The station bustled with life; the smell of heat and hints of smoke danced in the air. So many trains moved around me with mechanical precision. I found myself spinning unintentionally to take everything in from the all-window buildings to the cleanly organized trees along the central concrete pathway.

"I've never been so close to the castle before," Molly said to Mr. Walton. "Am I going to meet the king?" Her voice didn't sound as excited or animated as someone who wanted to meet the ruler of Iridion.

Mr. Walton chuckled lightly, which was a strange noise coming from his mouth. "Perhaps if you are proven to be a Senior Royal Crest Knight," the man replied.

A Royal Crest Knight. I had almost forgotten how I wouldn't be serving the Montgomerys here. Members with the Royal Crest brand were of the most elite and respected citizens of Iridion—an unattainable, laughable dream to Unfortunates. Where would I place among these Gifteds? Could I even make it to graduation?

Mr. Walton continued to lead us through the city.

"Where are we?" Molly demanded with a disapproving stare. "No Gifteds are wearing the military uniform."

Mr. Walton fiddled with his suit before answering. "We're currently in the financial sector. Most of the civilians you see here are businessmen. Couldn't expect everyone to graduate from Galdor like us."

Us, I thought. Like I was ranked with them.

"So, these people are below us," Molly clarified, her tone definitive instead of questioning. A nerve pulled; I couldn't help opening my mouth.

"Actually, I think they're above us. At least, the ones up there," I argued, gesturing to the tall buildings. It was a lame assertion but simply disagreeing would get under the Montgomery daughter's skin.

Molly turned to the me, ready to strike when Mr. Harris at the front chuckled loudly enough for the Imitation to snap her attention toward the instructor.

"What's so funny?"

"What's so funny is how you're addressing me in such a tone," Mr. Harris replied flatly. "I advise you to choose your words carefully around a Senior Royal Crest Knight."

Molly's mouth twitched, but she did not say anything against him.

We continued onward.

The Iridion Castle awaited, stretching against the morning sky. A solid black wall greeted us first, encasing the castle and Galdor Academy. The barrier must have been at least twelve feet tall like a daunting challenge. If two men stood on top of each other, the one above could *almost* reach the top if he had the determination—that is if the watchtower that poked out from behind the front wall didn't blare an alarm and slice his fingers off first.

The barrier was pristine, too, as though never touched, never broken or cracked from strain.

The rising sun didn't reach us as we walked left of the wall. As we approached the pointed black gate, which was the academy's only entrance, two Royal Crest Knights stood rigidly.

Though they wore armor and bore stone-cold faces, their attire lacked the same decorations of valor and of service that adorned Mr. Harris and Mr. Walton's uniforms. I recognized a similar insignia residing on their hearts, but the design did not shine with gold.

Mr. Walton somehow straightened his body even more so, but they weren't looking at him. Instead, their eyes fixated on Mr. Harris strolling up.

A sinking feeling eroded in my stomach as my eyes lowered to the ground. I fiddled with my fingers, resisting the urge to fold my hands together.

"Hello, boys," Mr. Harris greeted them with a smile.

"Mr. Harris," the left guard said. "New recruits?"

"Yes!" Mr. Harris responded enthusiastically. "Just arrived from Cherryville."

The two guards eyed me alongside Molly Montgomery with suspicion. I adjusted my stance, almost hiding behind Mr. Harris.

The left guard slowly lifted a walkie-talkie to his face. "West Watchtower, Front Gate here. We have some new recruits with Mr. Harris and Mr. Walton. Open Front Gate. Over."

A quick response crackled over the device. "West Watchtower opening Front Gate now. Over."

The black pointed gate squeaked as it separated.

To our immediate left stood the Iridion Castle, so close now that the structure devoured the very heavens. Galdor students weaved in and out of several doors along the castle's current visible side, most carrying books or pens or even backpacks. A swirl of jealousy formed inside my heart, the same jealousy I recalled when Neo surpassed his tenth birthday and still attended school. But here, now at Galdor Academy, could I have the chance among Gifted students? My promise to Valerie lingered in the back of my mind.

"Students are required to continue their education," Mr. Walton noted. "Mostly military tactics, Iridion history, royal etiquette, and of course, lessons on Gift technique."

A training field lay directly in front of me. Students ran along a track, and those enclosed on the field were stretching or exercising. The sheer number of Gifteds brought a chill up my spine.

"This is our fourth training field on campus," Mr. Walton gestured. "Prioritized for conditioning and defensive combat."

An instructor on the field shouted something I couldn't quite hear as two students fought against each other.

Mr. Walton pointed to our right. "The other three training fields are along the Southern Wall. You'll typically focus on your offensive combat and your Gift technique on those spaces."

An unusually playful squeal escaped Molly's lips while dread swirled within my stomach as an Avlis uprooted the earth to block another's attack.

"Right before the third training field is the storage building, and after the third training field is the infirmary."

He pointed to an open space in front of the third training field and infirmary where tall and narrow glass structures glistened in the mid-morning sun. "The Information Square is where you'll access mission details, daily positions, and rankings among your classmates."

We approached several larger buildings in the forefront of our vision.

The first three noticeably had no windows—three streamline black boxes. Mr. Walton flicked his wrist as he pointed to the first two buildings.

"These are the simulation labs. Simulations range from problem de-escalation to snuffing out a burning building." His casual tone did not match his words. "Most simulations will score your leadership, teamwork, and valor skills, so take each simulation seriously as if it's actually happening."

"Next door is the RC Exam Building," Mr. Walton continued. The third building was more compact compared to the simulation labs. "Students interested in becoming a Royal Crest Knight will have to pass the Royal Crest Exam. Testing is in this building, and though open to second year students, most complete the exam in their third year."

"I'll beat it my first year," Molly promised.

"That's highly improbable and also not permitted." Mr. Walton did not humor her. He continued his small tour, pointing to a tall but slender structure on our right that stood out for its small balconies and white exterior similar to the castle's material.

"Pay no mind to the instructor housing next to the RC Exam Building. Instructor offices are on the first and second floors, but you have Mr. Harris as your instructor. As a Senior Royal Crest Knight, he has a section of the palace where he resides instead."

An entire section of the palace to himself? The more I learned about Mr. Harris only raised more serious questions. How powerful was this Gifted? I couldn't come up with a proper answer. Perhaps the enigma of a madman was not meant be solved.

We walked up to the last buildings. Three identical buildings lined up beside each other facing three other identical buildings, the multiple consecutive windows indicating residency. "The student housing," Mr. Walton confirmed. "As first years, you'll live in this First Year Building here." The instructor brought them to the last building along the East Wall.

Mr. Walton mentioned a second watchtower along the East Wall and the dining hall that resided between the six residential halls.

"In the far-right corner are the servant quarters and the servant canteen. Causing trouble or disobeying orders can result in servant work as punishment."

I held back a sarcastic smile. Mr. Walton continued, "So keep that in mind at all times."

Was I supposed to fear this punishment as the other students did? *I've done nothing but servant work, punishment as you phrased, for the past eight years.* My lips formed a line as I struggled to keep my thoughts inward. How laughable.

"Oh, Nora will fit right in then," Molly teased.

"I hardly disobey orders," I hesitantly countered.

Molly rolled her eyes. *"Right."* She stretched the word in a doubtful tone. "You might not be violating any of the ULS now, but I'll be there when you do. And what *happens* when you violate those laws?"

My body bristled at the mention of the ULS; my throat tightened, unable to respond.

"Say any more about those laws," Mr. Harris intervened while staring forward, "and that'll be a month's worth of servant duty."

The threat silenced Molly, who crossed her arms as we entered the first-year building. An older woman waved politely from behind a desk in the lobby. Mr. Walton cleared his throat as he led us toward the center staircase.

"All students must be in their designated residence hall before 10:00 p.m. nightly and all students must be in the dining hall for breakfast before 7:00 a.m. daily. Ms. Carol is here to track your comings and goings. If you are late to either bed or breakfast, that can result in a three-day servant shift."

Molly didn't have any remarks. We continued upward, the floors incrementing from A onward.

We landed on the floor labeled D. Following Mr. Harris down a corridor filled with identical doors, we stopped at a door branded with the title D7.

"Remember D7," Mr. Walton said, "as this will be your first-year room at Galdor."

"Both of us?" Molly's eyes widened in shock before squinting toward my direction. "In the same room?"

My eyes were just as alarmed. I didn't like this setup either. When neither instructor said anything, Molly sighed and stretched out her hand in a giving gesture. "Fine," she spat, her fangs exposed. "I'll just lock the pet out at night."

Mr. Harris shook his head. "First years do not get locked doors," he said, but before Molly could object further, he pulled something out from his pocket.

"Your IDs," he handed each of us a card. "Keep this on you at all times. It'll identify you as a student and help you access the Information Square, cafeteria, and even some buildings."

Identity as a student meant this plastic was never leaving my side.

The photograph came from my most recent records, perhaps a year old. My name—as simple as "NORA"—was in large black letters at the left-hand corner. I also recognized my official title extension written underneath my name: "Property of Montgomery House."

A blight of anger festered within my soul. I still belonged to Gifteds here. I couldn't forget.

"Though we arrived early, the rest of your classmates should already be behind that door. I recommend meeting them before your first class."

He looked directly at me. "You're going to need allies. Friends even. Good luck."

Molly and I stood in frozen postures as Mr. Harris and Mr. Walton left. Friends? With Gifteds? The idea didn't feel real until this very moment.

As they disappeared, Molly snapped her attention toward me, exposing her forked tongue with a hiss. Flinching, I slammed into the wall. Her slit eyes rolled in disgust, "Don't introduce yourself alongside me. I don't associate with you. Got it?"

"Got it," I forced out instead of, "Yes, ma'am."

Molly turned and entered first, closing the door behind her.

I counted my heartbeats, but the quick thumping in my chest didn't waver. Apprehension prickled at the back of my neck as my hand reached outward. *Valerie, I wish I had an ounce of your strength.*

I twisted the knob.

CHAPTER SIX

Gifted Classmates

The room stretched out farther than expected. No decorations adorned the walls. Plain, identical beds lined the two opposing walls with a compact space in between each mattress for a lamp to reside on a small desk. One large window was directly at the end of the room, exposing the mid-morning sky.

What made the room most striking was its strange inhabitants—Gifted students, my new classmates. All eyes locked onto me, the newcomer. The intruder. I deviated from their attention by occupying myself with closing the door behind me.

My back instinctively pressed against the exit's safety. I was ten years old again when my body would become rigid as unknown guests arrived. My teeth would clench when those guests would expect service even though I was new and ignorant to their desires. *You're not here to serve anyone,* I urged. But my head stayed downward.

"Salutations."

The voice greeted me nearby. Glancing to my left, a boy stared back. He gestured me toward him.

Allies. Mr. Harris made it clear I needed to make allies for myself here. Another test perhaps? To see how well I mingled with Gifteds bent on killing first?

The young man in front of me had a youthful face that suggested he was younger, and his lanky arms and stream-lined body reminded me of the fishermen in Thunder Bay. The thought was odd, considering the only Gifteds there were city guards. I could still see the outline of the city guard flailing beneath me, powerlessly as Ms. Douglas's knife sank into his neck.

"Hi," I replied in a softer voice. Was I waving? Apparently so.

As I approached him, I noticed Molly standing near the window, her arms crossed over her chest but her back against the wall in a casually intimidating posture. She chatted with a blonde girl standing close to a tall male. The way the blonde girl locked arms with the tall boy indicated they were a couple. He remained rigidly quiet as the blonde girl waved her hand about and pulled her neck back in an exaggerated laugh to whatever Molly had said.

"Name?" he asked. No need to swap pleasantries, I guess. But the question still startled me. Gifteds didn't typically ask that question to their servants.

"Nora." My body bent into a small bow. My voice succeeded in being calm and fluent, though, so I could pass the action off as polite. "And you?"

"Kai Lancer," the boy introduced, dipping his head in return.

Kai. That had to be a fishing name.

"May I ask where you are from, Mr. Lancer?" I tried mimicking the formality Mrs. Montgomery would give new guests.

"No need for the formality as classmates," he assured with a gentle wave of his palm. "I'm from Stone Creek."

Stone Creek. I pictured the city on water immediately.

The city was to the south of Thunder Bay, directly on the ocean. During the summer seasons before my Choosing Ceremony, I would see the city move closer to land and become visible from the shoreline.

"Really?" I raised a surprised eyebrow, containing a wave of excitement that came with relatability. "I'm from Thunder Bay."

"Oh, Thunder Bay?" Kai's head tilted and eyes squinted. "Are your parents stationed there?"

Before I could come up with a response, a shadow loomed above. A weight rested itself on my right shoulder, and long fingers gripped my forearm as red hair cascaded down my face.

"You're so cute!" a tall girl proclaimed, squeezing onto my smaller frame. "I wish to know your name." She looked at Kai. "And your name!"

I remained perfectly still as I replied. "Nora, ma'am."

Kai stared above my head with curious eyes. "Kai Lancer."

"I'm Fern Fairaway." The tall girl twirled strands of red hair at the corners of my vision. *Fern* was certainly not a fishing name.

"Avlis then," Kai clarified.

"What gave it away?" The tall girl giggled.

Kai explained, "Well for starters, your name is Fern. It would not make sense for a family of any other Gift to name their child something related to plants. A rarer possibility is Nox, but you destroyed that theory immediately when you touched Nora's arm and she didn't die from poisoning. It was all a matter of narrowing down the options."

"So factual," Fern noted his dictation, but her tone was fascinated rather than sarcastic. "I couldn't be a Nox. No hugs." She squeezed my smaller frame again. "No fun."

"Yes," Kai agreed, looking at me with a reassuring look. He addressed me this time, "Avlis are known for their more personal, hands-on personalities."

I thought about the Avlis city guard threatening the shopkeeper. This girl was completely removed from that menace.

Fern gasped, pushing herself off me and taking a step back. "I apologize if you're uncomfortable. You're just so small and huggable!" The Avlis reached out and patted my head like I was a pet. A nerve rippled through my body as her fingers moved along my hairline. Her Gift could kill me at any misstep.

Was this how I made allies? By appearing small and huggable?

"So," Fern leaned forward with a smile. "Tell me what you think about the other classmates so far."

I faltered to answer as I looked around the room. "I haven't had a chance to meet anyone else, ma'am."

"Oh, stop with the pleasantries." Fern swatted the word away. "Tell me your immediate thoughts about those two over there instead."

Looking where Fern pointed, two dark-skinned recruits stood side by side, similar in features. Brother and sister perhaps. The presumed brother waved his arms about as he spoke with a cheeky grin on his face, relishing in a story I could only hear in fragments. The presumed sister nodded as she listened, her obsidian eyes fixated on every word even though she kept a neutral expression. I noticed the zigzag pattern on the presumed sister's scalp, the wavy edges along her hairline, the two tight braids that kept her hair together and then secured on the nap of her neck—a reasonable yet fashionable hairstyle.

"I think they are... brother and sister." I had little to evaluate.

"Very easily deduced," Kai agreed.

Fern leaned downward to whisper, "Leo introduced himself first and made an effort to point out his sister, Persephone. They're both..." The Avlis stopped herself, looking to Kai. "Can you guess what they are too?"

Kai stared for several seconds, the wheels clearly turning in his blue eyes.

"It's clear from their hands," he prompted. I noticed the distinct pattern along their fingers, too. Leo still waved his about, and Persephone kept hers folded in front of herself. Fern squinted in hopes of catching the significant details.

Kai continued, "He has lines along his fingers and palms, lighter from his natural skin tone. Do you see? And his sister—her lines are hardly noticeable, so much thinner than her brother's, which is fascinating." The Mare contemplated to himself. The wheels practically turned in his eyes as he tried to understand their differing line patterns.

"Which makes them *what* exactly?" Fern asked, leaning in further with a curious expression.

"Oh, they're Mati." Kai waved off any other possibility. "No doubt. It's so fascinating because their epidermis layer is incredibly fire-resistant, so they get those distinct lines using their ability over time."

"Excellent!" Fern clapped her hands with a squeal before Kai could spiral into more information. "You are correct once again! Oh, oh, do Nora. What is Nora?"

Both Gifteds turned their attention to me.

My nerves froze at the question. I wouldn't be able to avoid this question forever. *What do I say? Do I just agree with whatever Kai deduces?* I desperately wished Mr. Harris could give me an idea. But he was not here, and I hadn't thought about what to say to these Gifteds now that I was actually at Galdor Academy.

My heart drummed loudly in my ears as the two Gifteds stared and analyzed.

Tell them the truth, my first thought rang.

They can't hate you for being beneath them.

They won't see you as a threat that way.

They'll kill you if they know, another thought countered.

Kai had his analysis ready. "I originally thought Mati, but your hands aren't commonly marked, so I would say a Mare like myself. Most of the guards stationed in Thunder Bay are Mares, and I'm decently deceptive of my own Gift."

I would never be a Mare! My nose twitched, my only facial reaction in disgust.

Fern leaned forward, her green eyes glistening with anticipation. "Is he correct?"

Before I could formulate a response, a much louder and chirped voice cut me off.

"Greetings!"

A wide smile stretched across this new person's face, the blonde girl originally talking to Molly. Her black eyes searched my form.

"I'm Skylar Stanton." Her teeth were too white. "What's your name?"

Stepping back, I succeeded in keeping my voice steady. "Nora, ma'—. Nora."

"Nora…." Skylar let that word roll off her tongue like she had never heard that name before. "That's certainly not an Auran name. What is it, exactly?"

I faltered to respond, "It's a family name."

"But no House name?" Skylar's face was too close.

Not in the way you're asking. I refused to tell her I was property to a House instead.

"None that belong to me."

My quick response seemed to quench Skylar's curiosity as her gaze side-eyed to Fern before turning sharply to the rest of the room. "Attention, everyone!"

She now had an audience, waving and smiling like she was being praised for an unseen award. "Everyone hasn't been able to meet each other yet! As a reminder for those who don't know, I'm Skylar Stanton."

She intertwined her hands around the nearby tall boy's arm, the large diamond ring on her finger twinkling under the overhead lights. He briefly resisted her pull as she brought him forward to bask in the imaginary glory. "And this is Cal Hilfrey! Soon to be Stanton. We're both Auras from Galdor."

Skylar turned back around and grabbed my wrist. I helplessly followed her command. "You know everyone already, Nora?"

Unfamiliar faces blinked back. I glanced to the two Mati. "I haven't been formally introduced to Leo and Persephone yet, but I know they're both Mati."

"Did you know they're twins?" Skylar's fingers dug into my arm. She didn't wait for a response. "They don't have a House name either. You all can be friends."

Leo scoffed while Persephone crossed her arms at the comment.

"And what about her?" Skylar asked, pointing to Molly Montgomery. "You came in a little after her. Do you know her?"

Molly leaned forward and exposed her fangs. "Choose your words carefully, Unfortunate."

A crackle instead of a laugh erupted from Skylar's throat. "Harsh words!" She leaned closer to my face. "What are you going to say to that, Nora?"

She thought Molly was being mean instead of truthful. Staring into Skylar's dark eyes, I couldn't blink away. *Valerie, I need your bravery.*

Silence.

"It is as Miss Montgomery says," I finally said, "I am an Unfortunate."

Skylar lingered for several seconds—looking for the joke, the punchline—but when I simply stared back, her wide grin slowly fell into a mix of confusion and anger.

An undignified yell escaped Skylar's throat as she detached her hold on me immediately and backed away. Her nose wrinkled like she had a bad taste in her mouth, her act crumbling.

"*What?*" she screeched. The Gifted flicked her wrists like that would cleanse her fingertips from touching me.

She looked up to her fiancé for support, though Cal stepped back. His expression was familiar—on guard for her blowup. "How could this be?" Her white face burned a bright red.

The wind picked up in response to her outburst. A sudden gust rippled in my direction and through my body as Skylar's arms threw down to her sides.

She stormed over to Molly who turned wide-eyed and pressed against the far wall. "Is she your servant? Why is your servant here? What about the ULS?" Skylar demanded.

Molly's lips curled. "Oh, don't mention those laws or you'll be just like her for a month. Instructor orders. Says it's Divine jurisdiction."

Skylar visibly shook, silent for a heartbeat before sharply turning in my direction. As she ran up, I stepped backward. "Why did Mr. Harris invite you as a *student?*"

Cal reached out to the other Aura. "Skylar—"

"No!" She swatted him away, pointing her index finger at my face as she hurled toward me. "We worked *years* to get here, and I'll be downcast before I have an Unfortunate as a classmate!"

My palms planted against the wall as she hovered inches away. She could use her Gift to rip the air out of my lungs without ever clasping her hands around my throat. Her black eyes seeped into my face, desperate to consume information, to understand *why*.

"Look at you. Already shaking like a leaf. I don't blame you." She shook her head. "No. I don't. Because you're doing exactly what you're meant to. So why did Mr. Harris bring you here? Huh? What's so interesting about you?"

I held my breath, no longer trusting my words.

"Well, you must have done something *very* interesting," Skylar pressed. Her eyes still searched for an answer I wouldn't provide. I needed to keep my brief interaction with the Anti-Gifteds Movement close to my chest. It couldn't land in Gifted hands. Certainly not hers.

Kai wedged himself beside me, facing the Aura. "Leave her alone."

Skylar narrowed her eyes at him. "What? Are you going to confess that you're an Unfortunate too? You're lucky to have a last name at all."

She turned back and stared daggers at me before Kai could defend himself. "I guess we'll find out why at the combat exam." She stepped back. "Come along, Cal. I don't want to be anywhere near treachery any longer."

The two Auras walked toward the door. "Wait up!" Molly called out, running toward them.

Skylar stopped her. "Go hang out with *your* Unfortunate."

She slammed the door in Molly's face. But the Imitation persisted, opening the door and running down the hallway.

An exposed space opened around me as hesitation shifted through the air. "Are you okay?" asked Kai.

I inhaled sharply, my throat too clenched to even breathe. *When have you ever asked an Unfortunate that?*

Fern held her hands close to her chest, leaning backward. "So you really are an Unfortunate?"

I looked up to her, swallowing hard. "Yes," I whispered.

Several heartbeats passed. I hated this feeling. I had spent so much time clinging to the wall in hopes of passing by without incident. Now I was in the same position but at the center of baffled and harsh Gifted stares. Was this a chance or a death sentence?

Fern released the hold on herself, pointing to Kai. "Ha!" Her loud outburst sliced the silence; I hated how my body jumped. "You would have never guessed that! You said you could deduce your own Gift, and she wasn't a Mare at all!"

The Avlis shook her head and made a *tsk* sound. "That's one point against you, my friend." Fern outstretched her hand to me, and I pressed further into the wall. "And that's one point to Nora here."

I stared at her cheerful exterior as I fought off tears. My voice came out shakily, "I wasn't trying to trick anyone."

"Too late." Fern dismissed any doubt with the simple shake of her head.

"That's a point to Nora, and you're just going to have to prove yourself again Kai. I don't make the rules, sorry."

Fern closed the space, squishing herself shoulder to shoulder between me and Kai like we were well-established friends. Why was she treating me this way? This was wrong. I needed an outburst, a cringe, a hostility. Those atmospheres were familiar to me.

My back tensed as Fern held me there, the Gifted's playful demeanor foreign and doing little to comfort me.

CHAPTER SEVEN

Orientation

The first round of the combat exam was posted prominently at the Information Square.

I begrudgingly followed Fern and Kai through the academy grounds, arriving to an open space where tall glass-like structures stood upright from the dirt. The glass rectangles were placed within a small distance of each other and formed a large square. Galdor students stood in front of these glass structures both within and outside of the square, their eyes glancing about as if reading something I couldn't quite see yet.

"Here's a free one," Fern announced, jogging up to one of the glass rectangles quickly like someone else might get there first.

Kai and I followed. Fern's fingers tapped against the glass at random points, but nothing happened. The Avlis's jabbing became more insistent.

"Fern," Kai warned, reaching out to her arm. "You need to use one of these."

The Mare showed us a small card that had his name and photo prominently displayed on the front. He pressed the backside of his card to the glass where irregular black lines were drawn.

The clear glass surface transformed into a milky white color. I stood in awe as a small greeting read something I couldn't fully comprehend before the text faded away and replaced itself with a menu.

"How did you do that?" I whispered. I leaned forward to get a better look at Kai's card as he withdrew it from the glass.

"Our ID cards," Kai responded plainly. He tilted his head and squinted as I examined my own ID closely, turning it around in all directions. He explained further. "They're encoded with our information, which is stored on a database that gives us access to some of the buildings like the Info Square here."

I nodded even though most of Kai's words were lost to an Unfortunate like me. All I needed to know was his actions—press the black patterned backside to the glass.

Kai selected a button among the menu options, and a new image displayed itself on the screen. A large sheet of virtual paper repeated the button words at the top in all caps with the current date beside the header. Smaller text read out Kai's assignments for the day, explaining the first combat exam in detail. As Kai and Fern scanned the document, I remained in the background.

Kai pressed his index finger to the glass and moved in an upward gesture. The page adjusted as it scrolled to his command. Larger font read out classmate names below the combat exam's description.

"What does it say?" I asked.

Fern answered first, "Looks like I'm up against you!" She pointed at Kai with a squeal.

Kai made a *hmm* sound as he examined the screen.

Stepping forward to get a closer look, I could recognize my own name but hardly anything else. "Who am I against?" I squinted at the screen.

"It looks like…" Fern began, looking over at my name. A hesitation came with silence.

Kai finished for the Avlis, "You're against Skylar."

Skylar? *Skylar? SKYLAR?*

My heart pumped louder in my chest; nerves pointed my feet in preparation to flee. No, fleeing wouldn't do me any good. But what else could I possibly do? Scenarios played out in my head—all complete failures. I hardly catered to Auras. How could I possibly fight one?

"Easy now." Fern already had her long fingers wrapped around my upper arm, securing me into reality. "You'll be fine. It's the first combat exam. It's completely normal to be nervous."

I looked up and glared into the Avlis's eyes. "Give me an order."

"What?"

"Say it like you're giving me an order. Tell me what I need to do."

It was degrading, but so many times before I had catered to every Gifted's desire. Breaking out of that habit would be difficult. Maybe I could use it to my advantage here.

Fern paused. "You need to fight Skylar."

Taking a deep breath, I nodded earnestly. I had until the end of the week to even stand a chance against her. Four days to change a servant into a student.

"Hey, let's get lunch!" Fern encouraged, looking at the time marked on the glass structure. "We have our first classes in two hours."

Already?

"In Gift Techniques, it looks like." Kai scanned the Information Square. "I hope we discuss Isaac Winters!"

"Ooh, who's that?" Fern asked what we were both thinking.

"What?" Kai's voice raised an octave. "You've never heard of him?"

The Avlis shook her head as the Mare pressed a red button on the right upper-hand corner of the glass screen. All information faded.

The two Gifteds turned at the same time. Kai explained himself, "He's an Ice Mare! There's only a spare few every generation since it's so difficult to transition from one water state to another. And at a young age? It's unheard of."

"And his name is Isaac *Winters?*" Fern laughed.

"So that's actually a funny story!" Kai's hands extended to his sides in an excited gesture. His voice rose with each word. "His mother actually changed their House name to Winters when his Gift abilities got attention from Galdor."

Slowly, I followed the two Gifteds to the student canteen nearby as Kai analytically explain why Isaac Winters was at the forefront of his mind. The more Kai spoke, the more lost I became.

The only Mares I knew were the Crawfords, a modest Gifted family with no immediate heritage to Galdor Academy but who found themselves invited to the Montgomery home anyway for celebrations. And the only Mares in Thunder Bay were city guards who I, along with all other Unfortunates, tried avoiding at all costs.

So I stayed silent as we walked, my feet even sidestepping delicately to omit my sound of walking, as if I didn't exist there at all.

As we reached the door, my body and mind pushed me in two directions. Protocol required me to open the door for

Gifteds, but I wasn't fast enough to push through the two in front of me.

Kai touched the handle, pulling it open wide enough for us to all enter. I kept my head down as I passed, thanking him in a low whisper.

We approached a worker, undoubtedly an Unfortunate, watching as people scanned in. I watched as Kai pulled out his ID and scanned it. I did the same. Blending in was key.

I followed Fern and Kai to a line of their choosing, closer to their backs now that more Gifteds were condensed in this space.

Like clockwork, the students in front of us grabbed a tray. I reached out and took a tray after Fern and Kai.

Fern pointed at different foods through the glass as she spoke. The woman behind the counter, another Unfortunate wearing a uniform of kitchen attire, delicately placed the items on Fern's tray before handing it back to her.

The aroma flooded my senses at once, my stomach rumbling softly. I stared at the assortment of food at once, my eyes dancing around the options with questions bouncing around my mind. How much was I allowed to have? I could pick anything? Anything at all that I wanted? Was this free?

The Unfortunate stared at me with indifferent eyes. *When does she get to eat?*

"You're holding up the line," Kai warned in a whisper.

I slowly gave the Unfortunate my tray. "I would just like that, please," I pointed to a dish I almost recognized—noodles soaked in a warm broth, but there were a lot more decorations that belonged to Gifteds.

The Unfortunate handed back my tray in mechanical movements, looking to the next Gifted for his order. We moved along, some sections free for students to grab items and continue onward. Fern obnoxiously loaded her tray while Kai stared at each item meticulously before choosing what he deemed worthy. I kept my fingers at the edges of my tray.

We reached the end where small desserts were laid out in front of us. Fern took three cookies but one somehow landed on my tray. "You like chocolate chip?" she asked.

I stared at the cookie, remembering when I would make them for Melanie Montgomery on a stormy night. Valerie and I would steal one or two for ourselves. What was this Gifted's plan? Did she plan to be kind first so I would lose my guard? But I didn't see malice in her bouncy posture, and Mr. Harris's new mission for me was still at the forefront of my mind.

Nodding, I followed her outside of the line, now facing the dining area. Rows of long tables stretched out before us with large round tables dotting in between.

"Where should we sit?" Fern prompted to no one in particular.

"We're encouraged to sit with our classmates," replied Kai.

We spotted Skylar's bright blonde hair first, sitting center stage alongside Cal and Molly Montgomery. Her nose stayed in the air as she shouted her disdain. "What do these Unfortunates think they are? It's unbelievable! Inexcusable!"

A twist knotted in my stomach.

Her charcoal eyes caught sight of me first. She scoffed and looked away quickly. My very existence offended her.

I forced my attention elsewhere, finding the Mati siblings sitting at a round table by themselves. "How about them?" I gestured in their direction far away from Skylar.

Fern and Kai nodded, following me to the table. The action felt natural from all the times I acted as a guide around the Montgomery mansion.

Persephone noticed us first, bumping her brother with her shoulder. He looked up and flashed a confident smile. I forced a smile back, halting in front of them while Fern had already pulled her chair out. "May we sit with you?" I asked.

Leo scoffed, his hands partially covering his mouth. "Sure," he gestured to the chair in front of himself. Fire shot out from his fingertips.

Startled, my tray wobbled in my hands. My cookie fell from off the edge, landing on the freshly scorched table.

Persephone stood abruptly as Leo cursed, cupping his hands together. His sister held her arched fingers around his hands for several seconds.

"I have it under control, Persy," said Leo.

Persephone squinted her eyes but withdrew, resting her hands on the table.

I held the tray firmly now, staring at Leo with a bewildered expression. The Mati scoffed again as if someone had said something funny, flexing his fingers in front of himself as Persephone's shoulders tensed. "You can sit here if you dare," he said sarcastically.

Nothing dangerous happened this time.

I purposefully sat next to Persephone while Fern handed me one of her not-dropped cookies with a wink.

Fern and Kai sat slowly, all eyes on Leo who clasped his hands together in front of his face again. I noticed how close Persephone's hand was to mine; the light lines along her fingers and palms were clearer now. I'd never sat with Gifteds before. Even with Unfortunates, I only ate with my family once a month for the past eight years. Noah wasn't here to tell me when I could start. I kept my hands still anyway, waiting for someone to start eating first.

A hardy crunch broke the silence as Fern munched on one of the clean cookies.

I slowly reached out to my spoon and watched it sink into the brown broth.

"So are you finally ready to tell us how an Unfortunate gets here?" Leo's question drew all eyes toward me. The Gifteds shifted in their seats.

I stared at my utensil for several seconds.

"Mr. Harris invited me the same as everyone else," I decided to respond. My status as an Unfortunate was unavoidable, but I could still keep my experience with Ms. Douglas close to my chest. The Anti-Gifteds Movement was small. I didn't need to tell them Mr. Harris saw me as an appeasement to other Unfortunates.

"I don't buy that as the whole story." Leo crossed his arms. "There has to be something about you, something you're not telling us."

I held back a scoff. There was nothing about me, nothing special or spectacular. Nothing Gifted. But my simple existence at Galdor Academy bothered these Gifteds. I sat beside them rather than served them. My form forcibly etched in their minds as a person rather than property.

"What brings you here, then?" I redirected the conversation. "There must be something about you that Mr. Harris liked."

I took a calculated risk. The wide stretch of his smile and direct sarcasm told me he liked when people did the same. Please be right.

Leo's smile widened as he leaned back in his chair. He shrugged. "I guess we're not like most Gifteds. Are we, Persy?"

I was right.

Leo looked to his sister, but she didn't exchange the same glance. Leo continued, "Skylar already mentioned that we don't have a House name, so it shouldn't be a surprise that's why we're here. You can't earn a House name, a respectable one at least, in Norburn."

The mention of Norburn piqued Kai's interest as he looked up from his food. "Norburn?" Kai asked. "You're from the crime capital of Iridion?"

Leo leaned forward, smiling with nothing behind his eyes. "I promise you. My life isn't as death-defying or cool as you're imagining."

Kai waved his hand defensively. "I apologize. As a possible future ERS, I simply want to learn more about what it's like to live in a place like Norburn."

"Oh, is that why you're here?" Leo asked. "To become an ERS in a place like Norburn?"

Kai shook his head. "No, I plan to be an ERS or doctor in my own hometown of Stone Creek."

"Ah, you are indeed a smart guy then."

"I like to think I'm analytical, yes," Kai agreed.

Leo made a hmph sound. "What makes a Mare like you want to become a doctor in the first place?"

Kai fell silent, but he finally responded. "I know basic medical terminology and medical experience through my time with Dr. Hansen. She's taught me everything I know." He paused. "And it's a promising career path. It'll be enough money for my mother to finally take a rest from working long hours at sea."

"Most people want to become a Royal Crest Knight like Mr. Harris," Leo noted.

The thought of Mr. Harris deviated the conversation. "I'm sure that Skylar wants nothing more than to become Mr. Harris," commented Fern.

I flinched at the thought of Skylar as if her black eyes could cut through me now simply by talking about her.

The rest of the Gifted fell silent too.

"I'm not too worried about Skylar," Leo finally spoke. As he waved his arms about, Persephone's fingers visibly flexed. "She's a classic rude and arrogant heiress. She's all flash rather than anything else."

At least one of us felt that way.

"And how does she differ from you so far?" Fern asked.

Leo smiled again and raised his eyebrows, taken aback by the slicing comment. He placed a pretentious hand over his chest. "I am a classic rude and arrogant street rat."

He turned back to me, pointing an accusing finger this time. "So, Nora, I will ask you again. Why are you here?"

Because I'm in way over my head?

Before I could place my thoughts together, Fern interjected. "Well, I can tell you why I'm here!" She clapped her hands lightly together as if the question had been directed toward her the entire time. "I'm here because my mom is a retired Royal Crest Knight, and so I would like to follow in her footsteps, as the next great Fairaway Avlis."

Leo glanced from Fern back to me. He leaned forward with squinted eyes.

"You're going to have to figure out a story because people are going to ask questions, and they're not going to stop because you're not supposed to be here. Take it from someone who also doesn't belong here."

I looked straight into his eyes with all the courage and conviction I could possibly muster. I spoke slowly, "Mr. Harris invited me. That is all there is to say."

Leo rolled his eyes by the sheer mention of Mr. Harris once again.

"That man is quite the enigma," the Mati confessed. "To think the First Senior Royal Crest Knight invited an Unfortunate to Galdor Academy. It boggles the mind at what an accomplished man can do with his time."

"It really does," Kai started to go off on a tangent about the First Senior Royal Crest Knight and its position when Fern cut him off.

"Yeah, Mr. Harris is quite strange. I agree. You know my cousin Cassidy, she's a Fera too, a spider one! She communicates with spiders all the time. Anyway, we never see her without at least one spider around for company. I just, I don't see any spiders with Mr. Harris."

Everyone looked at her with blank expressions. I'd never had to cater to Feras, but I knew Imitations were similar for their affinity to an animal.

"That's nice, Fern," Leo spoke on the edge of a condescending voice like he was talking to a child rather than someone his own age.

But Fern kept smiling, unbothered.

"Well, whatever the reason is," Leo relentlessly looked back to me. "I'm sure I'll find out soon enough."

I didn't respond, unable to look at him anymore. He hunted for information like Skylar, but in a different way. His words were edged, sure, but his shoulders relaxed by his side, leaning toward me in interest rather than malice. Skylar was on the verge of pouncing at me for answers, her face twisted in disbelief and rage. Leo's hostility was guarded, perhaps often needing information for safety rather than instilling fear.

I looked to the food in front of me, knowing that if I stared at him too long, his interest would only grow. Even Persephone's quietly imposing stature told me my secrets would leak out all at once without ever having to say a word.

We sat in silence for what felt like an eternity until Fern finally picked up the conversation, "So what do you guys think about our first classes? The Gift Technique ones?"

Persephone glanced at her brother as if to say exactly how she felt about the Gift Technique classes. Leo glanced back at her with a gentle smile.

Kai was the first to respond. "They should be very educational. I was telling Fern how excited I was to see if we actually talk about Isaac Winters and all the other important Mares of history. And of course, Avlis and Mati history."

"In all honesty, that might be the class you best me in, Nora," Leo said.

The words fell from my lips. "What makes you say that?"

He looked at Persephone. "Let's just say Gift technique is not my strong suit."

I guess we will find out, I thought, but I kept my mouth shut.

"Speaking of which, it looks like it's about time," Kai said, standing up.

The other Gifteds followed quickly after. I jumped up with them.

"Any chance you know what the first class focuses on?" Leo looked at the Mare.

"Oh, this one shouldn't have a focus," Kai clarified. "A mandatory overview really."

The more I learned, the more agitated I became. Mr. Harris omitted a lot of useful information. Was this his way of forcing me to interact with my Gifted classmates? Or was he completely out of his depth just as I was?

CHAPTER EIGHT

Class in Session

———

Valerie and I always dreamed about going back to school. We would spend our sparse sleeping hours rereading the Montgomery recipe books in hopes of learning beyond those pages. We would keep handwritten notes from Gifted invitation letters, crudely replicate the words on the same piece of torn paper, and burn the evidence in the next morning's fireplace.

It was an unattainable dream even before the Choosing Ceremony. Unfortunate girls stayed in school until chosen, and I needed to be chosen. The Montgomerys handpicked me at ten years old and then handpicked Valerie three years later when she was thirteen.

I remember when Neo first started school. My choosing meant there was enough income to expand his learning. I wasn't sure how important his reading skills would be while he was training to become a fisherman, but that alone set him apart from most—set him apart from me.

On impulse, I swung the door open for the two Gifteds with me. Fern and Kai passed, nodding their heads in acknowledgment. I followed after them, my lungs clenching into a gasp as I faced a classroom once again.

Four curved rows ascended upward along the wall to my left, uniformly staring at the large blackboard at the front of the room. I could see the grey haze of erased chalk along the blackboard from years of scribbled notes being written, erased, and rewritten.

Fern jumped up the stairs to the fourth row, frantically waving to us as Kai walked along the first row. I hesitated, contemplating who I should follow. Fern would be fake upset if I didn't join her; Kai had no reason to be upset either way.

"Come along, Nora." Kai gestured, giving me my answer.

"Losers!" shouted Fern.

Kai sat down in the precisely centered chair, not looking up as he responded. "Students who sit at the front pay the most attention."

I sat two seats away, leaving an empty chair between us. The wooden desk frame bore scratch marks like a disobedient servant, and the chair, worn but comfortable, had held countless Gifted students before me.

Fern scrambled downward to the second row, sitting in the chair directly behind Kai's. The Mati siblings sat on the far right of the third row, and Skylar, Cal, and Molly sat along the left-most wall on the fourth row.

Molly's glare burned brighter alongside the cruel Aura.

Silence filled the classroom as Mr. Harris entered, his face stern but his movements sluggish, frustrated.

"Greeting, students," he said in a monotone voice, his eyes staring daggers into the wall. "I trust you all met each other already, but we must complete an overview of each Gift in preparation for your combat exam. After all, you'll be competing with them throughout your full three years."

Fern slouched into her chair as a sign of protest; Molly sighed; I could practically hear Skylar's eyes roll as she scoffed.

Mr. Harris squinted. "Trust me. If I could get a regular Royal Crest Knight to lecture you on this, I would."

He turned toward the board, writing and speaking out loud for my benefit.

"Aura, of the wind. Stanton and Hilfrey are the Auras in your class. You two aren't allowed to respond. What are Auran advantages?"

Kai shot his hand up, "Agility, flight, and long-range combat."

"Very good." Mr. Harris nodded as he wrote those three attributes on the board. "The ability to control air means your opponent can have an aerial view of a battle, separate themselves from it even, and attack from a farther vantage point than other Gifts. Great. What about Lancer's Gift?"

He wrote "Mare, of the water" next.

Kai raised his hand again, but Mr. Harris pointed upward to Persephone. "Fluidity, potential ice abilities..." she tried to find a third quality.

"Hard to drown," added Leo.

I bristled at the thought of Valerie who *wasn't* hard to drown; Kai snapped his attention upward in alarm while Persephone lightly hit her brother. Leo chuckled, winking at the Mare below.

Mr. Harris wrote the three phrases on the board anyway, starting to write an "A" when Kai interrupted his progress.

"Actually, I have a question before we continue," Kai blurted with excitement. "Are we going to be talking about any Ice Mares at all during this class?"

"Oh, there you go again, talking about Isaac Winters," Fern teased.

Skylar rolled her eyes. "Ugh, I do not need to hear that name right now."

"You know Isaac Winters?" Kai shouted.

"Know?" Skylar scoffed. "I spent way too much time with that Mare when we were younger. He's weirdly quiet, and his mother is crazy. Elevated status and changing your Gift name all for an Ice Mare child? Ridiculous."

She wrapped her hands around Cal's closest arm. "Did you like Isaac?"

Cal's eyes darted away at the sudden attention for a moment, half shrugging.

"You know Isaac Winters?" Kai repeated himself with complete disbelief.

"Wait…" Fern connected the dots. "Isaac is a *student?*"

"Yes?"

"Why would they be teaching about Isaac Winters in a Gift Technique class?" Fern demanded.

"It's just not common at all! And at his age?" Kai tried to defend himself. "He's been here for so long, I thought—"

"Lancer," Mr. Harris cut in. "Mr. Winters will not be discussed in this course, but you'll be tested on your own ice ability if you ever want to be an ERS."

Kai hesitated, staring at his fingers as he fiddled with them as if ice would form in front of him. It didn't. "Right," the Mare said in a low voice.

"Let's talk about Avlis, of the trees. Now Fairaway," Mr. Harris turned to Fern, "do not shout out any answers."

Fern slouched further in her chair.

"We typically see Avlis act more grounded than Auras," Skylar prompted, "using a lot more of their lower body when using their Gift. Avlis can also specialize in either earth or plant life, though earth comes more naturally to most." Her face scrunched, glancing upward in thought. "Do we need three?"

"No." Mr. Harris finished scribbling on the board. "Mati is the last elemental Gift, or of the flame. Advantages?"

Molly's snicker behind me twisted knots in my back, but no one said anything. I kept my gaze forward.

Leo spoke up, "Dexterity, full-body techniques, and unpredictability."

"How is unpredictability an advantage?" Skylar doubted.

"It's a disadvantage for the opponent."

An object hit my head; I flinched as a crumbled paper ball landed on the floor next to me. *Ignore it,* I thought. But it stayed within the corner of my eye as Skylar and Leo bickered about Mati techniques.

Their voices grew louder as I leaned down, picked up the ball, and opened it. One three letter word was scribbled in black ink, a word I recognized but needed to confirm.

"What does this say?" I leaned toward Kai for confirmation.

He took the paper from me, cringed, and then glanced from the note to the fourth row and back again. Fern perked up at Kai's sudden movements, leaning forward.

"What's that?" She snatched the crumbled paper from Kai.

"It says 'PET,'" Kai spoke quickly. "I'd just ignore—"

"Hey!" Fern swerved around and pointed straight at Molly. Skylar and Leo halted their argument for this new one. "No *snake* Imitation has any right calling others a pet!"

No, no, no, no. I focused all of my energy on remaining completely still as Molly hissed. "Oh, are you feeling empathetic to something other than a tree?" Molly stood up, arching her back. "She's still property of the Montgomery House, so *back off* Fairaway."

Leo fanned the flames. "Hey, Molly, if I cut your head off, would you still wriggle and twitch like a real snake?"

Molly snarled in his direction, baring her fangs.

"Enough!" The lights flickered as Mr. Harris's yell rippled through the lecture hall. All previous thoughts vanished from my mind as the entire class straightened and silenced.

"You're competing against each other to learn how to defend yourself in various scenarios. You'll also act like a team for the next three years. I suggest you start *now*."

He stared for several more heartbeats before moving on. "Now Imitation, of the animal." He wrote the Gift on the board. "Montgomery embodies the features and characteristics of a designated animal. In this case, a snake. Advantages?"

I waited several seconds before answering, "Miss Molly has her fangs, infrared sight, and sense of smell to her advantage as a snake Imitation."

The corner of Mr. Harris's mouth twitched in an encouraging smile. "And what about Imitations as a whole, Nora?"

His use of my name meant I needed to respond. I tried speaking louder. "Most Imitations have sharp teeth or claws, and each one is different so it's difficult to assume their actions."

I watched Mr. Harris transcribe my words onto the board in front of me; I appreciated each absentminded nod of his head as I spoke.

We continued to run through the rest of the Gifts.

"Makan, of the soul, seen in Prince Cassius of Iridion. He can transition between the visible and invisible plane.

"Lux, of the light, seen in our Head Minister Gabriel. He can see regardless of lighting and as minister, claims to see the Divine through his eyes.

"Nox, of the dark, seen in Princess Maya of Iridion. She is poisonous to the touch of all organic material.

"Fera, of the heart, seen through me. They can communicate and empathize with a designated animal.

"And Animus, of the mind. Known abilities include telekinesis and mind reading. But that Gift only runs in the royal family as seen in our first king, King Alston. No current members of the royal family have this Gift."

Mr. Harris clapped his hands to snap us back to attention. "That's all we need to review today. We'll focus on your advantages and hone your strengths for your first year, so keep that in mind for your first combat exam this Friday."

As several students stood to leave, Skylar outstretched her arm. "Mr. Harris, what *possible* advantage does an Unfortunate have that we should be aware of for the combat exam?"

A dread sank deeper into my chest, freezing my body in place.

"If you're still bitter about why I recruited an Unfortunate as a student, that is mine and Nora's business. She'll be expected to perform her best during the combat exam. The same is expected of you. Never underestimate your opponent, Stanton."

Skylar scoffed as she descended the steps, halting in front of me. Her relaxed posture didn't fool me. Anger festered within those black eyes.

I did my best to maintain eye contact, though every fiber in my being told me to look away, to look down, to become invisible. If only I was born a Makan.

"We'll see. Who knows what can happen during a combat exam. *Accidents* happen."

Nothing Gifteds ever did was an accident. *What would you do if you were with me now, Valerie?*

My voice started out shaky but become stern. "Well, me being here *isn't* an accident. And I won't be holding back either at the combat exam."

Skylar's face grew longer as her eyes widened, her head tilting as her body leaned backward.

I stared straight into her Gifted eyes, holding the stare for as long as I possibly could.

Skylar turned away first and charged toward the exit, refusing to acknowledge my presence any longer.

Once she, Molly, and Cal were out of the room, I finally breathed again, not realizing that I held my breath in the first place.

Four more days.

CHAPTER NINE

Uprooted Expectations

———

I awoke to the sunrise like clockwork. My body shot upright, running through the morning checklist until I recognized the plain walls as the dormitory instead of the Montgomery mansion.

Sighing, I leaned back, teetering on the edge of sleep and feeling my spine sink back into the soft pillow. I hesitated, contemplating the consequences, when Fern's arms stretched out gently in the bed beside me.

She let out a big yawn, bringing her hands back to her chest. Her eyes opened as she turned on her side to look at me. Small white flowers that weren't there when she fell asleep dotted her red hair.

"Good morning," she breathed.

A lump formed in my throat. It had been a long time since I awoke with another person. Now I was in a room with seven Gifteds.

She raised an eyebrow at my wide-eyed stare. "Better look away before your face stays like that permanently," Fern mumbled her words before rising. "You look like you've seen a ghost."

My eyes fluttered as I looked away.

An alarm blared on the far-right side of the room. Several Gifteds groaned at once, shifting in their beds. Skylar reached out to stop her alarm, taking only a breath before getting up and making her bed. I jumped out of bed too, occupying myself with the blanket.

Afterward, I opened the drawer installed in my desk. Mr. Harris's note from yesterday still greeted me here: "I guessed on size, but I'm sure they fit," signed with his signature. Wearing the pajamas from the drawer last night, I would say he had guessed correctly. I rummaged through, looking for an outfit that resembled anything Molly would wear during her training sessions.

Looking up for guidance, I noticed Skylar was already wearing her workout attire—a surprisingly simplistic black tank top with black form-fitting shorts, exposing her muscular arms. She tied her hair into a tight bun atop her head.

I looked through the drawer again, landing on something similar—a plain black T-shirt and grey leggings. I inhaled deeply, staring at the clothes for longer than I should have. Was I really doing this? Could I even do this? Anxiety bubbled in my chest. Valerie should have received this offer instead of me. She would have loud mouthed Skylar at first sight; she would have donned the workout clothes in the middle of the room if that forced Gifteds to look away. Simply my presence was bothersome. I hadn't earned any valid reasons for the constant side-glances.

I took another deep breath. This wasn't the time for second thoughts.

I still dressed in the communal bathroom down the hall, coming back to most of my fellow students already dressed and preparing to leave for breakfast. The only person still in bed was Leo, who held his covers close to his scrunched face.

Without saying anything, Skylar grabbed the air with her fingers and pulled back to her chest. Leo's blankets shot backward as a gust of wind blew them away. The Mati cursed in protest, punching in Skylar's direction. An ignition of bright red and yellow exploded from his fist in an upward motion, the heat washing over the room.

"Are you crazy?" Skylar yelled, stepping back in a defensive stance. "You could have burned me, you imbecile!"

The popcorn ceiling crackled.

Water flowed between Kai's curved fingers, but Persephone already stood over the property damage, her left palm held out fixed while her right arm gently rotated in a circular motion. The fire swayed in the direction of her right hand, stretching as Persephone's unseen force brought the flame to her hand. Once the fire hovered over her fingers, she slowly lowered her arms down. Near her chest, she covered her palm with her free hand. Grey smoke escaped through her fingertips until she clamped her hands together and the fire was completely extinguished.

All the while, Leo stood upright in his bed with a grizzled expression as Skylar screeched at him.

Fern leaned downward so Kai and I could hear her. "Breakfast?" she asked.

None of us looked away from the scene unfolding before us. "Yeah, that sounds good," we agreed at the same time.

***

Mr. Harris led the class at the fourth training field. We stretched in synchronized movements, extending our left leg out with our right knee bent and then switching sides.

I followed each command, watching the Gifteds around me for any reassurance of my movements.

"Okay!" Mr. Harris clapped his hands together. "Set up in pairs, preferably of the same Gift if you can, and practice forming and blocking simple attacks."

Skylar and Cal clapped their hands together immediately. Leo and Persephone naturally formed a pair; Kai turned to Molly with a reserved expression as Fern claimed me with a stern grip on my shoulder. I held down my flinch, inhaling the smell of fresh pine.

Mr. Harris was already upon us. "Since you're a special case, Nora, practice blocking Fern's simple attacks instead of throwing your own for now," he ordered.

His voice wasn't as low as I had wanted him to be, exposing my disadvantage to the class. Skylar rolled her eyes, "I'll go against the Unfortunate, Mr. Harris. She needs to defend against me after all."

"That won't be necessary, Stanton," Mr. Harris said, walking away to observe the class in full.

Fern broke the silence first, squealing a small, "Yes!" to herself and reaching out to my face with her hand. I stepped back too quickly at the sudden attack, falling down on my arm. The Avlis held her palm out with her eyebrows ruffled, "That was a high-five, Nora."

"Oh," was all I could let out.

"Maybe we should start out *basic,* basic," Fern prompted. "You need to keep your ground when someone comes your way instead of flinching—or falling."

She extended her arm out. I gingerly accepted her hand.

But Fern suddenly gasped, letting go of me in mid-air. Stumbling, I huffed as I gained my bearings. The Avlis shoved me closer to whisper, though her words came out as a sharp squeal. "Look over there! I think it's *him!*" She called out to Kai who held water out in front of him, "Kai, do you think it's him?"

We turned to where Fern was staring. A sea of other students greeted my attention.

Molly groaned irritably as Fern distracted her partner. "I do." Kai's voice hinted at curiosity.

I gave up my search. "Who are we looking at?"

"Right over there." Fern pointed obviously at a student setting up a space for himself, securing his hands in fingerless gloves. She harshly whispered, "It has to be Prince Cassius."

I watched the prince pick a staff from his duffel bag on the ground, idly spinning the object between his fingers while searching for something with his free hand. The staff disappeared and reappeared from my sight, but it never vanished. The prince's hand still clasped the object as it shifted from the visible and invisible planes.

"Using a weapon? It has to be," replied Kai, shaking his head. "A Makan can only do so much before becoming..." He teetered on a treacherous word, leaning in closer to us to say, "Useless."

"Hey, my sister is a Makan!" Fern defended, punching him in the arm. He winced, stumbling with the sudden action.

Useless? I thought. Like an Unfortunate? I watched him twirl the staff, flashing between visible and invisible, and found I wanted a weapon too.

"What's wrong with that?" I found myself asking.

The two Gifteds stared at me. "Let's just say he's first born but not first in line," Kai whispered back. "Princess Maya could disintegrate his weapon in a second."

Fern tried to hush his words by making a sharp *shh* sound. "Don't say that! He might hear you!"

But the Avlis's sudden and loud actions were enough to earn his attention. The prince's eyes locked on to me. I frantically looked away, glad to feel Fern's pull on my arm in the other direction. Subtle.

Fern stood firmly in front of me, the ground enclosing on her shoes. "We're going to work on your defensive instincts now," she explained, "but we're going to tell you exactly what to expect so you'll be fine."

I nodded.

Skylar was by far the loudest, praising herself for artful dodges or tactful attacks. I could see her perform in the corner of my vision and feel her eyes glance about my body as if I had a large red target painted on my back.

Fern's voice brought my attention back into focus. "I'm going to uproot the earth now."

I inhaled sharply as her foot kicked upward. The ground erupted upward as a solidified force; I stepped back, catching my balance.

"You're already light on your feet so that's good!" Fern encouraged with a smile. It felt genuine. "Okay, I'm going to throw some blocks at you, and you'll have to block them. Try using the back of your forearm. Don't forget to protect your face!"

I nodded again, my body tensing up in anticipation.

We stared at each other as Fern adjusted her stance, her left leg bent in a lunge formation while her right leg extended straight back. She rotated, pointing her left foot toward me. She brought her fists together slowly to show me her movements, pushing forward with her elbows bent.

The uprooted ground broke apart at the top, launching as her arms extended outward. It flew faster than I anticipated, grazing off my arm with a large thud before breaking into solid pieces like stone and hitting me in the face.

I spat dirt out of my mouth as Fern tried keeping a neutral expression. "What did I say about protecting your face?" she asked.

"I'll try to do better," I replied, placing my forearms out from my face in an awkward stance. I've only ever had to hold myself in this stance right before a beating. But I was able to fight back this time.

Fern nodded, adjusting her stance before launching another section of the uprooted earth.

Instinctively, my arm rotated to meet the projectile coming toward my chest. The block made impact with my forearm and broke apart more evenly. My feet dragged in the dirt as the momentum pushed me back a few inches.

"That was great!" Fern clapped her hands, jumping up and down.

My stance loosened as several of the other Gifteds looked our way. Fern didn't notice them. "No! Don't lose the stance now!" she spoke in an ecstatic voice. "Let's try again. This time two at a time."

Two at once? My shoulders started to slouch at the idea, but I forced myself to emulate my original stance as Fern waited.

The Avlis shot more forward. I followed their path, both successfully blocked. Another piece shot forward without warning. I inhaled, dodging. My feet stayed partially arched as I looked at Fern with a bewildered expression.

Her green eyes pierced through me. She jabbed her left and right fists; more layers of the uprooted earth cut through the air. My eyes searched frantically, blocking some and dodging others.

Dirt clung to my skin, but the more I dodged, the more Fern attacked until she ran out of material. My body stayed hunched and frozen in a defensive stance anyway. I slowly lowered my arms, cleaning them off.

The Avlis smiled, "You're a fast learner."

I wasn't sure how to respond properly to the compliment, so I remained quiet. Fern went back into her original stance, but her right leg bounced lightly. "We're going to try something different now," she said, her lips now in a smirk. "I'm going to attack you by uprooting the earth, and you'll remain light on your feet to dodge away."

So I'll be completely blind to your attacks, I thought. "Okay," I breathed, not entirely trusting that smile.

Fern bounced using her right foot. I watched her jerky movements in hopes of finding an indication of her attack. The Avlis swung her leg forward in a punt. The ground rumbled as it twisted and lifted by her command, solidified in taller and thicker slabs. I zigzagged, my weight on my toes, sprinting in short spurts. The earth's violent rumble was my only indication. The distance between us widened as Fern continued.

I jumped out of the way of another attack, but the wind suddenly held my right foot in the air by an unseen force. Unbalanced, I fell on my left side, forcing my forearm down first to take the brunt of the pressure.

Fern stopped abruptly.

Skylar's uncontrollable laughter echoed in my ears, bouncing in my skull.

"Nice going, Unfortunate!" she called.

Molly snickered along. I could feel the burn of curious eyes against my face as the insult rippled through the entire training field.

I stood upright.

Leaning forward while staring straight at the Aura, I ignored the consequences and yelled back. "You did that, you cheat!"

Skylar's face quickly twisted into rage. I flinched with a step backward, netted by Fern who stood in front of me, twisted her body to point at Skylar, and kicked her leg in one decisive blow. The Aura screamed as dirt sprayed and caked her body.

The wind picked up. But the air subsided quickly as Skylar lost all the red in her cheeks, and words drifted away from her lips. She stood there awestruck and started rapidly removing the dirt clumps from her hair like she was meeting the Divine.

I glanced to my right in time to see Prince Cassius approach. Several other students watched him near, too, bowing their heads in quick fluid motions as he passed. Fern straightened her own ponytail, and most of the Gifteds placed their arms behind their back in a rigid posture.

Prince Cassius's blue eyes twinkled brightly under the sun. "Are you okay?" he asked.

I stared blankly while Fern dipped her head. My eyes widened, trying to mimic her movement in a delayed reaction. "Fine, Your Highness," I stuttered, failing to meet his unwavering gaze.

My hands folded naturally at my waist. An awkward silence developed in the small space between us as the prince stared as though searching for something unseen.

"Your Highness," Skylar cut in, already lowered in a curtsey. The other Gifteds in sight bowed too as he turned. "What a pleasure, I—"

"You called her an Unfortunate," Prince Cassius said flatly.

Skylar faltered, her mouth agape. "Oh, I was just being high spirited, sir." She tried desperately to find the right words to save herself and fast. "I'm actually—"

But the prince already turned back to me, his eyebrows ruffled and eyes squinted. My shoulders tightened and scrunched up as he looked right through me.

"Are you the Unfortunate Mr. Harris recruited?" His voice was surprisingly soft like it was a title to be proud of.

My neck leaned forward in a deeper bow. "Yes, Your Highness."

"It's 'yes, sir' now," Kai spoke with one hand hiding his lips in Prince Cassius's direction. "You say 'Your Highness' in greeting, in passing, and in farewell."

I involuntarily jumped at the error, looking up with bulged eyes and speaking in an alarmed voice. "Yes, sir!"

A small laugh erupted from the prince's throat, his lips forming a smile.

"Your Highness," Mr. Harris's voice sounded startled as he approached. I glanced at my instructor with frantic eyes. Mr. Harris placed his hand over his heart and bowed quickly. "I didn't expect you to introduce yourself."

"It felt timely," replied the prince, keeping his gaze toward me.

Skylar's throat clenched in a gasp as she tried to find the right words to redeem herself, but nothing came out.

Mr. Harris glanced at the Aura and back to the prince with his lips in a straight line.

"Nora," Mr. Harris began, "this is Prince Cassius, First Born of the Third Auran Reign, House of Iridion. He'll act as your second point of contact for your time at Galdor Academy. He's been training much longer than the other students, and can help you learn just how to..." the instructor tried to find a delicate word, "...defend yourself against Gifteds."

I returned my focus to Prince Cassius, only to find that his had never left my face.

"If it's all the same to you, sir," Mr. Harris continued, looking to the prince, "I'd like to see how she reacts to her Gifted classmates before you two commence."

If it was the same to *him?* I couldn't train with someone that important. I wasn't even a palace servant before now. If I messed up at the royal level...

My hands clasped tighter together and my mouth kept wired shut.

The prince nodded. "You're the instructor," he agreed, one of his eyes closing. Did the Prince of Iridion just wink at me? "I'll be nearby if anything else escalates."

My lips formed to make the "s" sound in *sir* when I remembered what Kai had said.

"Your Highness," I bent my body in a small bow as he walked away, the shake in my voice unflattering.

Time stood still as everyone continued to stare. Skylar and Molly remained frozen in place, wide-eyed, their faces as red as Molly's hair. I took the opportunity to align my lips into a smirk before turning back to Fern for more drills—now under the prince's supervision.

Three more days until our combat exam.

CHAPTER TEN

Sinking Her Fangs

Three days dwindled into tomorrow, which dwindled into today—a repetition of classes and training in preparation.

Grey clouds covered the sky, hiding the sun. A water droplet smacked against my shoulder as I recoiled. *No. Not today.*

Mr. Harris greeted us at the third training field, the smallest of the training fields, which resided along the South Wall. Skylar and Cal were already there too, undoubtedly aware of their opponents. The Aura glared at me as I approached. I made a conscious effort this time to steady my pace and walk beside Fern instead of hiding behind her tall form. Prince Cassius worked idly in the background, but his eyes scanned in our direction.

Adding myself to the line facing Mr. Harris, I crossed my arms behind my back and mimicked standing at attention. An open space separated us from the First Senior Royal Crest Knight.

Mr. Harris wasted no time once we all arrived.

"Before you commence your first-year combat exam, remember that you can do almost anything necessary to win as long as your Gift remains within the training field borders. Do not kill each other during the first exam." He pointed to the lines cut into the dirt on either side of the space in front of us. "All fights will be completed when I blow my whistle, and the winner will be announced immediately."

"Let's get started with Fairaway verses Lancer."

"Yes!" Fern jumped in the air as she stepped out of formation. Mr. Harris gave her a disgruntled look. The Avlis tried to quickly adjust and imitate Kai's serious posture, but her excitement remained.

Both students faced each other.

Another droplet fell in front of my face.

Mr. Harris blew the whistle.

Fern's arms immediately swung upward. The grass beneath her feet followed her command, growing rapidly and wrapping around Kai's frame. The Mare managed to plant his right leg backward, and his right arm shot up toward the sky. Water sprang out of the soil, drying the ground out in the process. The liquid sliced through the vegetation like glass.

Fern hunched low, her forearms first crossed together, and then shakily separated. The earth ripped apart behind her.

Kai sprang forward.

The ground shifted under Fern's feet at the last second in a dodge. Striking air, Kai fell into a pit of Fern's design. The Avlis swung her fists in an upward motion, and the earth enclosed around him. Kai's head and part of his shoulders remained above ground.

Fern jumped in the air with a celebratory cheer. A white flower transformed in front of Kai's exposed face seemingly out of nowhere as he stared at her with a surprised expression. He couldn't calculate that fast enough.

Mr. Harris blew his whistle again. "Fairaway wins. Excellent work," he noted, writing something down on his clipboard. "Please release Lancer now."

Fern nodded, her fist connecting above her head and then separating as she lowered her arms to her chest. The ground rumbled as she moved, loosening and parting for Kai to free himself.

His defeat happened in under a minute. I stared for too long as Kai swatted the dirt off his clothes and walked back to the formation with his back slouched, his eyes downward in thought.

Fern, however, skipped back to the line, giggling as she gave me a wink.

Mr. Harris tapped the pencil in his hand, "Montgomery versus Persephone."

The two Gifteds stepped out and faced each other.

When Mr. Harris whistled, Persephone flattened her palm. A spark ignited in her hand, but the flame danced without burning the Mati's flesh.

Molly hovered, her head bobbing and weaving as the light reflected in her eyes. She hissed, exposing her fangs and lunging.

Persephone dodged, but Molly recoiled and lunged again, successfully biting into the Mati's upper arm.

Persephone grunted, and fire ignited along her arm in retaliation. Molly screamed, her entire body flailing as flames licked her face. The Imitation detached her fangs, her expression scrunching in disgust as bubbles distorted her lips.

Persephone winced as she tried to move her wounded limb in an upward direction. Her free arm extended in a quick fluid motion, and fire erupted to Persephone's height, circling the two Gifteds seemingly out of thin air.

On the sidelines, we all stepped back as the air swelled in a bright red hue. The flames licked the dried grass from the last combat, the rain not strong enough to dull its rage.

Molly shifted her head in a frantic search. *Her infrared sight,* I thought. Bright red, orange, and yellow must be rendering that part of her Imitation Gift useless.

Persephone wasted no time shifting to the offensive and pushing Molly to the ground. The two Gifteds collapsed on each other. Persephone held her fingers onto Molly's face, one hand on her forehead and the other around her throat. The Imitation struggled, her mouth open to let out a last-effort hiss.

Mr. Harris blew his whistle and scribbled more notes. "Excellent win, Persephone," he praised. "Disengage all fires."

Without moving, the flames shrank and dissipated, leaving the grass withered and a brown color. The two Gifteds remained in the same position as Molly continued to expose her fangs and wiggled in a futile display under Persephone's hold.

Mr. Harris whistled in a harsher, shrill octave.

The Mati backed away this time, outreaching her hand to Molly. The Imitation swatted the sportsmanship with a hiss, muttering a distasteful comment through her burn mark as she rose. Persephone gently held her own wound, gritting her teeth as smoke released from her fingers. After several seconds, the Mati removed her hand and revealed a red patch of skin.

The two Gifteds returned to the line formation.

"Reminder that you can check into the infirmary at any time after this exam," Mr. Harris noted. He gestured to the large white building to our immediate left without looking up from his clipboard.

The infirmary's red letters stared back at me.

Nora.

Nora.

"Nora!"

I snapped my attention to Mr. Harris. How long had the class been staring at me? Skylar was already standing in the open space, her faint snicker bouncing in my ear.

"You're up."

Stepping out, the white building remained at the corner of my vision. The sparse droplets became a light drizzle as a shiver ran down my spine.

No. Focus.

My orders were clear. I needed to fight Skylar. Recalling my impulse to chase after the Anti-Gifteds Movement only days earlier, my legs moved on their own here too. If my mind were to wander about the consequences too long, I would most certainly flee. This was no time to panic. *Easier said than done.*

The whistle sliced through my unsteady heart.

Skylar charged immediately. On instinct, I ran backward to avoid a collision, the sixth Unfortunate Law of Servitude branded along the edges of my mind. An Unfortunate cannot harm any Gifted under any jurisdiction.

But that was under Divine power. Mr. Harris assured me I had that jurisdiction. Even so, breaking out of that habit wouldn't be easy.

My foot skidded across the drawn line that denoted our combat exam space. Skylar snickered, jogging backward. A fake-out.

Taking a deep breath, I stepped back into position. Skylar watched with her hands on her hips.

Focus.

The Aura bent to the ground and jumped upward, her feet floating a little in the air. In an instant, I shrieked as my body launched from the ground. I rose, untethered.

Skylar dropped me from the sky; I fell onto my back with a large thud. A mix of dried dirt and mud sank into my clothes. I gasped, my body disconnected from my mind. *Get up!*

Skylar repeated the move, my body thrown effortlessly into the air and slammed into the dirt.

"I thought you would be at least interesting."

Thud.

"Not even a challenge. No surprise."

Thud.

I fell onto my stomach this time, my breaths short and rapid. My fingers clawed into the soil as I tried to rise.

"Honestly pathetic!"

Wind shot from Skylar's fist. I yelled, dodging and propelling myself forward.

Skylar gasped as I sailed by while throwing a punch, inches from the Aura's face. She stepped and leaned her body backward to dodge but barely succeeded, her expression twisted in surprise and disbelief.

Lifting her palms, a gust of wind followed her command, weakly throwing me in the air. I clumsily backflipped but succeeded in the landing.

I charged forward again. Skylar yelled in frustration, kicking her leg into the air. The wind underneath my right foot lifted me off balance. Before I could fall, another gust slammed into my chest, knocking me back to the ground.

I gasped for breath as my chest hit the earth, knocking all air from my lungs.

Mr. Harris blew the whistle. "Win for Stanton," he announced.

I gritted my teeth as I failed to move, flexing my fingers before regaining control of my arms. Lifting myself slowly, I noticed Skylar staring down at me. The Aura inhaled sharply, pulling lose strands of hair back into place. Her glare never left my form as she walked back to the formation next to Cal.

As I finally stood, the adrenaline of the combat wore off. I fought off the wobble in my legs while I made my way back into formation. My heart thumped loudly in my ears, the only indication that I was still alive.

As I rejoined Fern, the Avlis hunched down and clapped her hands together in a light tapping sound.

You did it, she mouthed.

I gave Fern a side-glance as to say, *I still lost,* but I immediately regretted the thought. What had I really expected fighting a Gifted? I've been trained my entire life to keep my head down and remember what my mother instilled years before my first Choosing Ceremony—how to talk to House guests to keep your safety, how to move out of a Gifted's way to keep your job, how to keep yourself so small and so compact and among the shadows that you hardly existed at all.

Yet, here I was, standing in line like I had eight years prior. Except now, these were Gifteds training for glory rather than Unfortunates following their mandate. I had lost against Skylar, but my forming bruises held a different meaning. Not of punishment but of…. I couldn't think of the right word. I rubbed my thumb gently against my aching chest. This pain felt earned rather than all the relentless times Molly pushed me down the stairs for laughs or when Mrs. Montgomery meticulously followed me around the house those grueling first few weeks, slapping my arm for completing tasks to the woman's dissatisfaction.

For a moment, I didn't notice the rain.

I watched my other classmates fight against each other. Kai regained his dignity by defeating Cal within a narrow margin. Leo's carefree movements challenged Skylar's sharp ones, but she managed to beat him quicker than I imagined.

The first of the loser brackets began. We could not prepare for our next opponent.

"Nora versus Montgomery," Mr. Harris declared.

I turned to my Gifted master as she stepped out. *Mr. Harris, you are a ruthless man.*

Hesitantly, I faced Molly. Insatiable black slits for eyes stared back.

I fixated my attention on her, waiting as she stalked forward.

Trying to emulate the Gifteds before her, I shifted my feet into a defensive stance.

Molly's mouth opened, revealing sharp fangs and a forked tongue. Closer. And closer. My back prickled, anticipating her attack as I had for so many years before.

She struck.

Against better instincts, my elbow connected with Molly's mouth. Hard.

The Imitation stumbled back. Did I draw blood? Yes, Molly's gums formed a dark red color.

I froze for a moment at the sight. I'd never defended myself against a Gifted, let alone my Gifted House before. I should be put to death for that.

A high-pitched hiss left her lips as she sprinted toward me again.

I tried mimicking Skylar's fluid movements, arching my back and weaving against Molly's open jaws. But the Gifted closed the space. Molly's hands clamped down on my cheeks. She pushed me to the ground, squeezing her hands together and crushing my skull.

My hands shot upward, pressing against the Imitation's neck. Molly's panted breath wetted my cheek, her long and pointed teeth hovering over my throat. Was I in the same position as Valerie when she died—struggling against a Gifted above her?

A hiss boiled from Molly's throat as she twisted her neck and attacked my exposed skin. I screamed, and a warm liquid cascaded down my shoulder as she bit down.

Tears formed in my eyes as the pain exploded, my fingers squeezing into Molly's neck, hoping she would release first. My arms shook violently with each passing second.

The shrill call of Mr. Harris's whistle ended the fight there, "There's no killing each other on the first day!"

A growl reverberated from Molly's throat as she irritably detached her fangs, pushing herself off me. Blood, *my* blood, caked her mouth. My arms collapsed onto my chest. I stayed immobile on the ground, looking up at the grey hue of the world. Rain sprayed against my cold face.

"Montgomery wins." Mr. Harris's voice felt far away. Black spots began dotting my vision, growing larger as my eyes fluttered. *Stay awake,* I urged. *Stay—*

CHAPTER ELEVEN

The Senior Circle

Bright lights suffocated my vision as I awoke. A whispered, "She's awake," floated through the air as the room squinted into focus.

White walls, white sheets, white tile—this new environment was completely void of color except for a flash of red hair to my right.

"Where am I?"

"Infirmary." Kai's voice came from the left.

Oh.

"Don't worry." Fern's delicate and decisive finger pushed a strand of hair away from my face. "You weren't out long."

"And it was more from stress and exhaustion than blood loss," Kai added.

Sitting up, I winced as I placed pressure on Molly's bite wound. Secure, white bandages wrapped around my arm. Panic must have consumed my expression as Fern began assuring me. "You should bounce back really quickly."

"Molly's bite marks didn't go far enough to cause any concern for permanent damage," Kai added the important information again. "Montgomery's tactic to dig into your arm was brilliant if you two weren't supposed to train together."

A brilliant attack indeed through Gifted eyes.

Opposing Gifteds had endured similar vicious consequences during matches against her in the past—splitting skin I had to clean, patch, and mend. I'd seen what she did to Valerie when defending my mistake. Venom blackened her brown skin. Examining my veins, Molly didn't do the same to me.

This was an act of uncharacteristic mercy—a final warning to what I had in store if I stayed here.

She did what she had to do to win. I removed any doubt of an alternative motive. *I need to do the same.*

Doubt seeped into that statement. But how?

"How did the rankings turn out?" I tried deviating my thoughts.

"You should have seen me against Cal!" boasted Fern. "I—"

"Yes," Kai interrupted her, "Fern did really well. Ranked herself fourth in the class." The Avlis posed herself at the compliment, but Kai ignored her as he continued.

"Persephone is currently in first, followed by Skylar, Leo, Fern, Molly, me, Cal, and then you."

Last place shouldn't have been a shock, but anger and embarrassment still tugged at my brain. "I have to move up in the rankings," I declared, shifting on the cot and slowly standing.

"You need to rest for at least a day," Kai opposed. A flinch rippled through my body as he grabbed my free arm.

I closed my eyes and slowly opened them. "Please get your hand off me."

He pulled away, and I could breathe again. Irritability bubbled in my chest.

Fern reached out for support as I stood, but I denied her as well.

"How do you expect to train like this?" asked Kai.

I huffed as I stood, my shoulder aching and almost bearable. The Unfortunate who mended me did her job well. "Hopefully I still have a prince willing to help me."

***

Other students purposefully positioned themselves a good distance away, even walking in an intentional semicircle past, some of their stares more obvious than others.

Two days after the combat exam, and my skin was almost completely scarred over. Bandages still hid Molly's bite mark from passing glances.

"Are you experienced at all with a weapon?" Prince Cassius asked, rummaging through his bag.

I snapped my attention to the prince, my throat clenched and mouth dry. Shaking my head, I communicated my inexperience.

"That's okay," he assured, taking out another staff noticeably shorter in size than the one he held. The prince examined this new weapon before handing it to me. "Usually, your bo staff will match your height, but it's not too far off. This will do for practice purposes."

A bo staff? I gingerly accepted the weapon, surprised by its lightness. It resembled a wooden broom without bristles, and I adjusted the staff to its full height. He was right; the end came to about my cheek.

Prince Cassius held his staff horizontally in front of himself, facing me. I mimicked his stance, my back tensing. Too many Gifteds watched us.

"Don't worry." The prince's blue eyes fixated on me, ignoring his surroundings. "Students outside your class don't know what you are. They think you're just the poor soul saddled with helping me—maybe a Lux forced to a supportive role."

What Kai said earlier that week lingered in my memory. Pointing out the prince's Gift in any capacity *in front of him* had to be off-limits. I remained silent, nodding and forcing my eyes to meet his.

"We'll stretch with the bo staff first so you can get more comfortable," he said, pulling his arms over his head, "and you can go easy with that shoulder wound."

I didn't respond, following along and extending my arms back to center. We did that repetitively ten times. I ignored my aching arm muscles.

Prince Cassius stopped; I halted.

"Cross your arms and hold for ten seconds," he instructed. The staff fully rotated by my command. We switched sides and held, a scorch developing in my shoulder with each rep.

The prince lost his stance as he moved the staff to one hand, gripping one end and extending the staff horizontally out to the side. I continued to mirror him throughout the stretch.

He came back to the start, holding the bo staff out from his chest. "Try and see if you can do this," he prompted, bringing his palms closer to the center of the staff underhanded.

I watched as he slowly rotated the staff in a circular motion. His arms crossed, rotated, and released in a methodical pattern; his stance straightened as he kept the staff centralized; his hands sped up after several rotations, twisting and turning over each other as the bo staff flowed gracefully over his fingers.

The prince stopped abruptly. "Give it a try." He smiled, motioning the actions again in slower, deliberate movements.

The staff wobbled in my loose grip, sloppily completing one rotation. He twirled the staff as he spoke. "This exercise helps gain balance. Get a feel for a few minutes."

I didn't respond, looking down at my hands. A second rotation was complete. I lost count of the prince's movements as he sped up again, though I was sure he wasn't counting anyway. A third rotation was complete.

My hands rotated faster. A fourth and fifth rotation were complete.

Prince Cassius repeated the exercise across from me as I twirled the staff faster and faster. Strange how my back tensed, apprehensive. Was I in the correct stance?

I faltered, my hands no longer near the center. The weapon slammed into the ground, clumsily falling from my fingers. I froze, locking eyes with the prince.

He stared back, chuckling softly. But he faltered, his staff fleeing from the scene in one rapid motion, victoriously spinning in the air and falling triumphantly in the grass several feet away.

We stared at its resting place.

My mouth twitched as a laugh bubbled from my lungs. I pressed a hand against my chest in hopes of subduing any insubordination to no avail. But I was not the only one. Prince Cassius failed to hold his laughter too. We giggled like children for several seconds, my face burning as more eyes looked our way. When was the last time I laughed like this? At all?

"If you want people to love you, you have to stand out." Prince Cassius shrugged with a grin as if joking, as though nothing embarrassing could bother him.

He stepped forward to retrieve his staff, but another figure was already jogging toward us. I straightened my posture as Mr. Harris approached, any humor void from his face.

"Ah, Mr. Harris," Prince Cassius greeted. "We were just getting started. Need her back already?"

"Your Highness," Mr. Harris bowed quickly, "we must get to the council room. An emergency meeting has been summoned. You're coming along too, Nora."

Me? I failed to hide my confusion.

Mr. Harris turned to leave, but the prince's face scrunched into a serious expression. "What for?"

Mr. Harris halted to a standstill, glancing in my direction.

Shouting erupted from the front gates. A crowd of uniformed soldiers forced a path toward the infirmary. Gifteds in crudely wrapped bandages were met by ERS doctors and nurses.

"That shall be discussed at the meeting." Mr. Harris chose his words carefully. He headed toward the castle, forcing us to run after him.

"No, you'll tell me now," the prince demanded. "I need to prepare myself for Princess Maya's angle."

We entered the castle.

"It would be wise to discuss details at the meeting."

"Mr. Harris." Prince Cassius's voice hardened. "You will tell me now."

Hesitantly, Mr. Harris replied. "There's been an attack. The largest government building holding Unfortunate records in Osthall has just been bombed."

An attack? Of Unfortunate records?

Mr. Harris turned a corner hard. We abruptly followed.

Prince Cassius didn't ask for more clarification. "You think the Anti-Gifteds Movement could do *that?*"

"We have reason to believe so, yes," Mr. Harris confirmed. "But that is what the meeting is for. Strange writing was also found at the scene that we can't fully explain."

Gifteds ran past us to see the scene outside.

Could Unfortunates really attack Gifteds so publicly?

No, it has always been the other way around. Always.

Sylvia Douglas plunged the knife deeper into the city guard's neck. Not always.

"Wait, Mr. Harris. I don't see the benefit of bringing Nora into a room full of angry Gifteds," Prince Cassius urged. I found myself falling behind, running in order to catch up to their urgency.

"She's not your responsibility, sir."

"Don't forget your place, Mr. Harris."

"I never do."

Mr. Harris and Prince Cassius halted, glaring at each other with stone-faced expressions.

My body jolted at the sudden stop.

Prince Cassius swallowed hard, looking away. "You understand this *attack*," he spat the words out like bile, "is an unprecedented course of action that will only put Nora in danger if we bring her into a room of the highest-ranking officials in the country."

Mr. Harris's jaw twitched. He leaned forward, his face softened into one of concern. "Sir, you know my place as the First Senior member, placed there by your father when he became sovereign."

Prince Cassius didn't respond.

"Then there's nothing to fear from the others," Mr. Harris continued, "they are Senior members, sure, but they're ranked lower than me *by the king himself.* That's not going to turn on its hat because of my crazy ideas, so what are you so fearful of, sir?"

Prince Cassius huffed, glancing to me and then back to Mr. Harris. He crossed his arms. "I've always supported you on this project of yours, but we both know my support means nothing compared to others in that room. Others you don't have. You can't act so recklessly."

"Your support is enough, sir," Mr. Harris promised with a soft smile. "And believe it or not, I do have an idea. One even Minister Gabriel cannot deny."

Did I have a say in this? I thought frantically as we made it to the Senior Cabinet Meeting Room. Prince Cassius was right. I didn't want to be in a room full of angry Gifteds, let alone the most powerful ones in the kingdom. But the stern expression on Mr. Harris's face told me this wasn't up for debate.

As we entered, the first thing I noticed was the darkness that decorated the walls. Tall and thick purple, white, and black drapes hung downward, designating the colors of the royal house. A large wooden circular table sat in the center of the meeting room where multiple Gifteds were already seated at their designated positions.

On a throne-like structure at the head of the table, which was elevated on a small stage, was King Daltus. Above his constituents, he sat, slightly slouched in his chair, silently watching over the other Gifteds.

Servants who typically lined the walls were not present here.

The cabinet members jumped up to the sound of the doors opening. They bowed quickly to Prince Cassius, but they addressed Mr. Harris.

"Mr. Harris," Mr. Walton acknowledged. "We were discussing recent developments."

"And where are those recent developments?" Mr. Harris asked immediately.

"Well, our sources are still fuzzy, but the Anti-Gifteds Movement has claimed responsibility for this act."

"Anything of Sylvia Douglas?"

I looked at Mr. Walton for an answer, the mention of Sylvia piquing my interest. *The Avlis in Thunder Bay struggled beneath her, beneath me.*

Mr. Walton shook his head.

The rest of the cabinet members remained standing as Mr. Harris took his place to the immediate right of King Daltus. I followed him with Prince Cassius close behind, my body wedged between the two as if that would hide me from view.

Princess Maya stood to the king's immediate left. A purple dress made from lightweight fabric hid her skin from exposure. White gloves poked out from her long sleeves, making her face the only exposed feature denoting a wax white color. Walking closer, I noticed how her straight blonde hair was almost an orange color compared to her brother's.

"Mr. Harris, this is no place for a first-year Mati student," said the man next to Princess Maya and across the table from us. He was a strikingly plump man with equally as striking large golden eyes, having a disgruntled look on his face as he stared at me.

"There goes the minister's Lux sight," Prince Cassius whispered seemingly to himself with an eye roll. Mr. Harris gave him a warning glance.

"Nora is not a Mati, Minister Gabriel," Mr. Harris clarified. "She needs to be here as the Unfortunate project I've talked about."

Minister Gabriel's wide face scrunched in disgust. "Unbelievable!" he shouted, "That's even worse! Why did you bring your pet project here, Mr. Harris? This is serious business regarding very dangerous Unfortunates, and you let her into this sacred place!"

Fear overwhelmed my senses as all Senior members leered in my direction, labeling me as Mr. Harris's pet project.

"Please be mindful of your status here," replied Mr. Harris. "As the First Senior member, I am allowed to bring whoever I deem necessary. And in this case, Nora needs to be here. If we are to understand this Anti-Gifteds Movement, we need an Unfortunate for an inside view. Don't you recall our previous meetings discussing my project?"

An inside view? I thought. What was Mr. Harris planning to do with me?

Prince Cassius gave Mr. Harris a side glance with an expression that read *This is a bad idea.* I wished I had the power to perform the same action.

"I still find this whole idea of yours ridiculous, Mr. Harris. I want that on record!" Minister Gabriel announced, grumbling to himself and shaking his head.

"It's *been* on record, Minister," Mr. Harris assured as several other Senior Royal Crest Knights mumbled to themselves. None outspokenly agreed with Minister Gabriel.

"And what is your plan of action again, Minister?" Mr. Harris pressed, looking at the minister with an almost bored expression as if he knew exactly what he was going to say. "What does the Head of the Church think is necessary for such an attack on our sacred land?"

Minister Gabriel puffed out his chest. "As the Head Minister of the Church of Iridion and Spiritual Advisor to the sovereign, I believe we must call for decisive action immediately. I'm suggesting restrictive action, an additional law to the Unfortunate Laws of Servitude."

Murmurs echoed throughout the room as several of the cabinet members discussed this prompted idea.

A new ULS? How many more did we need to obey?

Princess Maya stood next to Minister Gabriel across the table, her gloved hands folded gently over her body. Her glossed lips parted to say something when Prince Cassius spoke before her.

"You're always suggesting that," Prince Cassius said, crossing his arms. "There's no reason to be so harsh so quickly to all Unfortunates for several insurgents."

I turned my attention to the most rational person in the room. Advocating for Unfortunates? More and more, I understood why Mr. Harris trusted my training with the prince.

"Several insurgents!" Minister Gabriel repeated in a distraught tone. "Sir," he tried to compose himself, "with all due respect, it is important to make quick and decisive actions so these *insurgents* do not become an entire unified force against us. And from the looks of things, they have!"

Prince Cassius's lips formed a line, not responding.

Princess Maya jumped in. "Gentleman," she spoke in a respectfully soft voice. All cabinet members, including Minister Gabriel himself, quieted down to hear their princess speak.

She turned to her right. "Minister Gabriel, I admire your passion to protect our people. However, I also find it unwise to take drastic action so quickly when we have other options outside of adding a new law to the ULS."

Minister Gabriel matched Princess Maya's gentle tone. "And what other options do you have in mind, ma'am?"

The princess turned to me, her light blue eyes gleaming off the overhead chandelier. "What is your name, Unfortunate? I doubt you would like to be called as such."

My eyes bulged, lowering my head quickly in a jerked movement. I took a deep breath, relaxing my shoulders and remembering my training. "My name is Nora, Your Highness."

"Nora then." My name rolled off her tongue. Her eyes found Mr. Harris beside me.

"I believe Mr. Harris has a reason to bring Nora here outside of ruffling your feathers, Minister. What is your idea, Mr. Harris? Please speak now before we continue to squabble."

Mr. Harris's mouth twitched in a small smirk. He dipped his head to the princess. "I can never quite get anything past you. Can I, ma'am?" His playful expression shifted into a serious one as he looked upon the other cabinet members.

"Fellow Senior Royal Crest Knights, I understand you are uncomfortable with my new—what do you all call it—ah, yes my pet project. However, I think it behooves us to use this Unfortunate as a way to dismantle the Anti-Gifteds Movement."

"How do you suppose you're going to do that?" Mr. Walton piped in.

"The Anti-Gifteds Movement has a clear desire. They want change. Unlike most of you, I've actually encountered several members of the Anti-Gifteds Movement. I know how they think; I know how they operate. This is their first successful attack that has gained public attention. But what they don't know is change is happening now."

Mr. Harris gestured toward me. I was on display again, like I was standing in line for the Choosing Ceremony.

"Through Nora, we can show that their desires are already coming to fruition and effectively dismantle their whole purpose for existing."

The Senior Cabinet remained silent.

As those words sank in, I searched Mr. Harris's face for any indication—any indication at all—that my decision was my own.

"What exactly do you want me to do?" I heard myself asking out loud.

Mr. Harris continued speaking but kept his gaze at Minister Gabriel. "I propose that my first Unfortunate student and Iridion's first future Unfortunate soldier becomes our Unfortunate symbol against the Anti-Gifteds message. She will be interviewed, photographed, and documented as she succeeds here at Galdor Academy, and we can finally put this movement to rest."

An Unfortunate—

"What?" Minister Gabriel and Prince Cassius said at the same time.

"No. This is absolutely ridiculous, Mr. Harris!" Minister Gabriel shook his head.

Prince Cassius stepped forward. I flinched but remained motionless as he grabbed my wrist. "Mr. Harris, you did not discuss this idea with me."

I could feel the prince's gaze on me, but my own gaze was fixated on the floor. "Nora, you don't have to do this."

"We need an Unfortunate who is already moving against the tide."

"That isn't for you to decide for her."

"I'll do it." The words fell off my lips quickly. If this was what I needed to do to stay, to keep my promise to Valerie,

I would do anything. I looked up to the prince and then to Mr. Harris. "I'll do it."

Prince Cassius's grip tightened. I could feel his arm tremble. Or was that my arm? "Think about what you're saying."

"We only need a final verdict," Mr. Harris said.

All eyes slowly turned to the throne at the head of the table.

King Daltus had his middle finger pressed against his temple, securely holding his head in thought and staring at me with hollow eyes. After several heartbeats, he finally spoke.

"The Unfortunate shall be photographed while at Galdor Academy with the strict intent to discredit the Anti-Gifteds Movement. Anything that deters from that goal will fall solely on your shoulders, Mr. Harris."

Mr. Harris did not hesitate his response, "I understand."

"Then it is decided."

The decisive sound of a gavel sealed my new fate.

"What other business do you bring to this emergency meeting today?" King Daltus prompted.

A wave of anxiety swept the room. Mr. Harris's lips formed a frown. He shook his head, "I cannot explain it right now. The word 'DIVINER' was scribbled along the building's floor, but we have no way of knowing what that means."

Minister Gabriel scoffed with a disgruntled expression, "Trying to use the Divine for themselves. Unfortunate souls are downcast for a reason."

I bravely opened my mouth. "So we are to ignore it?"

Mr. Harris sighed. "For the time being, yes. We don't have enough information to know what the Diviner means or how that connects with the Anti-Gifteds Movement. No affiliated Unfortunates have been successfully contained."

My eyes squinted at the last comment. No Unfortunates were in custody? Was that because AGM members were able to evade capture? Or were all possible Unfortunate insurgents killed on sight? I didn't think I wanted the answer.

"Very well," King Daltus said after several heartbeats of silence. "If we have no new information, we shall proceed with Mr. Harris's plan of action using his Unfortunate student. All are dismissed."

Prince Cassius took a step forward. "Your Majesty—"

"I said dismissed." The king stared straight at his son with a stern expression.

The prince's jaw twitched.

"Cas," Princess Maya reached out.

"Don't call me that." He cut her off, letting go of my wrist and storming out of the meeting room.

My hand fell to my side. The princess's shoulders sank lower as the door slammed shut.

"Honestly that boy..." Minister Gabriel grumbled, his words trailing off before they became treacherous.

Mr. Harris sighed deeply. "He'll be okay, ma'am," he assured the princess.

Princess Maya's shoulders slouched, rendering her imperfect for a heartbeat.

She straightened her posture as she looked directly at me. "Let's get you prepared."

CHAPTER TWELVE

Black Box

"When you're inside the simulation lab, please be mindful of your surroundings." Mr. Harris spoke each word deliberately so the camera could better pick up the audio.

The air felt colder than usual here because of the anticipating simulation or because of the paint along my face, I couldn't decide.

"The entire purpose of this exercise is so you can get accustomed to how the simulation lab works and fulfill missions as if they're happening in real life. For this particular mission, there is a hostility between a shopkeeper and two Gifted civilians. These civilians have known records. Take that information as you see fit."

Two Gifteds with known criminal records. Our first simulation lab couldn't be more cut and dry regarding who was good and who was evil. I wondered if this was a normal simulation for first years. Mr. Harris had his own record for pushing boundaries. I doubted he would have made this assignment easy if there wasn't a blinking red light targeting his face.

"Your mission is to dismantle the hostility without increasing the conflict. If for some reason that mission fails, the next immediate source of action is to detain and arrest the two Gifteds with the least amount of property damage and Gifted casualties possible. The more damage caused, the lower your scores become *even* if you succeed in the mission."

Light on my feet, the other Gifteds around me were on edge as well. We had much more than the simulation lab ahead of us. Mr. Harris made it very clear that these cameras behind him and around us were here to stay.

We were under strict orders to avoid the cameras' gaze, but I could see them turn and press forward, closer to my face, examining every little facet of my body and my team members.

The Gifted students knew why cameras trailed our every move. The AGM was getting worse, and my purpose was revealed as dismantling their extremism. Mr. Harris didn't mention Sylvia Douglas, though, so I didn't either.

Leo stepped closer to Persephone, hiding his form as much as possible with his arms crossed and his face in a permanent scowl.

Standing next to me, Fern stood almost lifeless, her breathing shallow in an attempt to stay quiet. Her shoulders moved inward as she made herself smaller.

Kai, on the other side of me, had completely flipped personalities with Fern. He kept a determined façade, his nose higher in the air. Calculating, his eyes darted about without actually looking at the cameras to make sure he was still in frame.

Molly Montgomery secluded herself to the back of the formation. Arms crossed, her lips raised slightly to show her fangs.

Skylar was smiling wildly, flicking her wrist and flinging back her hair, doing any movement she possibly could that would attract the camera's attention toward her.

She even stepped in front of me now. The small whir of the camera focused from my frame in order to capture hers. I did not stop her.

"As a reminder, the suits you are currently wearing are embedded with technology that allows you to feel as though you are actually in that type of environment."

We all wore uniform tight suits, similar to the attire Molly Montgomery wore when she interviewed for Galdor Academy, and when Mr. Harris and I met.

"And that includes feeling any physical attack against you, including the moment up until death."

A dark silence filled the air, but Mr. Harris continued, "No different from any other simulation lab that you will experience. If one of your team members, including you, is killed in action, the simulation will end immediately in failure regardless of the mission's actual success.

"Please be mindful of all of this while you're inside the simulation lab and be mindful that you're not actually dying. You can feel like you're hurt, but you're not actually injured. Is that clear to everyone?"

We held back our hesitations. "Yes, sir!"

Mr. Harris nodded. "I will observe your progress from outside the lab itself, and I will not interrupt the lab until the mission is a success or failure. Good luck."

As we walked through the only entrance of the simulation lab, I finally understood why Gifteds called it the "Black Box." It wasn't just the exterior that was solid black in color. The inside of the simulation lab held the same hue. A large piece of two-sided glass along the wall obscured Mr. Harris and the cameras—unseen but watching closely.

My shoes sank a little into the ground. *Dirt.* Perfect for an Avlis.

After the doors closed, a loud whirring sound erupted from the ceiling as the simulation began.

Black walls fell away to reveal Galdor Square. The faceless models rendered into real-like faces. The scene would remind me of Thunder Bay if I was surrounded by Unfortunates selling seaside novelties. But scores of Gifteds passed by, shopping in Iridion's largest square.

Even though I knew these citizens were not real, I could still feel my body flinch as Gifted patrons walked past me.

In front of us formed two Gifteds as Mr. Harris described, already arguing with a shopkeeper who held his hands up defensively.

"What did you call me, old man?" the first Gifted demanded.

The timid shopkeeper stuttered, "Nothing… nothing. Just leave me alone, please."

Skylar started to step forward, but I spoke first.

"What's happening here?" I asked out loud. Not the best assertion, but it was enough for the two Gifteds to turn my way.

"We're just minding our own when this *old man* told us to leave," the first one said, a flame igniting in his palm.

"We demand respect!" the second chimed in, his curved nose and striking blue feathered hair indicating he was some sort of bird Imitation.

I stepped forward with my hand out toward the Mati. "There's no need to make a scene here," I found myself saying.

The Imitation Gifted scoffed. "Do you know who we are?"

"You haven't committed any crime yet." I stepped forward again. "How about we leave this shopkeeper alone, and you can go about your day."

The two Gifteds glanced at each other. A heartbeat passed.

"Fine," the Mati spit the word out like bile, closing his fist. The fire extinguished from his fingers.

They turned to leave. I could feel a hand grab my shoulder and I glanced over in time to see Skylar propel herself forward.

"You're going to let them off just like that?" she demanded. "What if one of them stole something?"

I flinched, not considering that possibility.

"Skylar, what are you doing?" asked Cal.

The two Gifteds turned back, the Mati reigniting the flame. "You *assuming* that I stole something from this old man?"

"Something is off about this simulation. It cannot be this simple," Skylar turned from her fiancé to the hostile Gifteds. "I simply find it very suspicious that the shopkeeper would call you out without reason to provoke him."

She raised her arm up in a quick motion. A gust of wind formed upward behind the two Gifteds as a warning.

"We're going to have to check your persons before we can let you go."

I reached out. "Wait—"

Heat enveloped my body as the Mati shot fire toward us. Skylar formed a wind wall, using both of her palms to push the fire upward. The nearby patrons scattered while the nearby shopkeepers tried to protect their merchandise.

Persephone stepped forward to assist Skylar, at the ready. She waved her arms upward to defuse the fire as it lifted into the air and became smoke.

The other Gifted charged me. My leg pivoted into a stance, but Fern shoved in front of me, lifting dirt upward into a solidified wall. The Imitation punched the structure; his hand sank inside. Fern clenched her fist in a rapid motion, and the Imitation screamed as the earth hardened around his hand. He struggled to free himself.

Kai swooped forward, water already formed between his hands. With a rotation of both wrists, the water shot outward and splashed the Imitation's face. He stumbled back.

Cal steadied himself next to Skylar as the Mati grew closer.

Skylar gritted her teeth as Cal added his own pressure. She forcefully pulled one of her arms away from its original target, screaming as she used enough energy to throw the Mati into a nearby stall. Flames ignited and spread.

Leo and Persephone moved toward the fire as the Mati struggled to free himself from the confines of the collapsed cloth roof.

Molly advanced toward the other Imitation. He opened his mouth to caw, yellow eyes fixated on his prey.

Kai redirected the water in his hands, aiming again at the Imitation's eyes. Molly stepped out on the offensive.

I caught sight of movement to my immediate left. The fire had reached the surrounding stalls, including the timid shopkeeper's. He held himself firmly on the ground, watching out in horror.

"Fern, I'm going to help the shopkeeper. Cover me," I said, running over before she could respond.

I reached out a shaky hand to him. "Sir, you need to evacuate this area."

He shook his head, his fear reminding me of an Unfortunate. His cloth roof began to erode away from the oncoming fire.

"Sir, now." I reached out again. "I'm going to grab your hand."

I grabbed his hand. He flinched but didn't retreat. Lifting him upward, I led him out of the stall as the stall collapsed in on itself. Encouraging him away, I yelled "Go!" as loudly as I could.

I didn't watch him disappear. "Persephone!" I called in her direction as the Mati Gifted emerged from the flames.

She hesitantly turned to me. "Stop the fire from spreading to any other stalls!"

I looked to Fern. "Fern! I need you to build a barrier so the culprits cannot get away."

"I'll try!" she called back.

Lowering herself to the ground completely, Fern rose slowly, her hands curled as she lifted an invisible weight.

A circular wall formed along the edges of the simulation lab, enclosing us in Galdor Square and part of the larger city.

"Skylar!" I turned to the Aura.

"I don't take orders from you!" she shouted back as she blasted a gust of wind at the Mati assailant who dodged.

Deviating my focus, I turned back to the Imitation assailant.

He shrieked as he sprang toward Molly.

Kai launched water at the Imitation's beak, clenching his fist. Small ice particles formed, but they weren't enough to solidify completely. He cursed under his breath as the two Imitations collided.

A caw and a hiss sliced through the bazaar.

Skylar's infuriated scream snapped my attention back to the final assailant… who was fleeing from the scene.

She ran after him first, and I found my feet sprinting in pursuit. He advanced toward the city, gaining ground.

"This one's mine!" Skylar yelled.

The Mati shot a quick blast of fire from behind himself without looking. I halted as the fire shot upward, zigzagging through a nearby building. The structure loosened and tilted.

My feet propelled forward.

"Skylar, wait!"

I pushed Skylar out of the way with all of my might as glass and concrete fell on top of me.

An ungodly weight crushed my lungs; my sight turned to black, blank, dead. The simulation environment fell back into darkness; I gasped desperately for air.

A loud buzzing sound erupted from above as a large X formed along my back.

I could hear Fern as she ran up, profusely apologizing. "Oh my gosh, Nora! I'm so sorry! It happened so fast—I... I need to work on using my Gift while running. I'm... *I'm so sorry.*"

I couldn't respond.

Skylar's form loomed overhead, pacing in frustration and cursing to herself. She shrieked in my direction, "Why did you do that, you idiot!"

Huffing, I managed to crane my neck up at her, my voice low. "Because we're a team?"

Running footsteps indicated that the rest of the team had arrived.

"Oh, so you're trying to take all the teamwork points too, huh? Ugh, I had him!" she yelled, stomping off.

I slowly sank my head back onto the ground. Feeling Fern's slender fingers push me back up into reality, I landed wobbly on my feet.

The only entrance was now open again. I could make out Mr. Harris's shadow as it faded in and out of my vision.

He's going to kill me, I thought. His reputation relied on my success in front of the cameras.

I forced my eyes open as I approached, my muscles aching as my body tried to regain its mobility.

"How was that?" I managed to say.

Mr. Harris shook his head slightly. "You're dismissed for the rest of the day."

My head drooped. "I'm fine."

"Your body needs rest after thinking it got crushed by falling concrete." Mr. Harris's monotone voice did not match his words. "But we managed to get great photos despite Skylar's decision to make things difficult."

I hyper-focused on keeping my body upright, but I still leaned at an angle. Fern and Kai stood by my side though, ready to support.

"Can I see them?" I asked. "The photos?"

Mr. Harris hesitated but gestured me forward. I walked the short distance to a nearby computer system set up against the glass of the simulation lab. Our figures in front of a rendering of the environment were already on screen.

"We're only keeping the photos of your success," Mr. Harris explained as he clicked through the gallery. "There's no need to publicize... yours and Skylar's squabbles."

Squabbles. I wished that word described the half of it.

He stopped. I recognized my form in a landscape photo, standing clearly in front of the Gifted students. The camera captured me mid-walk, my left leg forward and my arm slightly outreached. The two Gifted thugs stood opposing me, their expressions in a grimace while mine held stone-like. Determined.

I didn't recognize it as my own.

Mr. Harris changed to a different photograph—one of me mid-fight, my form almost blurred as I raced over to the burning tent. The next series of images caught my movements as I reached out to the shopkeeper and lifted him up, the fire nearing with each still frame.

I thought of the Gifted shopkeeper out of place in Thunder Bay. Had I appeared so confident then?

The next photograph zoomed closer to a side view of my face, my mouth open in mid-command, and my eyes trained on Persephone. I didn't remember the last time I saw myself so expressive.

Maybe this could work.

"These will go live later today," said Mr. Harris, "while you are resting."

I opened my mouth to say I was fine when the Mati siblings stepped forward. "We'll make sure she gets plenty of rest," Leo promised as Persephone hoisted me in the air. Mr. Harris raised an eyebrow.

My body was too weak to oppose as Persephone stepped toward the exit.

Awkward and hesitant, the rest of the team followed. My eyes adjusted to the sun's blaring light as we made it outside. My words jumbled incoherently as Persephone walked me toward the dormitories, her expression neutral as curious eyes followed our movements.

Persephone's pace quickened into a run. Leo jogged alongside her as my body bobbed up and down uncontrollably.

"Is he in our sight anymore?" Persephone asked her brother.

"Nope." Leo laughed, his cheeky smile widening. "We'll be in the clear when we ditch the others, though."

Straining became impossible at this point as Persephone's grip confined me in her swaying arms.

"Hey!" Fern's voice could be heard a little distance away.

"What are they doing?" Skylar called.

The castle doors closed behind us with a slam. Definitely not the dormitory as promised. *Where are we going?* I tried to yell, but my voice came out in mumbles. What could these Gifteds want with me?

A sudden fear spiked through my body, granting me enough energy to push Persephone's hand away in time to bite down on her finger.

She winced, her hand recoiling and yanking away. I spun out of her grasp as she abruptly stopped moving. Landing on the cold floor, I managed to spring back up on my feet in a defensive stance.

"Ah, we scared her," Leo said to his sister with a shake of his head. "Are you okay, Persy?" He examined the small indention of my teeth in her index finger.

"Just unexpected," Persephone assured. She looked to me. "I could have burned you."

"What are we doing here?" I demanded. "If you kill me here..." I tried to think of a threat that Gifteds would actually consider. "Mr. Harris will find out, and you don't want to ruin his project."

Leo raised an eyebrow with a startled expression. "*Kill* you?" His face scrunched deeper into confusion and concern. "Who said anything about killing you? What do you take us for?"

The two siblings looked at each other with the same look of disbelief. "Now get inside the vent." Persephone pointed to the low wall.

"What?" I huffed.

Persephone bent down and unscrewed the loose bolts, pulling the cover from its foundation. Leo gestured me forward as his sister crawled in first. "Quickly before the rest catch us," he urged.

The clanking sound that came with running piqued my attention down the hall. Out of sight but not for long.

With a sudden time limit, I found myself bending down and shoving myself through the open hole in the wall.

Persephone gently grabbed my forearms, helping me squeeze through and navigating the darkness. Leo crawled in last. The vent covering snapped back into place behind us.

After a few seconds of shifting, Persephone warned me of a drop. My body slid downward into a larger, unseen space. A soft crunch pressed against my leg as I sat down.

A dim flame illuminated from Persephone's ring finger. I watched the flame lower to the ground and then expand as it made contact with a string. Persephone continued, lighting several other candles until the world came back into focus.

An assortment of snacks, manufactured sweets, and ready-to-eat meals were piled hazardously in the area in which we sat.

"How do you have all of this?" I looked at all of the brands I noticed in the student canteen. "And *why?*"

Persephone immediately went for a bag of sunflower seeds. Leo scanned his treasures with his finger like he was both the claw machine and chooser.

"When you live in Norburn, you learn how to become a scavenger." Leo smiled, picking up a bag of peanuts and offering them to me. He unwrapped a lollypop for himself and popped it in his mouth. "The strict three meals leaves little for any fun, too."

I poured peanuts in my palm before eating them, sitting crisscross on the floor. The soft fire illuminated our faces in a warm hue.

I knew what it was like to be a scavenger. "Valerie and I always sneaked food when we knew it was safe," I began. "When we were younger, we would bake two extra cookies and eat them as fast as we could to avoid suspicion."

Melanie Montgomery never seemed to mind offering us cookies anyway when we baked them for her. Soon, she wouldn't be too young to understand why we had to refuse.

Leo swayed his arms absentmindedly in the snacks around him, the wraps making a collective crunching sound.

"Stop that," Persephone scolded in a whisper. "You're being distracting."

"I'm just *thinking*, Pers," Leo mocked a fake accent as a defense, pushing her lightly in the shoulder.

She teetered, pretending to fall down in a slow, dramatic action.

"Persy, nooooo," Leo dragged out in a whine. "You can't die. You're crushing all the chips!"

Persephone laughed—a soft, lighthearted chuckle that transformed her face into a glowing smile like she could use her Gift to brighten her very expression.

Leo tried lifting her off the ground without any actual effort placed in his movements, the vein in his neck even protruding as he faked struggling to pull her up.

"Get off me, you fool," Persephone snorted. She sat upright again. "You're spilling my sunflower seeds *everywhere*."

Leo rolled his eyes playfully, "Oh, we can get the Unfortunate to clean that up."

All the fun sucked out of my lungs as my breath hitched, my shoulders pulling back. Persephone's lips formed back into a line, her stare glaring into her brother. Even Leo placed his hand over his mouth, staring at me with raised eyebrows.

"Leo, that's not funny," Persephone said.

The Mati continued to stare at me, his entire body frozen as if stuck. "Nora, I am so sorry," he said in a low whisper.

I stuttered, "It's fine." It wasn't fine. But it wasn't the first time Gifteds made scathing comments about Unfortunates in my presence. They just never considered apologizing before.

"No, it's not!" Persephone's voice raised as she really hit her brother's shoulder. "What were you thinking?"

"I wasn't!"

"Clearly."

"I—" Leo struggled to find the words, again frozen in an awkward position, his mouth open. He looked back to me; his shoulders slouched. "I shouldn't have said that. Especially since we're hardly different from you."

My hand rubbed along my arm. No excuse for his actions. What was this feeling swirling alongside the pain in my chest?

"Hardly different how?" I pressed.

Leo glanced to his sister before responding. "Well, we don't have a House name to speak of for starters. That alone already lowers our status closer to Unfortunates."

Skylar pointed to the two siblings without any other introduction. *Don't worry, they don't have a House name either,* she'd said. Because House names are important—especially for someone as clearly superior as Skylar Stanton. "Property of Montgomery House" stamped my identity to Molly.

"And we've never had servants."

I looked up. "Not by choice I'm assuming."

"Right," Leo hesitated to continue, "Norburn doesn't have an annual Choosing Ceremony in the first place, but we could never afford one or have a home for upkeep."

I munched slower. "That sounds rough."

"Ah, we're here now." Leo waved his hand like what he said wasn't important. "Now—" as he clapped his hands together, a spark ignited and faded, "what should my punishment be as an apology?"

I raised my fingers to my chin in thought. "I shall take your finest delicacy."

"*Finest,* she says," Leo spoke out loud, immediately searching through the mounting pile. "Persy, what do you think is the finest delicacy we have in stock?"

I kept my posture straight and nose pointed as they looked for what was owed to me.

"Perfect." Leo held out something in his hands before tossing it my way.

Two mini chocolate cakes coated with icing could be seen through the clear wrapping.

As I opened the treat, a loud clattering sound erupted from behind us. The vent forcibly opened.

"They have to be here. Cal, you go first to confirm." Skylar's commanding voice echoed through the tunnel.

"What makes you say that?" asked Cal, his voice soft, cautious.

"Why are you disagreeing with me?"

"I'm not, Sky. I—"

"Fine, I'll do it." A meaty slap reverberated from the vent's entryway. Skylar huffed. "I swear you better be here or I'll be so *pissed.*"

My heartbeat quickened as Skylar crawled closer.

She inhaled, a gust of wind spiraling out of her mouth as she exhaled. The candle flames shuttered.

"Hey, don't put the lights out!" Leo yelled out.

"Aha!" Skylar popped out from the vent we came from, her shark-like grin and the candlelight hauntingly darkening her face. "I so called it. Cal! I was right! They're here!"

Cal lightly placed pressure on the vent as he entered.

"What is *this?*" Fern's voice hollered in a high-pitched squeal.

"Ugh!" Skylar grunted in protest. "I was hoping to get rid of them."

"Skylar, wait up!" Molly's voice ran toward us.

Skylar sighed as Cal appeared beside her.

Fern's body wrestled with the vent. "Stupid vent."

"Great, let's just have everyone stop by," said Leo sarcastically.

"Hey, guys!" Fern waved. "Is that food?"

The Avlis slid down to our position, her laughter bouncing off the walls as she buried herself in snacks.

The rest of the Gifteds followed, their bodies squishing up against us. My back pressed against the wall as they flooded in, drawing myself closer to Persephone as Molly entered the small space.

Fern's laughter grew louder as she examined each candy bar.

"Careful of the candles," warned Persephone.

"You're crushing all the food!" Leo cried.

"Stop pushing!" Skylar yelled.

"I'll stop pushing when you stop being disruptive!"

"Disruptive?"

"You heard me, princess!" Leo spat back. "You're disrupting now just as you were during the simulation lab because *you* wanted to be the center of attention. You couldn't stand being upstaged by an—"

A loud crashing sound interrupted their argument. The candle light extinguished us into darkness. Skylar gasped. "Get off me, Mati!"

"Me?" Leo scoffed. "*You're* the one crushing *my* body right now, princess!"

"Stop calling me that!"

They continued to yell, fighting to push away from the other but the space was too confined.

Kai popped his head in with a bewildered look. "Hey!" His shout echoed through the chamber. Skylar and Leo fell silent for a moment.

"Maybe we should all go to the cafeteria instead."

***

"Did you see me? I was like *whoosh*." Fern posed in the confines of her chair. "And then Kai," she pointed to him, "you swooped in like this." She crudely mimicked a Mare technique with her fingers. "Even Molly came in and showed that Imitation who was boss!"

I glanced toward my Gifted master at the other end of the table sitting next to Cal.

Fern slouched in her chair while looking up to the ceiling. "We honestly worked really well, you guys," she said with a sigh. She jolted upward as she tried to reenact the simulation.

The rest of us laughed along—except for Skylar who tried to act poised, Cal who kept his attention toward his tray, and Molly who mimicked Skylar.

Comfortable next to Fern, an airy and bubbly feeling blossomed inside my chest like an old wound flaring with each contraction of my diaphragm. The second time too after Prince Cassius.

Could I really be friends with Gifteds? The smile on my face betrayed my initial answer.

"Nora, what a beating!" Leo interjected. But he raised his glass as he said it as if offering a grand toast to someone more deserving. "But I have to hand it to you. That was quite the decision to push Skylar out of the way."

The laughing Gifteds lifted their drinks. "To pushing Skylar!" Fern joked.

Another eruption of laughter.

"No!" I countered quickly, noticing the twitch of Skylar's lips. "To becoming a team."

"To becoming a team!" they agreed.

We clanked our plastic cups.

This must be how Gifteds bonded—cheering in each other's success, celebrating each other's Gift techniques, relishing in their power. I was amidst their comradery. For a heartbeat, we were equals.

"Amazing as usual, Persephone," Leo said, grabbing his sister and squeezing her into a hug. "Always good at extinguishing fires."

She took the compliment by giving him a soft smile before looking at me. "It was the smart call," she said.

"Yes! Nora was the closest to disarming the conflict and then took action when she needed to!" Fern cheered.

My cheeks burned at the compliment. My lips quivered into a smile.

Leo nodded his head. "And that's impressive given your status."

Persephone lightly jabbed her brother for the comment. "Hey, that was a compliment this time."

"If only *someone*," Fern exaggeratedly bent her body toward Skylar, "didn't ruin the simulation and have us *fail*."

Skylar stopped eating, her eyes dangerously thin, but her body remained stationary.

"Fern, it's… it's fine," I muttered, reaching out and hoping she would get back into her chair in the correct position.

She did. But then she also strained even louder, "I would be fine if someone didn't ruin our mission."

Skylar's palm slammed into the table with a thud, her hair pushed forward from the momentum and feet hovering off the ground. "If you have something to say to me, you can say it to my face," she warned.

Fern crossed her arms. "You were the one who decided to make the simulation hard for us."

"The simulation is supposed to be a way to demonstrate our skills!" she defended for a second time. "There was no reason for it to be so quickly completed, especially by an *Unfortunate*. I did what made sense in the situation."

My shoulders slouched at her words. I knew the simulation was clear-cut. The quick photo op demanded it. But could the simulation lab possibly be rigged that much in my favor? Could an Unfortunate really defuse a situation between Gifteds so quickly?

"The mission was clear, Skylar," Kai reminded her.

"And we failed because you decided to interject and get one of your teammates killed," added Leo. "End of story."

I could feel the eyes of other students. "Guys, there's no need to argue here and draw attention to ourselves."

"We're not in a simulation anymore!" Skylar snapped. "You can stop pretending to be a leader."

"I never said—"

"I did what was best for this simulation. If the Unfortunate didn't put herself into unnecessary danger, we wouldn't have failed in the first place. I had that guy. We *would* have completed the mission."

Skylar landed back onto the ground, flinging her hair behind her as she walked away. I noticed the back-breaking stunts Cal did to avoid looking at me as he stepped away too.

If he couldn't bend air to his will, I would mistake him for an Unfortunate.

Molly jumped out of her chair to follow. A chill sliced through the air.

I sighed, slouching in my chair. If *we* were still divided, what did that mean for Mr. Harris's mission? For me?

CHAPTER THIRTEEN

Caliel

—

The Anti-Gifteds Movement attacked the city of Caliel two days after the crown announced their first Unfortunate soldier.

We watched the scene play out on TV. Flames licked the fragmented remains of the main Records Building, as ERS Mati and Mares tried to minimize the damage while Avlis broke apart and sorted through the concrete pieces that used to resemble King Alston's likeness.

A flash of red caught the camera's focus, and I had to turn away. I couldn't bear watching more Unfortunates die on screen—directly in front of me but hundreds of miles away.

This was what I wanted to prevent! Mr. Harris's plan did nothing. *I* did nothing.

"Where do you think they'll attack next?" Kai whispered aloud. "Corton? Northbrook? Galdor?"

Skylar's fists tightened by her side. She side-glanced in my direction, "Sure as hell won't be an Unfortunate city."

I ignored her stare, refusing to give her any ammunition.

"But Caliel is a mixed city," countered Kai. "There's a large population of Unfortunates there, too. The AGM risked attacking their own."

"Almost like nowhere is safe," Persephone added.

A slicing breeze crawled up my back, the hairs along my body standing up.

"Skylar." Cal placed his hand gently on her shoulder. Her muscles relaxed, pressing her back to his chest. "Nora didn't do this."

"Don't say her name casually. Call her the Unfortunate." Skylar bristled, but she remained in his gentle embrace. "Our family could have been there, Cal."

"They weren't," he reminded her.

Skylar's silence denoted her discomfort. Apprehension swirled in the air, familiar to Unfortunates but never among so many Gifteds.

"What would they be doing in Caliel?" Leo piped up. "Claiming another Unfortunate for the Stanton household?"

Cal shook his head in a warning gesture. Skylar rolled her eyes. "I don't have to explain my family to someone without a House name."

That lit the fuse in Leo. Fire reflected in his brown eyes.

But Skylar only offered a frown as Mr. Harris barged in without warning.

I noticed the tight structure of his face.

"Mr. Harris?" I asked. He swallowed hard.

"Nora, report. Now."

He headed back out of the door. Startled, I quickly followed.

Alone, Mr. Harris explained himself. "We need to chat with Ms. Sylvia Douglas."

I froze at the thought of seeing the Unfortunate again. *The city guard struggled underneath my feet.*

"Sylvia Douglas?" I shook my head. "Here? Does that mean—"

"She's been captured from Caliel." Mr. Harris was already speed-walking toward the castle.

I stepped forward, matching his speed.

What could possibly possess Mr. Harris to invite me along for this new misadventure?

My doubts came out all at once. "Why am I involved with this? Your plan was to enroll me here in hopes of invalidating the Anti-Gifteds Movement before they became something worse. They became something worse. What is there for you to gain from me being here now let alone bringing me along to what? An interrogation?"

Silence filled the space between us. An icy feeling crawled up my spine; I froze, anticipating an attack. I'd never spoken so freely in front of Gifteds, and this was the second or even third time my true feelings spilled out in front of Mr. Harris—a Gifted who had earned himself the highest position of power before royalty as the First Senior Royal Crest Knight. He could kill me right now, and no one would ever bat an eye.

"Sylvia Douglas only trusts other Unfortunates," Mr. Harris spoke rushed. "If I go in first, she'll be too focused on belittling me to spill secrets. But with another Unfortunate…"

He trailed off, looking at me with a serious expression, "… she might slip up."

From one Unfortunate to another.

She had bowed politely as she spoke like I would for Gifted guests. Her movements were fluid, calm. Fearless. But fearless like Valerie had deadly consequences. Surely Sylvia was not far from that fate.

I could feel the thin ice crack beneath my feet, but I asked anyway. "And what is there to gain from me staying at Galdor?" *Now that your plan is void,* I wanted to add.

Mr. Harris's jaw twitched. "Do you want to go back to the Montgomerys?"

"No."

My decision could not be so easily reversible. If I were to go back to the Montgomerys of my own volition, I would be walking into my grave. The bolded letters at the bottom of the Unfortunate Laws of Servitude wrote my fate long before I decided to go against it. Even if they didn't kill me right away, they would never allow such an embarrassing folly to happen again with their faithful servant. And I wasn't faithful anymore.

Mr. Harris's jaw twitched but this time in a smile. "Then you have everything to gain by staying until we find a new plan."

We. I liked the sound of *we.*

"Mr. Harris!" Prince Cassius's familiar voice called out. We turned in time to see the Makan prince approach, a grave expression on his face.

Mr. Harris halted, his jaw tightening at the sudden stop.

Prince Cassius's eyes glanced to me, squinting in confusion. "I heard that Walton captured an Anti-Gifteds Unfortunate. Are you questioning her now?"

"Yes, Your Highness," Mr. Harris spoke and bowed quickly.

"I'm coming along."

"There is no need for that, sir."

"We're a *team,* Peter. For better or for worse, your actions reflect on me. And my actions on you."

"Sir, we are not a—"

"I will talk to Sylvia Douglas if Prince Cassius comes along," I interjected quickly.

They both turned my way. The baffled expression on Mr. Harris's face was new. I recalled the way other Gifteds spoke about Makans behind his back. I liked how he countered Minister Gabriel's malicious proposal. *You wanted me to make allies, Mr. Harris.*

Prince Cassius's surprised look twitched into a pleased smile. We stared at the instructor expectantly.

After several seconds, Mr. Harris finally budged. "Hurry, sir. This cannot wait."

We followed Mr. Harris through the zigzag of hallways, approaching two Royal Crest Knights who stood guard in front of a solid wall.

Mr. Harris gestured his hand the way you would with a fly. "Mr. Peter Harris, First Senior Royal Crest Knight. Entry immediately with Prince Cassius Iridion and a first-year student of mine."

Without hesitation, the two guards took a grounded stance and lowered their hands toward the floor. The wall behind them rumbled as it adjusted to their command, lowering and revealing an open doorway.

Mr. Harris led us forward. No time for pleasantries.

We descended several flights of stairs, the air cooling as we traveled underground. Stone and brick replaced sleek marble. Overhead lights marked the way, rows of holding cells lining the walls until we finally arrived to a different hallway lined with small rooms.

Sylvia Douglas was on the other side of a two-sided glass. Dark strands clumped in a matted mess, pulling away from a low and loose bun. Pieces of her black cloak was torn away from a recent struggle, dried blood stuck to a laceration through her cheek, and purple splotches were already forming along her exposed skin. Did the Royal Crest Knights do this to her before capture?

Her body leaned back in her chair in a relaxed posture, eyes sharp.

"Why would the AGM attack a mixed city?" I asked. "Were..." I hesitated, "were Unfortunates hurt?"

Mr. Harris's jaw twitched. "It's worse than that. Something is not..." He didn't finish his sentence, rushing over and scanning his key card against the mechanism on the door. A green light illuminated with a beeping sound. Sylvia's posture straightened.

My fingers clasped the knob. "We're here if anything goes wrong," Mr. Harris assured as he held the door. He leaned down to whisper, "Ask about the Diviner."

I looked at him inquisitively but he didn't explain. Pulling forward, I entered the interrogation room.

Sylvia's mouth formed a wide sarcastic smile. "Ah, there's the Gifted puppet! Not a real girl yet, huh?" she asked.

A sharp pain sprouted from my heart at the harsh comment.

I inhaled sharply and forced my words to remain calm.

Closing the door behind me, I asked, "What makes an Unfortunate attack a mixed city like Caliel?"

Her smile stretched further, the skin around her wound tightening and causing a line of blood to drip down her face. "Do you know anything about Caliel?" she asked. "From the Great Book?"

"You know how to read from the Great Book *and* have a last name?" I tried matching her sarcasm. "Not much of an Unfortunate if you ask me."

"My Gifted House read to us every Sunday when we were supposed to have a day off and the night before our weekly lashing on Monday." Sylvia twisted her hand in a spinning motion. "The repetition solidifies Caliel in your mind."

My back straightened, my voice sincere. "I'm sorry they did that to you."

"Ah, we all have our stories. I am simply another link in a long chain of cruelty and constraint in this world. You can feel the metal against your wrists. Can't you?"

My body flinched involuntarily. The plaque that denoted the Unfortunate Laws of Servitude resided along the walls of my subconscious.

"Justice," Sylvia stretched out the word as she examined its pronunciation, "is what Caliel represents, the Auran word for the Divine. Surely you know the Divine, Nora."

The Divine. A twist tightened in my stomach at the association with the *Diviner* scribbled on rubble and carved in my mind. I forced my eyes to remain on Sylvia.

Stepping closer, I pulled the opposing chair out and sat down. "Is Caliel different from what the Church of Iridion teaches?"

Sylvia smiled and waved her hand carelessly. "For the most part, no actually. But let's find out."

I waited for her to continue.

"Caliel exacts justice on His people. He granted us Gifts to thrive with a simple catch." Sylvia held her index finger out. "If a Gifted defies Caliel or abuses the Gift granted..." Sylvia sucked her teeth disapprovingly, curling her index finger back. I nodded along.

"Then they shall be downcast to an Unfortunate soul," we finished in unison.

"You do know it!" Sylvia's playful voice didn't match her beaten physique.

"That is what is taught."

"Yes, but is that what happened?" Sylvia's face lost its smile. "I'm not entirely sure Gifteds know what justice means."

My frown deepened. "Did you belong to an Auran House?"

Sylvia scoffed, her eyes twinkling with a mischievous recognition. She answered looking at the two-mirror glass. "If you want to find out more about my past House, I'm afraid my papers burned in the city of Caliel."

I retracted as her eyes found mine. She continued through the interruption, "My Gifted House would remind us why we needed to be punished, needed to serve them in order to redeem ourselves. Gifteds don't care about justice."

Coins fell into Mr. Montgomery's open palms. A compensation for losing an Unfortunate the way you lose a commodity. I never did find the Gifteds who killed Valerie. I only found her lying unceremoniously in the street. Like trash. Like nothing.

Sylvia Douglas scoffed. "Gifted lives have done nothing but earn what they deserve."

I couldn't fight her on that sentiment. If I could give Valerie justice, I would without question.

"But Caliel is a mixed city," I managed to say. "Gifteds and Unfortunates live there. You could have hurt plenty of Unfortunates by attacking there. You would risk that to exact justice?"

"Unfortunates shouldn't have to die, but was their life any better before? You found a way to escape. That's what you're doing here, right? You grasped the first and most absurd chance you got because we both crave something better. Can you think of any Unfortunate who didn't?"

The bright red armband denoting her association with the Anti-Gifteds Movement shined brighter against the fluorescent light.

My nerves spiked as her dark brown eyes pierced through mine. "You can exact justice too. I can see it in your face.

Gifteds have hurt you. You've been an Unfortunate servant for your entire life too."

A smile stretched her face. "But I'm free from that life now. Don't you want that too? To be free?"

"We can finally be free!" Valerie squealed to release her excitement. Her imagination spilled out at once as she rambled about every possibility in our infinite future. I hushed her before that treachery fell on Gifted ears.

"Okay, okay!" Her voice elevated as our forms connected.

"Is that a yes, then?" I asked, a childish giggle escaping my lungs.

"I will if you make a promise with me."

I looked back to Sylvia Douglas. My words didn't feel like my own. "I am free."

Sylvia scoffed. "Nora, this new life of yours is fake. It's not real. You really think that Gifteds are going to allow you to stay here? Do you really think they would allow an Unfortunate to become a solider? Stand alongside them?"

Her body rose, demanding an answer.

I stood to match her.

"Really?" Valerie asked, a hopeful expression on her face.

I nodded. "Yes, really. We can leave on our next Sunday off."

Her warm hands clasped in mine. I had never felt lighter.

"I made a promise, just as I imagine you did to yourself."

"A promise? Yes, promises are powerful," Sylvia confessed, her eyes darkening. "If you're so into promises," she stepped forward in front of the table, "I promise that the next attack will be on Thunder Bay."

Stepping back, I brought my hands closer to my chest.

"You would hurt your own people to get to me?" I asked. "Did-did you attack Caliel because of *me?*"

"To make a statement, absolutely." Sylvia Douglas did not hesitate. "Gifted sympathizers like you are the worst kinds of Unfortunates. Perpetuating that life... doesn't deserve my mercy."

The door swung open; Sylvia lunged at me.

Prince Cassius pushed me back while Mr. Harris grabbed Sylvia. Her voice escalated to a yell. "We'll exact justice on all of your kind! The Diviner will take care of the rest!"

Sylvia's body slammed into the wall with a loud crack.

"What is the Diviner?" Mr. Harris bellowed.

"*Peter,*" her head rotated toward him, "I'm not telling you *shit.*"

"Sit down!" he ordered, pulling her off the wall and shoving her into the chair.

Her body flowed like liquid to his command, but her smile remained.

"You will tell me what the Diviner is right now!" Mr. Harris slammed his hands onto the table.

"Mr. Harris let's not be hasty." Prince Cassius tried stepping in between the two. The prince turned invisible for a flash as Mr. Harris bypassed him and beelined for Sylvia.

"Several of my men were killed during their attack! By something else—something that happened inside of them. A bright light and then they died without wounds! *Who* or *what* is the Diviner?"

Sylvia squinted her eyes. "I'm the Diviner for all you know."

Mr. Harris pointed a hand toward Sylvia's face. She pushed her head back to avoid his touch.

"Mr. Harris—" Prince Cassius began, but his voice was drowned out by Sylvia Douglas's screaming.

Sylvia's body twisted as she struggled against an invisible bind. The florescent lights flickered overhead.

My shaking body pressed against the cool glass, my hands cupped to my ears as a disorientating ringing sound split my skull and drowned my thoughts.

The prince backed away too, his own body shifting in and out of the invisible plane as Sylvia's screams grew louder. He leaned closer to me so I could hear him say, "It's not me."

"*Who* or *what* is the Diviner?" Mr. Harris demanded again.

Several agonizing heartbeats passed as the Unfortunate continued to thrash in her seat.

"Stop!" Prince Cassius and I said at the same time.

My arm shot out. "You're killing her!" But the prince grabbed my hand before I could reach Mr. Harris. He shook his head.

The florescent lights slowly illuminated again, and the ringing stopped. As Sylvia's screaming ceased, she held her face in her hands. Was she...

The Unfortunate sobbed, the rise and fall of her chest inconsistent but alive. My shoulders slouched in relief as Sylvia breathed. The Gifteds remained still.

"Nora, I think you're done here," Mr. Harris breathed.

"I'm not going anywhere!" I countered. "You could have killed her!"

Sylvia's lungs contracted into a dry laughter. "Like you all give a damn about my life." She shook her head, looking up at Mr. Harris. "I don't fear the Divine like you do. But I would fear the Diviner if I was you. Someone is walking in Caliel's footsteps. And He's exacting justice on all Gifteds who defy Him."

Mr. Harris's jaw tightened. "Nora, it's time for you to go," he demanded.

I stepped forward anyway, but Mr. Harris snapped his neck toward me, his eyes slicing through my mind. Prince Cassius blocked my path with his arm.

My body shook violently at the image of her bruised body in front of me. I stepped away, becoming smaller than ever before.

"You too, Your Highness," said Mr. Harris.

Prince Cassius's expression flared. "Are you *ordering* me to leave?" The prince dared Mr. Harris to repeat himself.

The First Senior Royal Crest Knight did. "Yes. My plan for Nora has failed again, and I need answers for what happened to my men."

"I can be here for answers too, sir."

"Sir," Mr. Harris said, exasperated. "Once I have a better understanding of the situation, you will be the *first* informed. I need to interrogate the criminal personally."

Prince Cassius lingered, his eyes squinted and jaw twitched as if in thought. He glanced in my direction and then back to Mr. Harris. "The first informed," the prince strained.

Mr. Harris nodded. "Yes, Your Highness."

The door clicked as I opened it. "Run along, Gifted puppet." Sylvia's voice felt far away, her laugh fading in and out like I was once again witnessing what had happened earlier.

As we left the interrogation room and stepped away from Mr. Harris and Sylvia Douglas, the floor swayed under my feet. Nausea flooded my senses; I reached out to the wall and was caught by another force entirely.

"Easy," Prince Cassius warned, "you're okay. Sometimes Mr. Harris's Gift can linger, but I haven't seen him this intense in years."

I tried speaking but a miserable groan came out instead. An unbearable ache festered within my soul; anger and sorrow consumed my veins. It was just one thing after another around these Gifteds. The Montgomerys were easier to handle, easier to understand.

Forcing my legs forward, I clenched my teeth *hard* to restrain my thoughts. Prince Cassius stepped back to walk alongside me. "It's okay. You're just experiencing his emotions. He doesn't lose focus often, so it can be jarring at first."

I kept my mouth wired shut, nodding instead and keeping myself composed enough to exit the lower prison floor physically unscathed. Prince Cassius offered to walk me back to the barracks; I managed a small and simple, "No, thank you."

When he was safely out of sight, my pace quickened from a walk to a run and then a sprint, Sylvia's laughter and shriek jumbling together in my head.

CHAPTER FOURTEEN

The Diviner Task Force

Fern clapped her hands as Kai pressed his ID against one of the portals at the Information Square. "I wonder what our assignments are going to be today!" she cheered.

I wished I could match her enthusiasm. After what had happened yesterday, any cheeriness no longer resided within me. Sylvia Douglas threatened my hometown to hurt me. How could I explain that to a Gifted who had never had to fear for their life?

When they pried about Mr. Harris's whereabouts last night, I didn't indulge. They didn't ask again now.

A wave of whispers from nearby students piqued my interest. I watched as they glanced at the other glass structures for reassurance.

"Do you see that?" I asked.

Fern stopped bouncing. Kai turned to the nearest portal and gasped.

My shoulders drew closer to my chest. "What is it?"

Fern and I looked at what Kai was gawking at. My skin bristled with goosebumps as my eyes caught sight of an older student with light blond hair that waved at his shoulders. Puffs of smoke escaped his lips as he breathed even though the weather was still well into autumn. His arms crossed over his chest as his eyes scanned over the pop-up ad on his portal.

"Is that—"

Isaac Winters extended his hand to click out of the message.

"Wait!" Fern reached out. He turned, his face expressionless as Fern stumbled over to his side. "I want to read this." She pointed and began reading before he could respond.

"Kai, get over here!" Fern encouraged, gesturing with her hand. Kai's feet sank into the earth by Fern's command. As though on an invisible string, the Avlis took hold with a clenched fist. The Mare yelled as his body lunged forward until he was at Fern's side.

I approached by my own free will. "What does it say?"

"It says that Mr. Harris is creating a task force of some kind," Fern replied.

"A task force?" Did this have to do with Sylvia Douglas?

"Yes, a task force to go against the Diviner."

My back straightened at the mention of the Diviner. What did Sylvia say after I left? What did Mr. Harris do to her?

I swallowed hard but didn't say anything.

"Why didn't we get this?" Fern looked back at Isaac. Kai jolted as Isaac's head shifted.

"I imagine it's because you're first years," Isaac guessed, shrugging lightly.

"You're factual," Fern randomly commented with a smile. "Like my friend Kai Lancer. He's very smart and is also a Mare."

Kai brightened to a red hue as Isaac looked at him. He hit her arm with enough panic to also shoot water from his water bottle and into her face. Ignoring his actions, Kai quickly said, "Sorry for bothering you, Mr. Winters."

Isaac scrunched at the formal title, evening out into a neutral expression after a heartbeat. Kai pushed Fern away.

First years, I thought as we walked away.

No, this had to be more than a technicality. *You really think that Gifteds are going to allow you to stay here? Do you really think they would allow an Unfortunate to become a solider?* Sylvia Douglas's words stuck to my conscience like a tumor.

Mr. Harris was already on thin ice bringing me to Galdor. And after the Anti-Gifteds Movement attacked another city... King Daltus's gaze flashed behind my eyes.

I needed to prove my worth more than ever. For Mr. Harris's gambit. For Valerie's promise.

It was time for the morning run. As Fern teased Kai about meeting his hero, I made a beeline toward Mr. Harris. I stomped over with my fist clench like a child, but I didn't care. This was too important to care. We didn't exchange a smile or greeting.

"I see you're creating a task force." I tried standing taller, placing my hands on my hips.

He continued writing on his clipboard as if I wasn't there.

"Mr. Harris, I think it behooves us to let me be on this task force of yours."

Mr. Harris scoffed. His pencil pressed down harder on the paper. "I will do no such thing."

His tone was final, but I refused to yield.

"Mr. Harris." I stepped forward as he began to walk away, drilling to the other students. I tried speaking above him. "After what happened with my little public stunt, I think it's important that we still work together. This could be my new purpose."

"This is not your new purpose." Mr. Harris finally looked at me. "It's too dangerous for..."

"For what? An Unfortunate?"

"For *first years*," Mr. Harris finished. "No first year is allowed to be on any task force. You're too inexperienced."

"Unfortunates are not allowed at a school for Gifteds either. This shouldn't be difficult to arrange."

"I'm not going to rearrange anything, Nora. I will not put your life in danger."

A voice I almost didn't recognize as my own shouted back. "My life is already in danger! My life has always been in danger!"

Valerie's blood pooled around her head.

I inhaled sharply. "This is no different."

"You're not getting assigned to the Diviner task force, and that is final. More insubordination will only serve to punish you."

"I don't fear servant work like the other students do," I countered with narrowed eyes. "What do I need to do to help you?"

"There is nothing you can do."

"What do I need—"

"I only let people who can defeat me on the task force," Mr. Harris cut me off again. He turned away, scribbling on his clipboard. As if I wasn't a threat. As if I was nothing.

I only need to defeat you. I thought. *Very well.*

I charged him.

Mr. Harris turned swiftly in time with my own movements, his hand lightly grabbing my extended arm and twirling me around. He didn't fight back. He didn't punch. He didn't scream. He simply let go. I spun a full rotation before gaining back my bearings.

Several curious eyes turned to our direction. Scattered questions floated through the air.

"What is she doing?"

"What's happening?"

"Did she just—"

Mr. Harris squinted his eyes in a warning look.

No, I thought, launching again.

Mr. Harris adjusted his position, right outside of my grasp. In mid-stride, he tripped my feet. My upper body fell forward; my arms shot out to break the fall. I flipped back to my feet and turned toward Mr. Harris again.

"Fight me!" I yelled.

By this time, the Gifted students stopped their own exercises to witness the show—all stunned and unsure how to act.

"I will do no such thing, Nora."

The rise and fall of my chest grew faster and more irregular. *Calm down,* a part of my brain urged, but I didn't know how to conceal my true feelings anymore. Especially around Mr. Harris.

A hand lightly pressed my shoulder. I snapped my attention to Prince Cassius.

"Your Highness." Mr. Harris sighed as if relieved. "Please take her away for personal training. She needs to learn better offensive combat, and I don't want to see her until she's cooled down."

My neck snapped back to Mr. Harris at the comment, but the prince's grip tightened, lightly pushing me away from the instructor. I walked with the prince in silence. I didn't want to see Mr. Harris anymore either.

***

We moved through the Iridion castle in silence, stopping on the first floor near the classrooms.

A royal guard opened the door in front of us, and we entered.

A large indoor training space greeted us. Monkey bars arched at an incredible height, twisting and turning along the ceiling. Brave Imitation and Avlis students dangled there, their fists clenched white and their focus concentrated ahead. An Avlis dropped downward—caught by the swallowing grass below. Auras danced along the top, lightly touching the bars as they tested their abilities. Several Mares practiced control along the large pool near the back center of the complex. Others hovered their hands over the pool's edge for a moment to capture a sample for their own sparring matches playing out nearby. Along the walls, I could see students practicing in designated rooms through a long clear glass. A Mati thrashed his body to dodge a machine-produced fire, collecting another in his hands and dissipating its fury before anticipating the next one.

Prince Cassius led me to a room offset from the main gym area that had the words, "PERSONAL TRAINING | PRINCE CASSIUS" engraved on the wall next to the door. The windowless room separated us from the world.

Inside, the floor was padded in a light blue color, and white plain walls replaced the castle marble. On the far-right side of the room was an array of weapons powerful Gifteds didn't use.

"Offensive combat today. Since your wounds have healed up a lot more since the last time we trained, let's continue with the bo staff," the prince said, walking over to the array of weapons.

I pressed against the doorframe, unmoving. Helpless adrenaline still thumped loudly in my chest; frustration and embarrassment burned in my expression. What seemingly gave me new worth beyond a servant was in jeopardy—the very idea twisted in my stomach like a knife.

"Nora?" Prince Cassius held out the bo staff.

Why even bother with me? my thoughts screamed. *I'm a failed pet project. Useless and worthless. Nothing more.*

Who was I fooling? I was never anything more.

I flinched as Prince Cassius gently brushed his thumb across my cheek. When did he eliminate the space between us? When did I start crying? More tears fell down my face like rain. Humiliation urgently tried to wipe them away, but the prince didn't back away from me.

"Do you need a moment before we get started?" he asked.

My head shook as I sniffled. I forced the words out, "You have to teach me how to defeat Mr. Harris."

Prince Cassius registered the question. A scoff cracked his concerned expression. "You're asking a Makan how to defeat a Senior Crest Knight?"

"Sure," I pressed, my lips twitching into a small smile to match his. "What's wrong with that, sir?"

"Nothing, nothing," he assured me, scoffing again and looking at the floor with an unexpected cheeky smile. The prince looked back up to meet my glistened eyes. "It's one hell of a request is all."

He stepped back to offer the bo staff again. "Let's get started then. The most important thing to remember is Gifteds are so used to their Gift, they'll underestimate those they deem lesser."

I accepted the weapon. "Guess that works since I'm not a Gifted."

"I much prefer you as an Unfortunate," Prince Cassius agreed, adjusting his footing toward me. We started stretching. "You're more valuable that way."

A doubtful huff escaped my chest. My eyes widened at the mistake. "I'm sorry, sir. Please forgive me for the outbursts."

The prince shrugged. "You may speak freely here, Nora."

Exposed by his sight on my form, I bit my lip. "Mr. Harris won't let me on the Diviner task force."

The prince's movements faltered for a moment. "So you *attacked* him?"

Heat flushed my face confronting that decision. "He said if I could beat him, I could be placed on the team."

"That's Mr. Harris for you," Prince Cassius chuckled to himself, shaking his head as we switched to a new warm-up. "You're motivated at the very least. That's important. I'm sure he will come around when you prove your skills to him."

That wasn't a bad idea, I thought.

"Or attack him again," the prince teased, "whichever comes first, right?"

I scoffed. "Right."

We stretched for several minutes, mimicking the same movements we practiced out in the training field when we first trained together. It was the first time I laughed hard in a while, but no laughter bubbled inside of me now.

"Let's start with the fundamental offense and defense," the prince said, adjusting his staff to the horizontal position. "You can be the first to strike."

The wooden staff wobbled hesitantly in my unsteady hands.

"Like this," he commented, adjusting his staff into the vertical position with one hand toward the center and the other hand gripping the end. "Start with a downward strike in this position."

My staff slowly lowered, connecting with the prince's staff positioned horizontally to block his face.

His eyebrows furrowed. "What *was* that, Nora? Don't hold out on me now. Try again."

Adjusting my stance, I brought the staff down faster. A smacking sound erupted as the staffs collided. "Perfect, now hold your position," he instructed.

I did as the prince lowered his arms, his staff still ready to defend. "Now shift your grip and strike upward."

My hands shifted and pushed upward to strike. A loud snapping sound followed.

"Alright, now you block as I do the same."

I steadied my stance and grip as I blocked his strikes. We switched back and forth several more times, my movements becoming fluid and natural.

"You've got the hang of it," the prince confirmed with a small smile. "Let's try stabbing."

Stabbing? I thought with alarm. Prince Cassius's staff lightly jabbed the center of my chest.

With my mouth agape in humorous shock, my hand instinctively tried pushing it away. He withdrew before I could. "You weren't paying attention."

"I apologize, sir."

"Then let's see you block the attack." Prince Cassius lunged forward. I stumbled back as his staff pressed into my stomach.

He made a *tsk* sound. "Moving backward is almost always a disadvantage. If you parry, try moving to the side instead."

I nodded, stepping forward.

I watched his movements, jolting prematurely as I tried to jump to the side, defending myself poorly. Another jab near my heart.

My body temperature rose. We tried again. My body shifted to the left, my staff angled diagonally like a shield.

We held our position. "Great. What do you plan to do next?"

I examined our situation. He stood in a lowered lunge, his staff poking outward and leaving his body exposed.

I lightly prodded along his rib cage.

"Great," he encouraged. I withdrew. "Again."

We practiced striking and stabbing, our moves becoming more elaborate as we practiced.

"Are you ready to spar?" he asked.

I hesitated. "As I'll ever be, sir."

"Alright." The prince held the staff next to him. "Ground rules: no notes or advice. We'll simply play out a scenario, and you'll have to think on your feet. Whoever makes first contact with the other wins. Ready?"

I shifted one foot toward him with the other pointing to the side. One hand firmly held the end of the staff while the other hand gripped the center.

"Ready, sir."

Prince Cassius charged with an upward strike.

As I blocked, the prince switched into a downward strike. My movements were slower, but I managed to block, the vibration from contact loosening my grip. I regained form as he attacked again, our staffs crossing into an X formation.

He adjusted his hands, pushing down on my weapon. My body forcibly moved downward. I glanced up in time to see Prince Cassius swipe at my head from my right. I ducked, hopping to my right to avoid another attack.

Twirling the staff in my hands, I stepped backward. Prince Cassius spun the staff through his fingers at a faster pace, stepping forward. He changed stances to face sideways, crossing one leg behind the other and crossing his arms.

He held the staff with one hand behind himself, slightly bent. Gripping his hands over the other at the end of the staff, he smacked downward.

I parried again. He spun low as he rose, nearly tripping me in the process. Jumping up, I swung toward Prince Cassius's chest. He jumped off his left foot to dodge, but he landed too late. My staff burrowed into his stomach.

Prince Cassius smiled brightly. "You did it!"

I withdrew, but my initial smile quickly vanished.

"You may speak freely, Nora," he reminded me.

"I still don't think Mr. Harris is gonna let me on the task force."

Prince Cassius's shoulders slouched. "Let's take a break."

I didn't respond as we sat down on the bench against the far right of the room near the weapons.

We drank water in silence. Prince Cassius spoke first. "So why do you want to be on the task force so badly?"

I sighed, refusing to look up. "I failed. I was... I was supposed to come here because I made a promise to someone. And I'm failing that promise to her."

Prince Cassius's lips formed a line. He carefully selected his words as he spoke. "I don't understand exactly what you're going through, but I do understand what it's like to feel like a failure, especially around Gifteds."

I turned to face him. "Do you really?"

"Yes!" It was his turn to look away, his hands out in front of him as he spoke. "My entire life has been nothing but trying to prove myself to other people. My citizens, my sister, my parents, my royal court, even to myself. I don't know what it's like to be an Unfortunate, but I do know what people say about Makans."

As his voice elevated, pieces of his waving arms flickered in and out of the visible plane. I recalled what Kai had said when we first noticed Prince Cassius on the training field. *A Makan can only do so much. Useless even.*

"I'm sorry you have to hear that," I finally said.

"I'm used to it," Prince Cassius tried to joke, running his fingers through his hair. "I'm only on the task force because I'm technically higher ranking than Mr. Harris—though that often doesn't matter. But at the end of the day, my title still exists, even if I am also a Makan. I just have to prove that I'm worthy of being that title."

We sat in that weight.

"Your sister seems to care about you," I tried to encourage.

"My sister is one of the most powerful Gifteds in this world and she doesn't even use it. She refuses!" He threw his hands up in the air in defeat.

So that was not the right thing to say, I thought.

"She wears gloves to hide her skin so she doesn't poison others. It infuriates me! I..." He trailed off, his voice lowering. "I just want to be as powerful as her because that's all they care about."

I tried a different approach. "Well, you're a fantastic teacher. I'm sure others know how much work you're putting into prove yourself to them. Mr. Harris wouldn't include you in the fold for my training otherwise."

Prince Cassius smiled. He adjusted his hair as he spoke. "I'm sorry for just blurting out my own emotions on you."

"You can speak freely here, sir."

The prince paused. "You can stop calling me sir when it's just us."

We locked eyes. His blue eyes were a lot darker close up, the color of crashing waves at the center of a sea.

He playfully squinted. "Are you sure you're an Unfortunate?"

I squinted back in confusion, my voice faltering without looking away. "Why would I be anything else?"

"You're just incredibly bright is all," the prince had his answer ready. "You're different from what I'm used to, you know?"

I did. He was completely different from any Gifted I was used to. We were deemed useless; two powerless people wanting to prove ourselves otherwise.

I realized my intense stare and how close his face was to mine and looked away first, trying to say anything at all to distract myself.

"Has Mr. Harris told you anything? What other information did he get out of Sylvia Douglas?" I found myself asking.

He sighed. "Nothing useful I'm afraid."

My throat clenched as I thought about Sylvia's threat. "Do you think she's going to... actually hurt Thunder Bay because of me?"

"I wouldn't discredit the AGM or the Diviner now," the prince replied honestly. "But maybe we can refuge your family before anything like that can happen."

"Can we save the entire bay?"

Prince Cassius smiled sheepishly. "We can certainly try."

Trying seemed to be the best we both could do right now.

"How about this." Prince Cassius leaned forward with a serious expression. "If you want to prove to Mr. Harris that you are worthy of being a student here—that you are worthy of being on the Diviner task force—what's stopping you from doing a recon mission?"

"A recon mission?"

"Yeah, take destiny in your own hands, Nora!" he encouraged. "It can be a simple recon mission to prove yourself. You could go after the Diviner yourself first without doing anything too dangerous. You could get information about the Diviner and report back! Mr. Harris would have no choice but to include you in the fold."

"I don't know," I said, trying to shake the idea off to no avail. "I don't know how I could even do that."

"All the information you need is freely accessible on Mr. Harris's ID card," the prince clarified.

I gave him a bewildered look. "You're encouraging me to go behind Mr. Harris's back?"

"It's clear from yesterday that you and Mr. Harris are not on the *best* terms," he said delicately. The prince shook his head. "Attacking him this morning didn't help either."

My shoulders slouched at the reminder of my actions. The prince was right. I needed to stay in Mr. Harris's good graces if I was going to stay here and be useful. I couldn't forsake my promise now.

But stealing Mr. Harris's ID card? Going off campus without permission? Could I even pull something like that off? The gleam in Prince Cassius's eyes said I could.

"Would you be coming with me?" I asked.

His smile faltered. "They don't usually notice when I disappear, but Mr. Harris would get suspicious if I missed a task force meeting."

The idea dwindled from my mind.

He leaned toward me, a cheeky smile reforming on his face. "But have you forgotten that I can become invisible?"

CHAPTER FIFTEEN

His Dance and Their Begrudging Truce

"When I said you need to be a little braver sometimes, Nora, this is not what I meant," Leo said.

I fiddled with the candy wrapper in my hands, thankful I couldn't hear the downpour inside the vent. After winning Fern over almost immediately and gaining Kai's favor after tailoring to his goal as an ERS, I thought asking the twins would be a little easier. Of my Gifted classmates, these four were the only ones I could reasonably trust.

"It'll be a simple recon mission. Nothing more, nothing less," I attested. "This can prove we're meant to be here and be on the Diviner task force."

"You can't *attack* a Senior Knight and then go behind his back," Leo continued, gesturing to himself and his sister. "That's something *we* would do in Norburn, and we're not in Norburn anymore."

I remained silent, watching the candle light. I tried piecing my words together.

As I did, Persephone slowly leaned toward her brother. "Leo."

He refused to look at his sister for several seconds, shaking his head and keeping his nose in the air like Skylar. "*Leo*," she repeated in a slower, haunted voice, "it's a simple task. I'm going to say yes and you'll have no choice."

Leo's shoulders slouched, exasperated. He waved his arms at her, the chaos bringing about a crescendo of wrappers.

Persephone straightened back to her sitting position with a smirk on her face before looking at me and nodding.

"We will help." Leo pointed a finger up at his sister as if in warning. "But *only* when it comes to stealing Mr. Harris's ID. We've come too far to do anything more to ruffle his feathers."

"Thank you," I breathed.

Confidence swelled within me—a new feeling that was becoming more and more frequent. Was this how Gifteds felt all the time?

"Then it's settled." I clapped my hands together. "Let's go steal Mr. Harris's ID!"

***

Prince Cassius, Persephone, and I all waited outside of Mr. Harris's office during our lunch break.

"Remember," Prince Cassius whispered, "keep your thoughts and emotions as blank as possible. He's the First Senior Knight for a reason. Unlike other Feras, he's just listed as one."

"His animal isn't specified?" Persephone asked.

The prince shook his head. "Could be a security measure, but I have a suspicion that he can read *our* emotions, so keep your feelings as completely neutral as possible whenever you're close to him."

I remembered when Mr. Harris's emotions poured out and became my own when he was torturing Sylvia Douglas. Was she still alive below my feet? It wasn't long ago that she held a Gifted below her feet.

I shook off my spiraling thoughts. "This cannot fail," I said, looking at the two Gifteds between me. Prince Cassius and Persephone nodded.

The latch on the door snapped open, and Mr. Harris stepped out into the hallway. The three of us pressed ourselves against the wall behind the left-hand side corner, my hand tightening around Prince Cassius's hand.

On cue, Leo walked out from the other side of the hallway away from us, walking toward Mr. Harris.

Leo intercepted him, colliding with Mr. Harris as if by accident. The clipboard and pen fell softly onto the carpeted floor. "Oh, my apologizes, Mr. Harris!" Leo said, bending down with the instructor to assist him. They both arose as Leo continued to pat the instructor, apologizing again.

"It's fine, Leo." Mr. Harris's voice was quieter. "Looking for something on me?"

"No, I was just going on a walk, exploring the castle." Leo didn't hesitate, stepping to walk away when Mr. Harris grabbed his arm.

Silence filled the space. I could practically see Mr. Harris's eyes squint.

My thoughts began to race. Could Mr. Harris already be onto us? I quickly tried to think of nothing as Prince Cassius had advised.

"You're not going off to your secret hiding place. Are you?" Mr. Harris asked.

"You know about that?"

"Of course I do. I didn't choose you and Persephone when I found you in Norburn because you were upstanding citizens."

"Well, that's exactly where I'm going. You caught me." Leo laughed, his footsteps nearing our end of the hallway.

Prince Cassius lifted us from the invisible plane as Leo turned the corner. He jolted as we became visible to him, but instead of saying anything, he shook his head to Persephone.

"It's not on his person," she whispered.

"That's why we have a plan B." Prince Cassius and I shared a glance. "Don't let go."

I couldn't feel my body go into the invisible plane. Everything was still in my view. Did Prince Cassius see the world the same as the rest of us?

We moved unseen through the open hallway. Several students and Royal Crest Knights passed us without incident when they would have at least done the simple gesture of acknowledging Prince Cassius if they could see him.

Leo and Persephone walked out as the hallway cleared. Persephone took a pin out of her black curls, picking the lock to his office. A clicking sound met her approving smile. She pushed the door open, and we entered.

The prince closed the door behind us. Persephone and Leo stood guard outside of the room, far enough away from the door and speaking to each other nearby to avoid suspicion.

Prince Cassius and I let go of each other. He began rummaging through Mr. Harris's office with ease, opening the nearby drawer next to the desk but finding nothing. He closed it and then opened the next row underneath.

I tried to follow his lead by looking through a small white cabinet at the left-hand corner of the room, avoiding the nearby window fogged from the rain.

Looking at a delicate tea set on the highest platform, I opened the tea kettle and looked inside as if it would be hiding there. Finding nothing, I moved downward. Prince Cassius was already at the other corner of the room, moving through an identical cabinet.

"Anything yet?" I found myself asking, my voice shaking.

"Not yet," he replied, not looking at me as he turned toward a small wooden organizer on Mr. Harris's desk.

His fingers thumbed through the papers.

"Found it." Prince Cassius smiled, holding up a white square with Mr. Harris's face on it.

Leo's voice bled through the door. "Hi again, Mr. Harris!" His voice boomed as a warning to us.

I froze, eyes widened. Exchanging pleasantries, it was clear that the siblings couldn't keep him distracted for long.

The knob twisted.

Prince Cassius shoved the ID back into its place before pushing me against the wall nearest to us, his hand firmly over my mouth. He pressed his body against mine, wedging me there as the door swung open. My heartbeat thumped loudly against his.

Mr. Harris entered.

My back instinctively bristled as the weight of his feet moved closer to us. I silenced myself as best as I could as my heartbeat quickened. I tried desperately to concentrate on anything but Prince Cassius's breath falling against my forehead. I stared at the darkness of his chest as if it was a black screen.

Moments passed until Mr. Harris slid away, moving things along his desk in search of something.

Panic seeped into my brain.

Several agonizing minutes passed.

Finally, I could hear the door swing open, closed, and then lock on the other side.

We remained still as Mr. Harris's footsteps receded down the hallway.

Prince Cassius stepped back, taking his hand away from my mouth. "I'm sorry," he apologized. "I had to think quickly before we were caught."

I fumbled over my words. "It's okay. Is the ID still there?"

Prince Cassius turned and looked through the organizer again. He held up the ID. "Yes."

I sighed in relief.

We exited the office as quietly as possible. Leo and Persephone were no longer in the hallway.

He held my hand again. We delicately moved through the castle under the prince's power, far away from Mr. Harris's office and any suspicion that we had been there before.

The Information Square was too public for using Mr. Harris's ID. The number of servants, Knights, and Gifted delegates dwindled until the hallways were completely void of human life.

He opened a seemingly common door, but as I entered, dark grey pillows and clean sheets denoted a bedroom. *His* bedroom. Trinkets decorated plush furniture, so clean and orderly that either he hardly used anything here or the castle Unfortunates did their jobs perfectly.

A large window displayed the grey haze of the world. Rain pelted against the glass, sending a shiver down my spine.

My hand fell back to my side as Prince Cassius reached into his pocket and lifted out nothing between his fingertips. The ID appeared before our eyes as he switched it to the visible plane.

A small glass structure sat on the nearby desk. Pressing Mr. Harris's ID against the portal glass, we accessed the First Senior Royal Crest Knight's account.

A greeting for Mr. Harris popped up on the screen before displaying the instructor's home screen.

Along the left side was our names and faces. Our designated rankings were in smaller font next to our names. I walked closer to the prince, stifling a flinch as a low thunder rolled overhead. I didn't know what I would do if it was raining in Norburn tomorrow.

Two green plus signs with the number five in large text caught my attention.

"What does that say?" I pointed curiously.

"It says that Mr. Harris gave you five points for leadership and valor skills. Must have been for the simulation lab."

More confidence swelled within my heart.

A red minus sign with the number eight in large text resided next to Skylar's photo. "Looks like Skylar lost big points for her teamwork skills."

A new pop-up window greeted the prince. He read it with a frown. "The Diviner task force folder is locked," he explained, exiting out and moving through folders faster than I could comprehend. "I'm going to check his history to see if we can find any insight. Mr. Harris mentioned something about searching through Norburn in our last meeting, but we haven't acted on it yet."

Prince Cassius continued, "Since Norburn is known for its criminal activity, it does make sense for us to search there for a mysterious terrorist."

"Is that all we have to go on?"

The prince nodded, searching more before finally speaking. "Okay, so there's several mentions of the Lilac District in Norburn."

I nodded as the prince continued to frantically type. Harsh wind pierced the silence, and I rubbed the goosebumps along my arm.

"Done," he finally said. "I've used Mr. Harris's administration to place your team on a night patrol in Osthall." He displayed the screen. "That way it registers as Mr. Harris placing the mission himself. You should pass the gate guards easily."

"Why not a mission in Norburn directly?" I asked.

"It's too risky to post you there as first years. Patrols through Norburn are rare, and when they do, it's restricted to third years or Royal Crest Knights because of its reputation. A patrol through Osthall is pretty normal for first and second years since it's the second largest city in Iridion after Galdor. You'll avoid suspicion with this fake assignment. You'll just take the train to Osthall and then directly toward Norburn."

I nodded again. "Sounds like a plan."

The prince logged out of Mr. Harris's account, turning the ID invisible in his hands and tucking it back into his pocket. The mission was now written plainly on the daily activities page.

"Confirmation. You're set. Good luck, Nora." Prince Cassius gave me an encouraging smile.

"We could really use your power on this mission."

Prince Cassius scoffed lightly. "You don't need me. You've brought your team together, and they'll be your best asset moving forward. You can do this without a Makan like me."

I gave him a pained look. "We wouldn't have gotten the ID in the first place without a Makan like you."

He scoffed again, ruffling his fingers through his hair. "I guess not." He finally looked directly at me. "But someone recently got points for her leadership and valor skills."

My temperature rose at the praise, unsure how to respond.

A white flash collided with a dreadful thunder so sudden and loud I involuntarily screamed, stepping closer and bumping into the prince. I wanted to apologize, but my teeth gritted together as my heart beat pounded faster in my chest. I remained motionless, paralyzed, as the Choosing Ceremony forced its way to the forefront of my mind.

Prince Cassius hovered around my frame, close enough I could feel the fabric of his clothes along my cheek but open enough for me to step away if I needed to.

Slowly, he held his hand out to me. "Would you dance with me, Nora?"

"What?" I managed to ask in between unsteady breaths.

"Dance with me," he repeated. "It'll distract you from the Choosing Ceremony and calm your nerves."

My voice came out as a whisper. "You know about that?"

The prince shrugged as his hands reached out for mine, leading them upward to his shoulders before slowly wrapping his hands around my waist. "I see it all the time in the palace Unfortunates—how fearful they become over seemingly nothing. For you, is it the rain perhaps? Was it raining at your Choosing Ceremony?"

I nodded, my eyes fluttering from his face to my feet.

"Seems like I'm the only one who actually cares enough to ask and comfort." He sighed, looking away for a moment before changing the subject. "We're going to do something simple. Mirror my movements."

I kept my gaze downward, stepping to my right as he stepped to his left, stepping backward as he stepped forward, my left, upward, and repeat...

"Easy, right?" he asked.

Thunder rumbled above; I inhaled sharply.

"Look at me. Focus on me," Prince Cassius whispered.

I did, concentrating on his eyes—the same dark blue coloring of the world. Except a twinkle resided in his gaze unlike the storm outside. The sound of rain softened as the prince hummed a low tune; the Choosing Ceremony washed away as I danced in his warm embrace. Not huddled or crammed. Safe. Secure. *The way I felt around you.*

I nodded in agreement.

We danced for more heartbeats than I could count. He slowed to a stop, and we lingered there for a couple more seconds until he let go and stepped back.

"Now go prove yourself," Prince Cassius said. "I'll get the ID back before Mr. Harris notices, and I'll make sure he stays unsuspecting."

Right. I ignored other desires, concentrating instead on the mission as it became more real with each passing second. I dipped my head to him. "Thank you, Your Highness."

***

A flush still warmed my cheeks as I entered the dorm.

I didn't register the muffled yelling until all Gifteds abruptly silenced and turned in my direction.

My smile faltered into a line as Skylar and Molly slunk forward, their backs hunched to pounce and eyes trained on their prey. Tension dampened the air; Fern held her hands tightly against her mouth, her own eyes so wide they might pop out.

"*Nora*," Molly dragged out my name as the two Gifteds crept forward.

Their shadows suffocated my form, my body wedged between them and the closed door.

"Come on. Leave her alone," Leo warned, fire licking his fingers. Persephone bristled and stepped closer to him.

"We're just going to have a quick chat," Skylar assured. She reached out and grabbed the doorknob, effectively cutting off any escape. Her dark stare bore into me, but she addressed Leo this time. "Unless you want to die from carbon monoxide, back down, Mati."

Leo's fingers curled; Persephone wrapped her hand around his and snuffed the flame.

I successfully hid my terror behind a blank, almost clueless façade. I'd had eight years of practice.

"Fern told us you're planning a recon mission," Skylar prompted.

"Nora, I am so sorry. It slipped—"

"Quiet," Skylar waved her hand behind herself. "Do you think you'll get all the glory if this works? We want to be on a task force as first years just as much as you do. You think you can take that leverage away from us?"

I swallowed hard. "I'm not taking anything from either of you."

The usual ticks that would push Molly away brought her closer to me instead.

"You still belong to me. Understand?" Molly pressed a firm hand along the wall closest to my healing shoulder and leaned down. Her slit eyes consumed my vision. "Regardless of what Mr. Harris says, your actions still embarrass my family."

Her hand jumped to my hip, the other clutching my mouth and muffling my scream. Molly pressed my face against the door as I squirmed, her hiss paralyzing me in place like I was back at the Montgomery mansion.

My arms were scrunched together near my chest. Pushing the Imitation away became futile.

"Molly!" Fern yelled. Skylar whipped around with her hand out, a powerful gust throwing the other Gifteds to the ground.

Fern sprung up; the plant on her desk morphed wildly within seconds and curled behind her form. Water spiraled around Kai's torso, and fire burned brightly where Leo and Persephone stood. Skylar held a lunged pose facing the other Gifteds with her palms open.

Cal stepped out from his corner near Fern, his hands by his side. "Let the Unfortunate go, Skylar."

"We'll let her go in just a moment."

"Sky."

"What is wrong with you lately?" she demanded with a pained expression. *"I said a moment."*

Molly's forked tongue brushed against my exposed neck. "We're coming along for this little mission of yours, or we're telling Mr. Harris that you're going behind his back. Got it?"

All the theatrics for not bringing them into the fold? I managed to nod my head despite Molly's best efforts.

The Imitation's black mouth moved from my neck to my face, adjusting her hand from my mouth to below my ear. I involuntarily whimpered as her tongue grazed along my cheek, soiling any comfort left over from Prince Cassius's dance.

"I missed your fear," Molly whispered. "It suits you, especially when you were with that other Unfortunate girl. Do you remember when I almost tore her hand off? Your fear was intoxicating."

No. My hand clamped onto Molly's wrist so hard my knuckles whitened. I pushed myself off the wall, creating enough space between us to step forward. My other hand found her neck, gaining momentum to push her to the ground. I straddled her, both of us trembling against the other.

I tried screaming at her—payback for the combat exam—but the words choked in my throat as air depleted from my lungs.

"Skylar!" I'd never heard Cal yell before.

I gasped as breath came back to me.

"You're not allowed to fight me!" Skylar yelled.

"You kill her now and you don't get your task force."

After several heartbeats, Skylar cursed, throwing her hands up. A cutting wind knocked me off Molly. The Imitation continued to squirm and spit on the ground until Fern wrapped foliage around Molly's limbs and subdued her.

As I stood, Persephone held my arms in place. Cal was closer to his fiancée now, his hand outreached but not touching Skylar.

Anger seeped from every pore. We huffed at each other, our teeth gritted like animals. I certainly wasn't that sheepish servant girl anymore.

"Where is this recon mission, Nora?" Fern asked, concern betraying her expression. Could changing the subject really undo what just happened?

"Norburn," I replied shortly. "We leave tonight."

The twins shared a side glance.

"Persy, we can't. We can't." Leo shook his head at her even though she didn't say anything.

"What is it?" I demanded.

Leo looked down as Persephone spoke in a slow and calming voice. "That's close to home is all."

"Close to home?" Leo scoffed. "That's a district away, Persy. How close do you have to be before considering it home?"

"I've never considered it home."

Leo crossed his arms. "I don't want to go back there, Pers. Especially if Skylar is going."

Skylar gave him a scowl that he returned. "Careful, princess," Leo warned, "you don't look very regal right now."

Cal threw his arm out as Skylar did, redirecting her attack toward the far wall. He finally grabbed her forearm, "Sky."

"Get off of me!" she yelled, tearing her arm away from him, but she didn't attack again. Skylar inhaled a deep sigh, her fists flexing at her side and gaze downward. "You're pathetic, Cal."

His chest rose as he inhaled sharply, but he didn't refute her claim. Silence claimed the room.

Any confidence I'd had before was replaced with an impending dread. If I was forced to sneak out of Galdor with Skylar and Molly, I could use all the allies I could get. I needed Leo and Persephone. So much for bringing the team together.

Persephone finally spoke up, "Guess you'll stay behind and cover for us, Leo."

Flames ignited with Leo's disapproving grunt, rising from his forearm and quickly dissipating at his shoulder. Persephone stared at him with an aura of authority.

"Not this again," Leo spat before sighing. "*Fine.* You know I can't let you go in alone."

He groaned his opposition a second time before turning to me. All Gifted eyes fell on me again as he asked, "What's the plan?"

I looked out at the divided room, focusing directly on Skylar. "If I tell you, you can't ruin it like you did in the Black Box."

Skylar pointed an accusing finger, but Cal held her back. She huffed.

I continued, "It's strictly a recon mission. Can I trust that you both will stick to recon *only*? We don't know what the Diviner is capable of, but we know he's dangerous beyond our familiarity."

Just saying that out loud dampened the air with dread. But there wasn't any turning back now. We all had something to gain and lose from this mission.

"Don't talk to us like that—" Molly began, struggling against the vines.

"*Yes,*" Skylar crossed her arms, leering down to the Imitation. "We'll stick to recon only."

Too many emotions swirled in Skylar's dark eyes as she looked up at me. Ambition and determination struck me the most—a common ground we could silently agree on.

Okay, I thought. *A begrudging truce was better than none.*

CHAPTER SIXTEEN

Hidden in the Lilac District

Night approached faster than I realized. The rain clouds drifted south, away from Norburn.

We'd all dressed in dark student uniforms, the material skin tight and elastic like what we used in the simulation lab.

Kai explained that the word RECRUIT was stamped in white along our hearts with our last names visible underneath.

The Mati twins and I didn't have a family name, so it simply read our first names.

The western watchtower's lights looked down upon us as we approached the gated entrance. Two Royal Crest Knights stood guard, halting us.

"State your business," the left one said, holding out his hand out.

Kai held his ID forward. "Kai Lancer with the rest of Mr. Harris's first-year class. We are on our way to a night patrol in Osthall as given by our instructor."

The Royal Crest Knight pressed down on the walkie-talkie he had resting on his chest. "West Watchtower. This is the West Gate. I have Mr. Harris's first-year class requesting an exit for a night patrol in Osthall. Request for confirmation. Over."

There was a reply of static as the West Watchtower looked through its records of a nightly patrol.

After a minute, a response echoed through the walkie-talkie. "This is the West Watchtower. Request confirmation approval. Over."

A loud beeping sound I recognized from first entering Galdor Academy blared as the gates pulled back at the watchtowers command. The two Royal Crest Knights parted for us.

We stepped through without incident.

A cold chill ran down my back.

Galdor's city lights gleamed as Gifteds enjoyed the civilian nightlife. We walked along the neatly laid sidewalk as Gifteds chatted and laughed on their way to some bar or party or their homes.

We passed Galdor Square, and I recognized the space from the simulation lab. A long emptiness reached out for a mile. The bazaar had since been closed down for the night, the shops lifted, and their shopkeepers calling it a night.

We approached the train station, a denser mix of Gifteds than I expected at this hour. Bypassing the expense of a ticket because of our fake patrol, we entered the train without incident.

We sat down in our train car, the sign above the doors reading: "Next Stop: OSTHALL."

I reiterated the plan. "When we get to Osthall, we will redirect to the F10 train that goes toward Norburn."

They nodded in acknowledgment.

I looked at the rest of my classmates, Sylvia's warning fading in and out of my subconscious. *Do you really think they would allow an Unfortunate to become a solider? Stand alongside them?*

Several Gifteds here wanted to be alongside me. Others were here for their own gain. I watched Skylar and Molly chat with each other a few rows away from me.

Fern nudged me with an encouraging smile. "I'm sorry again for spilling. I was just so... nothing can be an excuse, huh?"

At least this wasn't the first time a Gifted stumbled through an apology around me. "As long as we focus on recon, we should be fine," I managed. Skylar and Molly had something to lose from failure too. That alone should keep them in check.

Looking outside, Galdor shrank into a bright light as we traveled toward the Crime Capital of Iridion.

A pitch-black night greeted us as the train doors opened at its final destination. The train station was a far cry from the buzzing atmosphere of Galdor. The lights that weren't shattered overhead flickered in and out, the only sign of life struggling to stay that way. The station must not have seen maintenance in years. Shadows danced about at the corners of my vision. I hoped they were only my imagination.

Leo walked off the train first, followed by his sister. The platform was cracked as we stepped off—either by time or by an Avlis, I couldn't be sure.

"Home sweet home," Leo said sarcastically, shaking his head.

The words, "WELCOME TO NORBURN" were printed on a large sign, but *"welcome"* and *"to"* were covered with "LEAVE" in bright red letters.

"We're trying to reach the Lilac District," Kai reminded the group, glancing up at an old map of Norburn painted on the brick wall. Spray paint scribbled and overlapped each other as people claimed and lost territory. A thick layer of black paint obscured the bottom left corner of the map. Kai's eyebrows ruffled, "I don't see it here."

"That's because the Lilac District is technically located here." Leo pointed to the black mark. "But hardly anyone sets foot there after the Lady Lilacs were taken down."

"Lady... Lilacs?" we all asked.

"Yeah, an all-women gang that resided on the southwest side of town. They specialized in taking down romantic and domestic abusers. They were done in what? A decade ago by the royal guard?" He looked over to Persephone for help but continued. "Almost all Lilacs were taken away to prison.

The rest scattered and renounced their association. Since the conflict happened for several years before their leader was captured, both sides destroyed everything they possibly could to defeat the other. It's so worn down now that hardly anyone acknowledges it."

I crossed my arms. "Then it's the perfect place for someone to lay low."

I was silently thankful that Mr. Harris's intel was becoming more credible by the moment. Now all that was left to do was scope out the Diviner and report back.

The siblings led the way as we entered the city limits.

Worn down was an understatement. Most buildings leaned on top of each other in unrestful slumber; cockroaches scurried between concrete and glass pieces that littered the ground; pipes jutted and twisted toward the night sky; the wind howled and screamed in our ears as it zigzagged through overgrown streets.

My muscles tensed at every shadow, anticipating a strike that never came.

Leo made a *hmm* sound as he and Persephone stopped in their tracks. We did the same. "What is it?" Kai whispered.

The Mati brother pointed to a nearby warehouse. "That building over there is more intact than the others. If I were to stay here, I would choose the most accommodating place."

Could an abandoned warehouse count as accommodating?

We approached the slab that resembled a door. Skylar raised her hand, her palm open.

"Don't," Kai warned her before she could summon her Gift. "The structure is still hazardous. If you use your Gift, you might do more than simply swing the door open."

Skylar gestured to use her Gift anyway, but everyone's glare reminded her of our begrudging truce. She let her arms fall to her sides.

Persephone and Cal worked together to pull the door open with their bare hands instead. Rust rubbed against concrete as the door slid from one side to the other. Darkness greeted us, though the open hole where the ceiling should have been allowed a crescent moon to gleam dimly at the immediate surroundings.

Most of the space was empty as far as we could see. A crunching sound erupted as I stepped on glass. "Careful where you step," I advised as we made our way toward the center of the abandoned warehouse.

My foot stepped onto something elevated from the ground and soft. Not glass.

I looked down and picked up a dirty book. I couldn't read its spine, but the contents scribbled out dates with logged entries I couldn't comprehend even in the moonlight.

"Kai, look at this."

He stood in front of me. I handed the book over to him, but he shook his head as he flipped through the pages. "It's just an old log book for the inventory."

No dice.

I sighed. I guess it couldn't be that easy.

"Where do you expect to find the Diviner in this?" Skylar crossed her arms and leaned toward Cal, her voice echoing through the building.

I fumbled, my voice softer. "That's the entire point of recon. We—"

Kai cut me off, "Quiet!"

A gust of wind rustled through the open infrastructure. The only entrance slammed shut. Darkness developed our sight.

"Did you do that?" I shakily asked Skylar.

She shook her head. "Cal?"

He shook his head no.

"Molly," I turned to her, "can you see anything?"

"I don't take orders from an Unfortunate," the Imitation hissed.

"Molly!" Skylar yelled.

"I don't—" Molly searched around frantically. "On the railing!"

Leo punched in the direction she pointed, a flame erupting upward. A black-cloaked figure illuminated above us, his smooth white mask hiding his identity.

Leo tried again, his flame expanding and more violent than before. The masked Gifted shot his hands out, the fire rolling back against the air. *An Aura.*

Persephone stood firmly next to her brother, holding her left hand out and circling her right hand to concentrate Leo's Gift toward the target. Leo gritted his teeth, his hand shaking.

The masked Gifted snapped his hands apart, air pulling the flames at either side of him. Leo yelled as wind forced him closer. Persephone grabbed her brother's hand and steadied him.

Crossing his arms over his head, the masked Gifted released them violently to his sides. A strong gust of wind knocked us back. I slammed into the far wall. Molly winced next to me.

"Cal!" Skylar shrieked to my right.

My breath hitched as I turned to see Cal's body faced upward to the sky, a metal rod sticking out of his stomach.

His hands curled, blood pouring onto the floor. Fern and Skylar hovered over his trembling body; Skylar repeatedly said, "I'm sorry," in a shrill voice I didn't recognize as her own.

No.

The masked Gifted clenched his fist, a red glow igniting underneath his black attire. He pulled his arm back, a flame forming from his knuckles. *A Mati?* But he was an Aura before. How could he switch Gifts?

Fire ignited downward toward Persephone, Leo, and Kai who had held their ground at the center of the warehouse. Persephone waved her hand, deflecting as fast as she could. The flame redirected toward the left, a puddle of spilled oil erupting into flame and illuminating the warehouse in a bright red heat.

"I'm out of here!" Molly yelled, beelining toward the exit. My body struggled to stand, still shocked from the wall's initial impact.

"Molly, no!" I tried following her on instinct.

The masked Gifted jumped down from the railing, grabbing her before she could escape. I stopped dead in my tracks.

Molly screamed as she struggled against his grasp. Her fangs bit down on air. He held her neck steady in an extended pose. A red and black light ignited brighter than any fire, burning my eyes.

I turned away; Molly screamed until the light faded and ceased.

I turned back in time to see Molly slump over on the ground, unmoving.

My breath hitched as he looked up, the nearby flames reflecting in his white mask.

"Fall back," I ordered.

The masked Gifted lunged forward. Persephone stepped in first. Fire followed her right hook. Dodging, the masked Gifted curled his hand as he absorbed Persephone's flame. She held her arm out, as it throbbed uncontrollably and her teeth gritted. They held at a standstill for a heartbeat. His fingers curled tighter into a ball. Twisting his wrist, he shot the flame back at her.

She gasped as her body was thrown toward the consuming fire. Persephone held her palms out, igniting a flame quickly enough to propel her off course and fall near a pillar.

Leo weaved into the fight in his sister's place. The masked Gifted grabbed his wrist, dug his nails inward, and lit the fuse. Leo screamed as fire ripped through his right arm, burning him from the inside.

As Leo fell to his knees, Kai ran forward to the Mati's aid. *No.*

"I can't pull him out by force!" Skylar's voice cried behind me. She looked up to Fern pleadingly. "Do you know how to bend metal?"

Fern's hands were unsteady in front of her, her face twisted in horror. "I-I-I can try."

The masked Gifted stepped toward us. I needed to hold him off as long as I possibly could.

I sprinted in his direction, but he deviated off course to avoid me. Gritting my teeth, I followed, reaching out my hand and catching his sleeve. The masked Gifted tried pulling away. My fingers gripped harder in anticipation of an attack—of fire to ignite my skin.

He brought me closer instead, bringing me face-to-face with the white mask. With both hands on my shoulder, he pushed me downward.

"No!" I yelled, side swiping my feet and successfully tripping him. A bead clattered to the floor as it spilled from his possession—bright red in color with a black oval shape swirling in the center like a familiar eye staring straight at me. The masked Gifted frantically tried capturing the bead as it bounced away, but it cracked open, its color completely distinguishing into grey.

My body shot upward, positioning myself in front of Fern and Skylar again, my arms raised toward my face.

He stood up too, his eyes unseen but glaring through me regardless. My nerves bristled, expecting fire or any Gift at all now that he'd changed from an Aura. For several heartbeats, we remained motionless.

Why wasn't he using his Gift against me? Could he know I was an Unfortunate just by sight alone? And even if he could somehow know I was an Unfortunate... his caution would not be wasted. I couldn't let him hurt anyone else.

I roundhouse kicked. His fingers wrapped around my ankle, redirecting my aim. I spun, landing clumsily on my toes. But I landed nonetheless, propelling myself forward to intercept him before he could move past me.

My elbow connected with his neck, his mask falling to the floor. Black cloth covered his face underneath. Close enough to hear his rapid breath, I twisted my leg back to lock his leg into place. My elbow connected with his cheek, but he untangled himself, kicking the back of my leg.

I stumbled forward, falling onto my face. Broken glass dug into my lip; the metallic taste of blood lined my mouth.

He picked up his mask as I reached for a nearby rod, its end sharpened from years of erosion.

I forced my body upward, slashing the masked Gifted while he had his back turned. He yelled, clamping his hand onto his right side. Not the deep laceration I had intended but successful nonetheless.

With one hand, he hastily cauterized the wound. With the other, he turned back to me and grabbed the rod, holding me there.

The rod in his left hand burned red as it melted between his fingers. I gasped as he threw me aside. More glass impaled my left palm. Screaming, my hand shook side to side violently as blood spilled out of the wound. *I tried, Valerie. I tried being as brave as you.*

But he didn't go after me.

Skylar yelled, a heavy force of wind blocking the masked Gifted's advances. He struggled to push through, his hands covering his hidden face. He slowly curled his hand inward, crushing something. A green glow erupted beneath his black attire. With the same hand, he lifted his arm upward.

Cal screamed as the metal rod started splitting in half, digging into either side of his ribs. More blood splattered on the ground. Fern screamed through gritted teeth, her shuddering fingers trying to press together to no avail.

Skylar faltered as she turned to her fiancé's cries. *The masked Gifted was an Avlis now?*

The masked Gifted grabbed Skylar as she was distracted, the earth splitting the concrete and lifting them upward to the skyline. Fern swiped her hand across her chest. The earth structure crumbled, but the masked Gifted and Skylar were gone.

I cursed, scanning the wreckage of the warehouse. Fern shakily bent down over Cal's body. Molly lay motionless at the entryway. Persephone and Kai struggled to subdue Leo, who was squirming on the floor, holding his burnt and smoking flesh as fire erupted from his every scream.

My legs raced toward the exit before I could understand the consequences, before anyone could protest or even follow me.

I frantically looked up to the rooftops for any sign at all. Skylar's protests echoed through the empty streets, but I couldn't see her. Instead, I ran after her cursing.

The commotion led me to an abandoned apartment building. As I entered, her screams cut out at once. I stopped mid-stride at the base of the staircase. Silence pierced the air.

I slowly ascended, hoping for any indication of their position, for any indication that Skylar was alive. The stairs stopped abruptly at the fifth floor, the rest missing. I entered the fifth-floor hallway, noticing two doors ajar unlike the others.

Tiptoeing closer, my heartbeat thumped loudly in my ears.

I hovered in front of the door, holding my breath as I looked inward. Skylar was on the ground, her hands and feet carelessly tied to a chair leg. Tape covered her mouth.

A violent crashing sound exploded from my right. I snapped my attention to see the masked Gifted in the next room, his back to me as he violently rummaged around for something unseen. He held his cut wound in his free hand, huffing.

I squeezed into the room with Skylar, my index finger on my lips. Her muffled cries grew louder as she noticed me, violently shaking in her restraints. Wind rattled the open windows.

I looked around the room for anything that could help me break or untie the knots. Searching the nearest drawer, I pulled it open and found a pair of old scissors—not ideal but a possibility.

As I picked it up, the hair along my neck stood up. I twisted around.

The masked Gifted stared at me through the doorway.

I stepped in front of Skylar, my hands clasped around the scissors as my only defense.

The masked Gifted stepped into the room. My voice came out as shakily as the scissors rattling in front of me. "Are you the Diviner?"

Before he could answer, a cold chill swept the hallway, the same chill I had felt when we left Galdor Academy.

The entrance wall intersecting with the right wall began to frost over in a blue hue. My body jerked involuntarily at the sudden drop in temperature. The wooden floor of the hallway entrance splintered and cracked.

Isaac Winters stepped into the doorframe.

The masked Gifted stood between us, his head tilted as if in thought. As the ice continued to consume the fragile infrastructure of the room as his choices dwindled.

I jolted as he sprinted to my immediate left, avoiding the consuming ice and jumping out of the nearest window. Running over and looking down, I noticed a half-formed vine descended from the outer wall.

The masked Gifted had vanished.

I fell to my knees, dropping the scissors as the rise and fall of my chest suffocated me.

What have I done?

CHAPTER SEVENTEEN

A Princess's Pardon

I looked down at the rusty scissors. Tears swelled in my eyes, falling down onto the floor like rain.

Grabbing the weapon, I turned. "Isaac, help me untie Skylar."

The Aura screamed something unknown behind the tape, but she didn't struggle as I pulled on one of the ropes and tried cutting into it.

Isaac walked behind Skylar, slowly grabbing one of the ropes behind her arms. Ice developed around his fingers, and the material splintered apart.

"Are you okay?" I asked as we freed her. "Did he do anything to you?"

Without moving her hand at all, I lost my footing and slammed into the nearest wall opposite of Skylar as wind swirled around her.

"He wasn't able to do anything!" Skylar yelled, standing up. "But I have to go after him *right now.*"

She charged the open window. I leaned up but my body wouldn't stand. "Wait, it's too dangerous now!"

Isaac held his hand up; ice crystalized around Skylar's feet. She fell forward.

Sitting on her palms, she shouted. A stormy wind cracked the wall and violently shifted the old furniture around the room. Isaac held his hand out to the open window, sealing it with a thick slab of ice.

"Let me go!" Skylar demanded, shooting up from the ground and staring straight through my Unfortunate soul. Her hands balled into fists. "This entire mission is a complete *failure!* I can't believe this is happening. This is all your fault! If Cal—if Cal is..."

She stopped herself, her lips quivering and limbs shivering.

I struggled to find the words myself. The childish thing to do was spitting back in Skylar's face. Tell her that she forced *my* hand to get here. But I couldn't. Not when she looked human.

I couldn't say anything to fix what I'd done. To Cal. To Leo. Even to Molly. No way could I take back my actions against them.

"How did you know where to find us?" Skylar turned toward Isaac, who stared back blankly.

He pointed in my direction. "Your initial fascination with a task force, and then seeing you leave for a night patrol was suspicious at best. I've been stuck at Galdor long enough to know Mr. Harris would never assign anything to a first-year class so early."

My nerves spiked at the thought of Mr. Harris.

I swallowed hard. "Where is Mr. Harris?"

"He and the other Royal Crest Knights are already at the abandoned warehouse tending to your classmates. We shall rendezvous with him there."

My feet stuck to the ground. I wasn't ready to face him or whatever waited at that warehouse. *We should have run away together when we had the chance, Valerie.* But running away was not an option anymore.

We walked the empty streets of the Lilac District in silence toward the abandoned warehouse, now lit with artificial light.

Royal Crest Knights were posted outside, all whispering and contacting each other through walkie-talkies. The door was wide open as we arrived.

I hesitated at the entrance.

A gust of wind tripped my feet. I stumbled forward as Skylar walked past with more urgency.

The fire had been extinguished, and Mr. Harris stood near the center of the warehouse, his back turned to me.

Leo's agonizing grunts pushed my sight toward him. Kai and another medical personnel were wrapping his right arm in gauze. I could see the blisters and bubbles of his dark skin. Persephone held his left hand, her face twisted in worry.

My legs continued forward against my will, my footsteps quiet. I didn't want Mr. Harris to turn around. I didn't want him to ever turn around.

A stretcher lay before him. He spoke something unknown to the medical ERS at the helm who adjusted the patient's arm.

Molly.

I was close enough now to see Mr. Harris hold his hand against Molly's cheek. Her eyes were closed, and her body remained still.

"She's breathing but unconscious," the ERS explained.

"We'll find out what happened to her when she's awake," Mr. Harris said. "If our suspicions are correct, she's the first to stay alive this long after an encounter. Take her to the infirmary and check for any injuries immediately."

The ERS nodded and propelled the stretcher forward.

Skylar's voice hitched in her throat at the sight of another stretcher near a pipe that jutted out to the sky, a red liquid drying on the floor. Something tall hid underneath a white sheet.

She ran over, screaming out his name.

Mr. Harris turned at her cries. His face visibly hardened as we locked eyes. His glare froze me in place.

The back of my hair stood up as I anticipated a strike. I deserved it. He could kill me right now and I would deserve it.

"I take full responsibility, Mr. Harris." I forced the words out through my clenched throat.

Mr. Harris didn't say anything for several heartbeats. "What attacked your team? Do you have a description?"

The words fell out as my nerves spiked, recalling the events. "I didn't see their face. They were wearing a white mask and black clothes, but the build suggests male—"

Mr. Harris grabbed my shoulders, steadying me. "Was it an all-white mask?"

I nodded.

Mr. Harris's focus was elsewhere, lost in thought. "Was there any—any bright lights you saw?"

I nodded again. "He did something to Molly. And he… he changed his Gift right in front of us."

Mr. Harris released me and stepped back.

"Is that what the Diviner means?" I asked.

His jaw tightened, giving me my answer. The Diviner and the masked figure were one and the same.

Mr. Harris finally looked at me. "Nora, you are condemned to classroom and servant duty indefinitely until the Senior Circle can figure out what to do with you."

He turned away.

I had expected an argument, his face red with anger and his words laced with venom. For a chasm to form instead…

I opened my mouth to say something useful, but Mr. Harris interrupted me.

"Dismissed."

Isaac stepped forward to escort me, waiting.

I didn't have enough energy to fight him. My feet dragged out of the warehouse, a dark and heavy feeling enveloping my chest, my lungs, and my very being.

***

Mr. Harris kept to his word.

Alone in the lecture hall, I irritably tapped the pencil in my hand as a regular Royal Crest Knight relished in the history of Iridion. Mr. Leka was startled at the beginning of our lesson when a large textbook landed on my desk and I told him how I couldn't fully read along.

But Mr. Leka persisted, drawing a crude map of Iridion on the board and using it as his guide. He extended his arms and began pulling them inward like he was trying to crush the map with his mind. Not a Gift he could possess.

"So King Alston was able to unite the kingdom underneath his rule because of his unique Animus ability."

I tried following along. I had dreamed of following along at school, but I couldn't now. My mind wandered to what happened yesterday. The Diviner stuck to my skin.

And that strange light when the Diviner grabbed Molly. The bright red hue, the black center. It all reminded me of her eyes, but why?

Mr. Harris said she was the first to survive. What did the Diviner do that you can't come back from?

"With that power, King Alston formed the Kingdom of Iridion. What's interesting is how an Animus is only present in the royal family, so his Gift had been bestowed to him by Caliel to lead us."

"Caliel?" I blurted.

"Sorry, force of habit. Auran translation," Mr. Leka apologized, "by the *Divine* to lead us."

The reminder of Sylvia's rude words echoed in my mind. She had told me this new life was fake. But my bruises were real. Cal, Leo, Molly, and Skylar's screams were real. Not that I could face them now. I looked around the empty lecture hall.

What could this mean for Mr. Harris? He was already on thin ice for bringing an Unfortunate to Galdor Academy and then held responsible for my public failure. Damnit. The only reason I even left the academy was to help him, but all I did was doom us both.

"...how we haven't seen an Animus in about three hundred years. Let's hope that—"

"What is an Animus again?"

Mr. Leka tapped his pen on his shoulder at the second outburst. He pointed to King Alston on the board, his drawing as elegant as an elementary student's rendition. "An Animus is of the mind, which means that they are capable of both reading minds and moving objects with their minds."

I cursed to myself. The Diviner couldn't be an Animus then.

"Has there ever been..." I paused as I tried to find the right words, "a Gifted who could... change their Gift on a whim?"

Mr. Leka stared at me for too long. His face slowly scrunched into a confused expression. "I don't understand the question."

I played with my fingers as I spoke. "Has there ever been a Gifted that can be *bestowed* more than one Gift?"

Mr. Leka looked at his drawing for an answer. "Not any I'm aware of…"

A knock interrupted our lecture. Mr. Leka took the interruption with stride.

"Come in," he encouraged.

I jumped at the sight of Princess Maya as she entered the classroom. "I'm sorry to interrupt." She spoke in a soft and thoughtful voice.

Her smile brightened the room. A bright light like when Molly thrashed in the Diviner's grasp.

"Oh, I thought Mr. Harris would be with you. My apologies," she said.

"Oh, no apologies at all, Your Highness!" Mr. Leka extended his entire body forward in a bow.

Princess Maya waved her gloved hand out. "At ease, Mr. Leka. I was hoping to find a guard for my afternoon walk. Since he's not here, would you like to accompany me, Nora?"

My eyes widened. "You want me to accompany you, Your Highness?" I asked politely.

"Indeed." She nodded her head. "I do believe if Mr. Harris is not here, he might be squabbling with Minister Gabriel. Or perhaps training the unharmed students."

Her comment sliced my nerves.

"I don't think I have the experience to guard you properly, ma'am. Why not take Mr. Leka?"

"Oh, that won't be a problem," Princess Maya insisted. "We're not even leaving the Grounds. Promise."

Mr. Leka and I exchanged an uncertain look.

"It's settled." Princess Maya clapped her hands together before anyone could object. She stepped out of the room, and I jumped out of my seat to follow her.

"Careful," she warned, stepping away as I ran out to her. A flash of heat radiated off her body, my only warning to her poisonous skin. "You don't want to get too close to me. Nox, remember?"

I recalled how Kai mentioned that Princess Maya could melt Prince Cassius's bo staff with one touch.

"I apologize, ma'am." I bowed my head softly while taking a step back, a space forming between us.

"No need to apologize," she assured as we walked down the hallway.

We didn't say anything for several minutes while Royal Crest Knights, students, and Unfortunate servants alike all bowed to her as we passed, their backs instinctively pressing toward the walls to avoid her touch.

We made it out to the Grounds.

The princess reached her hands out to the bright light with a sigh. "It's such a beautiful day out today."

"It is indeed, ma'am."

We walked down the Southern Wall near the student dormitories. She adjusted her clothes, overlaying her light pink long sleeve dress onto her gloves. "I'm so glad it's cooler out. Sometimes when it's too hot," Princess Maya fanned her face, "it's hard for me to take a stroll without completely burning up."

"Winter is fast approaching, ma'am."

Princess Maya's lips pouted in concern as we passed the East Watchtower. She didn't press as we moved toward the open space that divided the academy from the Servant Quarters and the Servant Canteen.

The princess deviated as though following an invisible barrier. She looked out to the wooden L-shaped building that denoted the Servant Quarters.

"I must admit, Nora, you're the most unusual Unfortunate I have ever encountered."

"I apologize if I disappoint you, ma'am."

"Not necessarily disappoint," she countered, turning toward me. Her eyes were the same blue color as her brother's. "All my life, I've simply wished to be an Unfortunate, someone who causes no harm to others. But recently, between you and this Anti-Gifteds Movement... you are the most *dangerous* Unfortunate I've ever seen."

A jolt rippled throughout my body. I recalled how Prince Cassius had ranted about his sister holding a powerful Gift but refusing to use it. But did she really want to be an Unfortunate? Someone with no power at all? The idea burned me to my very core.

"You wouldn't be the Princess of Iridion if you held no power, ma'am."

"Perhaps not," she agreed, running her hands through her straight blonde hair. "But I wouldn't have to take such precautions around other people if I was something other than a Nox. I'm happy with my position, don't ever think otherwise. I just..."

The princess stopped twiddling with her hair, her eyes looking down in thought. "I just wish I could connect with people the way other Gifteds and even Unfortunates can."

Could she be talking about her brother?

We walked along the South Wall where the third training field was located, where I had first attempted attacking Gifteds in the combat exam.

Now one was dead, another had their right arm severely burned, and the other...

I couldn't figure out what the Diviner had done to her.

"I must admit, Nora," Princess Maya interrupted my thoughts, looking upward to the sky, "I didn't go to your classroom to see if Mr. Harris would take me on my afternoon walk. I actually wanted to talk to *you*. In private."

"You did, ma'am?"

"Yes." Princess Maya folded one gloved hand over the other. "Due to recent actions, I have decided to pardon you, Nora. I shall push the Senior Circle to do the same in your favor."

My eyebrows ruffled, unable to hide my confusion. No. I didn't deserve forgiveness so easily. Skylar rightfully blamed me for the recon disaster; Fern and Kai rightfully avoided my path; Persephone was too busy assisting her brother to show me any real disdain; and I refused to visit Molly if and when she awoke.

"You should forgive Mr. Harris. He had nothing to do with this."

"Oh, you shouldn't worry about Mr. Harris," Princess Maya assured. "He's in deep water, surely, but he has a strong relationship with the king. It wanes every now and then, but..." She trailed off again. "I doubt the king would ever replace him as the First Senior Knight."

So Mr. Harris was safe. I allowed myself to sigh in relief.

"Why would you do that for me then, ma'am?"

"I believe everyone has the ability to do good and to be given second chances."

"I've had more than one second chance to prove myself, ma'am."

"Perhaps, but I see the potential Mr. Harris and Prince Cassius chat about. It would be a shame for you to return to servant life with so much happening in the kingdom." Princess Maya hesitated, fiddling with her hair again. "May I share with you something personal, Nora?"

"Of course, ma'am."

Princess Maya smiled softly, pushing her hair behind her ear. The sunlight bounced off her porcelain skin, her exposed face revealing small freckles along her cheeks and nose. "The first time I got to see my brother—or at least remember seeing him—was at my fourteenth birthday party. He had run off for doing something *unfavorable...* when I was a baby and he was six years old."

I waited for her to continue.

"But he came back as a birthday present to me. And I was so happy to finally meet him for the first time. I'd always pictured what he looked like, how he sounded, what he did. I had never been so happy before in my life. I could practically hug him if I could. When he first arrived back, he had a hardship in adjusting back to royal life. But I can see he's getting happier every day. I think this new attitude partially has to do with you and Mr. Harris. Training you gives him more purpose than ever before."

My thoughts conflicted at her confession. I couldn't possibly be valuable enough to keep now, and Prince Cassius wasn't popular enough to warrant my stay because I was entertaining to him. But if that *did* mean I could stay... would I take the opportunity?

The memory of his dance flourished in my mind. *Was it a betrayal to you if I said I enjoyed that comfort, enjoyed his presence?*

"We cannot keep that purpose if you're sent back to the Montgomerys," Princess Maya continued.

I flinched at the idea of going back to the Montgomery mansion. The threat of returning loomed over me constantly.

"That Montgomery Imitation student... Molly, right?" Princess Maya went on. "She's still recovering?"

I nodded, my throat clenched and mouth dry.

"Excellent. We can leverage that if need be since you still technically belong to her and her family."

You still belong to me. Yesterday, Molly was threatening my life. Now, she was fighting for her own. A sickening relief relaxed my shoulders. She couldn't do anything to me while she was helpless.

We progressed in silence, the weight of Princess Maya's words bouncing in my mind. I didn't deserve to be pardoned so quickly and by someone so forgiving. Could someone who wished to be an Unfortunate have an ulterior motive?

I couldn't explore that possibility as we neared the West Wall where the West Gate resided. I had led my classmates out of Galdor Academy and into an ill-fated mission. Its black points shined beneath the sun.

I looked away immediately.

"Please forgive me, ma'am. I do believe I have servant duty about now," I said, not quite sure what the time was. But I needed to leave. I needed to get as far as I could from this gate.

"Oh my, I understand," said Princess Maya. "I do not mean to take you away from your duties. Continue exhibiting persistence and bravery, Nora. You can relax knowing that you have a princess in your corner."

A small frown betrayed my neutral expression. "Ma'am?"

"Hmm?"

"Permission to speak freely, ma'am."

"Granted."

"Why *do* I have a princess in my corner?"

Princess Maya and I stared at each other.

"I have already explained myself, Nora," she replied politely. "But if you're still doubting yourself, that tells me you have compassion in your heart. Most Gifteds lack that in themselves. You know what you did was wrong, and you know you need to do better in the future. Truly, I believe you belong here. You keep surprising us." She laughed cheekily. "Even if it's in the wrong direction sometimes."

Her words coupled with her laughter calmed my nerves, even if it was just for a second.

"Thank you, Your Highness." I bowed before walking toward the servant canteen, my mind still buzzing with more questions than answers.

CHAPTER EIGHTEEN

Sorting the Facts

———

An Unfortunate servant handed me a dish. I washed it. I sent it off to the next servant to dry.

Get.

Wash.

Send.

Repeat.

No clocks were visible from my position inside the servant canteen kitchen, but the tension in my legs told me I had been standing still for a couple of hours.

When was the last time my fingers were so pruned and wrinkled from washing and cleaning? I had been so used to my hands being this way before... seeing them now was foreign, rough, and gross.

The door swung open, as it often did. Servants crisscrossed in and out to their duties, but a wave of servants whispered to each other. They frantically moved out of the way in a flurry.

I stared at a plate for too long, watching the soapy water drip downward. *How many times did you encourage me to betray the Montgomerys beneath the ruckus of clanking dishes?*

"Nora."

A pain ripped at my heart at the sound of my name. His voice wasn't yours.

I turned to see Mr. Harris. My nerves spiked with dread. "I need you to come with me," he said flatly, his almond eyes narrowed.

He didn't wait for an answer, walking away. Panicking, I removed my apron and handed it to the Unfortunate closest to me. I hesitantly followed him outside, the coming and going servants watching our every move.

We walked in silence through the Grounds. We didn't speak as we entered the Iridion Castle. We didn't look at each other as Mr. Harris instructed the guards to open the hidden underground staircase, and we continued in silence as we walked downward. Gold encrusted decorations on a white marble wall were swapped out for bare brick.

What were we doing down here? Seeing Sylvia Douglas? Was she still down here? That meant her twisted promise couldn't be fulfilled. Thunder Bay could live peacefully another day.

Sylvia Douglas was sitting with her knees close to her chest in one of the holding cells. Her back straightened as we caught sight of each other, but Mr. Harris walked forward without even a side-glance. The Anti-Gifteds Movement rebel kept her eyes trained on me the entire time until we passed the cell and I couldn't see her anymore.

Several rows down, Mr. Harris opened a wooden door that was different from the other metal ones that led to a jail cell.

Inside was a laughably miniature version of the Senior Circle round table. But what was more unexpected were the faces staring back at me.

Almost all of my classmates were in this confined space, looking toward their leader.

No. It was too early to confront them. What did you say to the people that you'd doomed? I froze in place. My lips remained sealed, teeth clenched together.

Princess Maya, Prince Cassius, Isaac Winters, and several other Royal Crest Knights I didn't recognize were also in attendance. They must be part of the Diviner task force, I realized. Why else would I be brought here? This might be the most quiet and secluded part of the castle besides Leo's hiding place.

The prince sat so far back at the left corner of the room, most of his form was hidden. He was as far away from his sister as possible as she sat at the head of the table. No one sat to his immediate right, but he patted the open seat on his immediate left. We hadn't spoken since I executed the mission that went terribly wrong.

You can do this, I encouraged myself. *You have to do this.*

I slowly walked over, sitting between him and Fern. The Avlis held her hands close to her face, her usual gleaming green eyes vacant. She'd watched Cal die in front of her, watched as a metal she couldn't bend split his torso apart.

Skylar glared at me from across the table. I leaned closer to Prince Cassius, looking at him as if that would block out the others around me.

"I'm sorry," I whispered quickly. His thumb rubbed my jawline. "I wasn't able to keep things from escalating in Norburn. I'm sorry if you're in trouble because of me. I—"

"Hey, don't worry about me," Prince Cassius cut me off before I could spiral. "What you did was brave—a worthy shot regardless of the outcome. You don't need to carry the world by yourself."

Mr. Harris took his seat at the front of the table with Princess Maya; Prince Cassius withdrew as Mr. Harris's eyes flickered in a subtle squint.

I was startled to see Molly here. She kept her gaze on the wooden table to Mr. Harris's left and diagonal from me. She didn't antagonize me the same way she did at the Montgomery mansion. She didn't say anything at all. The wooden table was more important.

"Stop staring at her if you're not going to say anything!" Skylar cut in. Startled, I turned toward her with wide eyes, my mouth agape.

"I'm sorry," I said quickly. "I don't know what to say other than I'm sorry."

Molly's head lifted to look at me. My muscles tensed, fearful of her slit eyes. But her pupils were circular, human, and their red bright color now a dark brown. Molly's hair, which was always a raging red color as a result of her albino snake features, was now faded into a more natural orange hue. Even her skin clung to her bones and organs as if it didn't belong to her, and hair was forming along her arms. She shivered, trembling and holding herself for comfort. Kai secured the blanket around her. I was so used to reading Molly as a vicious ticking time bomb that I couldn't read her coddled like a child.

What did the Diviner do to her?

I forced my question out. "Where's Leo?" The Mati twins were not present.

"Leo's still recovering in the infirmary," Kai answered first. "He's not allowed to sleep unless someone is there to make sure he doesn't go into any shock. Persephone is by his side."

"Will he recover?" I dared to ask.

Kai thought about the question for a second, my thoughts poisoned with terrible possibilities. "There's no reason to believe otherwise at the moment. But we're not quite sure what his scarring means for him and his future at Galdor Academy."

My lips formed a line. Could scarring effect his Gift?

"Right," Mr. Harris prompted. "Let's begin. I've gathered you all here so we can try and fit together this complex puzzle."

Kai stood up at the front of the room behind Mr. Harris and Princess Maya where a large white board covered the wall. He glanced at Isaac Winters, visibly trying to maintain the same neutral expression.

"Nora." Mr. Harris's voice was detached. I squirmed in my seat as all eyes turned toward me. "Tell us about your first encounter with the Anti-Gifteds Movement."

The Gifted classmates leaned forward, their eyebrows ruffled.

"Sorry," Skylar spoke first, appalled. *"First encounter?"*

I opened my mouth to defend myself, but nothing came out in time.

Fern adjusted in her seat, withdrawing from me. Kai stared for too long. Molly shivered in her cot.

"Are you a traitor to your country?" demanded Skylar.

"Miss Stanton," Mr. Harris cut in. She immediately pulled back in her chair, her expression unnaturally softening in his direction. "The only reason you are here is because Nora pursued the Diviner and compromised you. *Stand down.*"

Skylar swallowed hard, blinking a few times as if fighting off tears. She quickly recovered, standing to attention and looking at me expectantly.

I avoided her gaze, looking to Kai instead.

Sylvia Douglas in a room nearby flashed in my mind. She held her head high now as she did then. I remembered how she bowed politely to me in Thunder Bay.

"I was confronted by an Unfortunate named Sylvia Douglas and several others who harassed and even managed to kill a city guard. She said, 'From one Unfortunate to another' to me," I pointed to Mr. Harris, "before you showed up."

Kai started writing on the board in front of us. Prince Cassius leaned in, pointing out Sylvia's circled full name and then some words next to my hometown's namesake underneath.

"Yes, originally a small faction of Unfortunates sought equality by any means necessary," agreed Mr. Harris. "I thought we had more time to contain them before anything worse happened." He shook his head. "What a fallacy."

Yes, but if Mr. Harris didn't think there would be enough time, would he have offered me a place at Galdor Academy? I fumbled at the sudden thought, forcing the conversation forward. "The first large-scale AGM attack happened in Osthall."

Princess Maya nodded. "The central government building in Osthall was bombed. The facility held almost all of the records and documentation of Osthall's Unfortunate population. The Diviner was written on one of the only standing walls. At the time, we didn't know what this meant. But it was clear from here that the AGM was more organized than ever."

As she spoke, Kai wrote out the new information on the board. He connected the first encounter to his circled "AGM #1" bubble with an arrow. He wrote, "What is the Diviner?" and "AGM are organized" underneath the destruction of Osthall.

Kai crouched as he wrote at the center bottom of the white board. He wrote out the words, "THE DIVINER" in all caps followed by the short caption, "Unknown terrorist."

Kai pointed an arrow from the first AGM attack to the Diviner's alias.

I recalled their first large-scale strike perfectly. Moments before, I was training to redeem myself after the first combat exam. I was laughing, the first in a long time. Looking to Prince Cassius now, his stern glare at the board made me question if it ever happened in the first place.

"That's when we were informed about the AGM threat and how you were going to be photographed alongside us," Fern noted.

King Daltus's neutral stare sliced through me.

"Against my advice," Prince Cassius mentioned, staring down Mr. Harris. "Mr. Harris cast Nora as an Unfortunate symbol, something to use to discredit the Anti-Gifteds Movement's entire desires."

"It was a reasonable plan given the circumstances," Mr. Harris defended. "The king had the final say and agreed."

"But I warned you that it would be dangerous," countered Prince Cassius. "Almost like it was doomed to fail from the beginning."

A thick silence filled the small room. Could that be true? Could Mr. Harris know that his proposal to make me a symbol, a solider in the first place, would fail? I glanced to Prince Cassius's serious face. Could he be implying that Mr. Harris was *working* for the Anti-Gifteds Movement?

Princess Maya held her gloved hands out to the two Gifteds. "What's in the past is in the past," she interjected. "Instead of pointing fingers, now is the time to sort out the facts."

The princess looked to Mr. Harris with a gentle nod. "Nora became an Unfortunate spokesperson of sorts. What happened after that?"

Mr. Harris hesitated before explaining. "The AGM attacked again, this time in Caliel. Another government building holding Unfortunate documents was destroyed, and the statue of King Alston outside of the Justice Building was forcibly demolished."

Forcibly demolished was a professional way of saying violent Unfortunates blew it the fuck up.

Kai wrote "AGM #2" on the board, circling his words and writing "Caliel" underneath.

"It was the first physical Diviner appearance," Mr. Harris continued. "We couldn't confirm at the time until *your* carelessness—"

He glanced my way and stopped himself before continuing, his eyes drifting away into an unseen memory. "He... my men were collapsing underneath his touch. I didn't understand it. A bright light and then... falling. They all died unexplainably."

I remembered when Mr. Harris barged into Sylvia's interrogation. He screamed at her, demanded she explain why his men were dying without any physical injuries. She screamed back, *We'll exact justice on all of your kind! The Diviner will take care of the rest!*

I forced my attention to Molly who didn't hold my gaze. How was she alive when so many others died? I regretted the question immediately. The Imitation before me didn't look alive.

"Miss Montgomery is the first Gifted to survive," Mr. Harris said, looking to Molly.

Molly dug half of her face into the blanket. "I felt anguish," she whispered, "and then nothing at all. Like my soul had been ripped out of my chest."

I flinched, looking down. Prince Cassius's warm hand lightly squeezed my wrist as if to tell me it was okay, but that couldn't be further from the truth. I'd always hated Molly. She attacked me at every turn because she could, and when she wasn't doing that, she was threatening to tear me to pieces. Looking at her shiver beneath blankets, I pitied her. I actually pitied her.

Mr. Harris looked to the group. "When Miss Montgomery came to, we could finally confirm what the Diviner did to Gifteds and why he's able to change Gifts." His jaw tightened, struggling to get the words out.

"He can take away a person's Gift."

An audible and collective gasp erupted from the table. Molly sank deeper in her chair.

The Gifteds all frantically glanced to each other, their questions thrown out and blending together. I tried closing the space between me and Fern, reaching my hand out so she could see my effort to console her. I didn't dare touch a Gifted right now. Not when their Gifts were at the most temperamental.

Princess Maya stood up first, waving her fingers downward. "Please settle down."

But panic continued to envelop the room.

Prince Cassius stood from his chair, his arm recoiling and pressing his side at the sudden and violent rise. In a louder, more commanding voice, he yelled, "Silence!"

Everyone quieted at once, but worry still clung to the air.

The prince sat back down, followed hesitantly by his sister.

"This development is concerning, yes, but it's an important one," said Mr. Harris. "We have to assume that if the Diviner can take a Gift away, he can use it for himself. Hence why he's able to change Gifts."

Mr. Harris waited for panic to take over the room again, but we remained quiet. He continued, "The next appearance was when my first-year class went rogue in Norburn."

Kai transcribed the new information on the board, nearing the right side when circling "Norburn discovery." He took it upon himself to write my three scarring mistakes: "Cal's death, Molly's downcastment, and Leo's burn."

"I need every detail of what happened in that warehouse," Mr. Harris ordered.

I inhaled sharply. *You can do this.*

"He changed Gifts in front of us," Fern started the conversation. "He was an Aura at first and then shifted into a Mati somehow."

Kai counted on his fingers. "Aura, Mati, and then an Avlis."

"Did he use the same Gift as the perpetrator?" a female Royal Crest Knights asked.

Kai shook his head first. "Leo used fire, and the Diviner blocked as an Aura. He then changed into a Mati to defend against Leo and Persephone..." He contemplated the events. "He did change into an Avlis, but he didn't attack Fern. He changed into an Avlis to hurt Cal and then confront Skylar. I don't have enough concrete evidence to support or deny that idea as of right now. But for a first contact, no he did not. Mr. Harris?"

Mr. Harris blinked rapidly as he remembered his first Diviner encounter. After almost a minute of silence, Mr. Harris shook his head. "No. It's more like he changed Gifts when he needed to rather than who he was fighting."

Kai transcribed the confirmation on the board, pointing the "Norburn discovery" bubble to "THE DIVINER." He wrote two important questions: "How does the Diviner change Gifts? How does he take Gifts away?"

"He crushed something in his hands," I said my thoughts out loud, clenching my fist to mimic what I saw. "It can't be on a whim. Another entity must be involved."

"Like what?"

The red orb shattered on the ground in my mind. "Something small enough to fit in his palm. One fell on the floor and turned grey when it cracked."

"A glow emitted from his palm before he changed Gifts," Skylar piped up as Kai pointed an arrow from "How does the Diviner change Gifts?" to "THE DIVINER," lining the arrow with "Crushed entity? What entity?"

"He also didn't use his Gift against me," I voiced. "I don't understand why."

"He could have heard Molly call you an Unfortunate," Kai recalled. "Perhaps he didn't want to harm an Unfortunate the same way he does Gifteds since he's associated with the Anti-Gifteds Movement."

"But I'm clearly not a member of the Anti-Gifteds Movement," I argued. "He has no real reason to avoid using a Gift the way he did with me."

"I agree with Kai," added Prince Cassius. "What does the Diviner have to gain by killing a possible ally?"

A clump formed in my throat. It was easier to discredit my fellow classmate than the Prince of Iridion.

A strange idea formed in my head. I turned back to Kai. "Is it really possible to know a person's Gift by sight?"

All of the Gifteds scrunched their faces in a doubtful expression. "Like when I guessed yours?" Kai asked. "Or like the minister who sees the Divine's light?"

"No, no guessing. You both thought I was a Mati. Is it possible for a Gifted to *know*? To see a person's inner Gift somehow?"

"That seems unlikely," Mr. Harris denoted quickly.

"But he also went after Molly and Skylar," I pressed. Looking at Molly again, I chose my words carefully. "It makes sense for him to target her before she could escape, but Skylar is a different story. She hadn't used her Gift against him yet, and she was the farthest away from him. He would have no idea she was an Aura until she defended herself."

Skylar shifted in her seat.

I continued, "Why was he so adamant kidnapping her and not me or Fern or anyone else he came into close contact with? He wanted Skylar. *Her* Gift."

Silence filled the room, seeping doubt into my words. "That might be my imagination." I fiddled with my fingers.

"I would say there isn't enough evidence to make that claim just yet," Kai said, but he wrote the possibility on the board in smaller font anyway.

"That leaves us with our latest update," Mr. Harris changed the subject. "Ebony Nique has escaped containment in Ironcrest."

All Gifteds jolted. "Ebony *Nique?*" Skylar asked in disbelief.

"The media will no doubt report this attack soon. We have reason to believe that the Anti-Gifteds Movement aided in her escape and bombed the nearby military base as well."

Kai wrote out her name on the board along with her prison photo. I glanced around at their worried faces. "Who is Ebony Nique?" I asked.

"A Mute serial killer," Prince Cassius leaned in. "She posed as Unfortunate servants and then killed the Gifted Houses."

Skylar shivered, and she gritted her teeth. "We were terrified for months that she would infiltrate the Stanton House. We have thirty-two servants, so she could replace any one of them."

"Unfortunates that killed Gifteds *could* align themselves with another Gifted killer, but that idea seemed risky. Do you think she has a connection to the Diviner himself?" I asked.

Mr. Harris responded. "Ebony Nique has a strong religious foundation. When finally apprehended, she rationalized her actions through the will of the Divine. If there's a *Diviner* out there, it's safe to assume that Ebony Nique would want to be with that person."

"But these attacks happened years after she was placed into maximum security prison," said Prince Cassius. "How would she get word of the Diviner?"

"Guards?" Mr. Harris suggested. "They could easily talk about the attacks with Ebony listening in, or even worse, the two could have known each other before she was captured."

"That seems like a stretch to assume, Mr. Harris."

"I agree," replied Mr. Harris. "But it's unlikely that the Anti-Gifteds Movement would target her otherwise. They share no love for Gifteds, so what is the point of breaking a Gifted out of jail that could easily kill or even ignore them entirely?

"This leads me to two possibilities. Either the Diviner and Ebony Nique knew each other prior to her capture, and she's been playing the long game for the past five years. Or the Diviner is quite possibly the leader of the Anti-Gifteds Movement and ordered the attack to gain a dangerous ally.

"They both act in the Divine's will. The Divine downcasts Gifteds into Unfortunate souls when a Gifted goes against His will. The Diviner has the same ability. Ebony Nique believes she's acting in the Divine's will when she kills Gifteds. The two are too similar to ignore."

After a long pause, the prince was the first to speak. "Can we get any more information from Sylvia Douglas?"

Mr. Harris shook his head irritability. "Ms. Douglas is a dead end now. We won't be able to get any new information out of her since she's been in our custody since the second AGM attack. She's open for standing trial. Anywhere but in Caliel."

Frustration seeped through my body. The more we learned, the more we didn't understand. The Diviner could take a person's Gift, but we didn't know how. The Diviner could change Gifts, but we didn't know how. Ebony Nique was important to the Anti-Gifteds Movement, but we didn't know how. The Diviner wore all black with a featureless white mask, but we didn't know his identity.

We stared at Kai's creation on the board for several minutes in silence, watching the arrows connect and intersect in a web of complex twist and turns.

Two new lingering questions remained, unspoken but well-understood among the task force. Where would the Anti-Gifteds Movement and the Diviner attack next? And how could we possibly prepare for it?

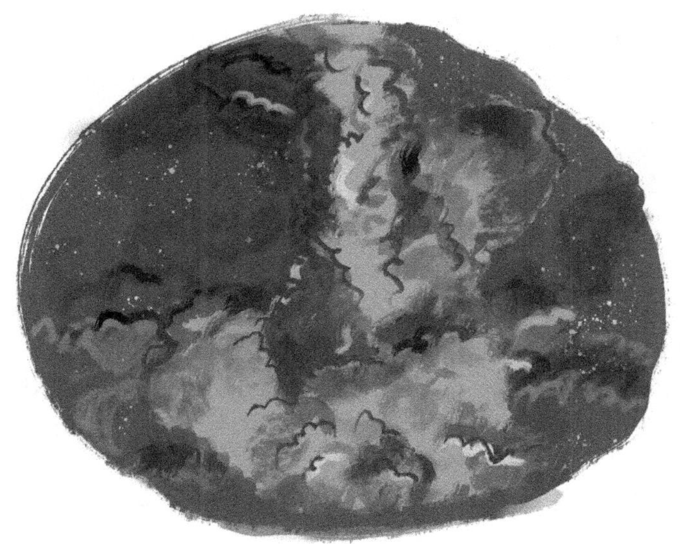

CHAPTER NINETEEN

The Galdor Square Massacre

We received our answer two days later.

At first, I was thankful that an outside disturbance jerked me away from reoccurring nightmares. The warehouse had cast an endless darkness. Fern cried out first, but the more I ran, the more the warehouse expanded outward. I could never reach them, and the world shifted to fire, a blackened sky, a faceless blood smeared mask…

My classmates shot up from their beds too, alerted by the high-pitched alarm emitting from the ceiling. Could Leo hear the same alert from the infirmary?

Persephone was the first to stand, peering out the window opposite of the door.

"Holy shit."

We stood up and moved toward her.

Dark shadows danced crudely in the open streets at Galdor Square. Multitudes of Gifteds could not be seen, but their Gifts visibly clashed, masking any sense of civilized order. Waves of burning embers floated to the sky from a careless Mati, illuminating the chaos.

The front door swung open so abruptly that we all flinched.

My nerves sliced down my back at Mr. Harris's grave expression. Behind him, the hallway flashed in a bright red hue, spilling into the room.

"What's going on?" Skylar demanded.

Mr. Harris pulled his hair back from his face before responding. I noticed his lips quivered ever so slightly, but the rest of his body was stiff, serious. "There's a riot," he said shortly.

The coals of his eyes glanced to me.

I shivered, "The Diviner?"

Mr. Harris hesitated. "It's at least the Anti-Gifteds Movement, but civilian Gifteds and Unfortunates are killing each other too."

Mr. Harris glanced at me again, stopping himself as though wanting to say more, but he couldn't in front of Unfortunate ears.

His face became rigid. "All capable recruits are required to report!" he blurted, straightening his posture. "Your job is to follow orders and protect the kingdom. You wanted to prove yourself? Get dressed in your patrol outfits now or get out of Galdor!"

Startled, we raced to our dressers and changed. Skylar began a single-file line to exit. I ran behind Fern at the back of the line.

"Report to Training Field Number Four immediately," Mr. Harris ordered. "All except Miss Montgomery. You are to report to the infirmary and stay there."

Molly didn't object. As the rest of the class flooded into the hallway, Mr. Harris grabbed my forearm.

"Yes, sir?"

"You can't go on this operation," he replied flatly. "Too risky for an Unfortunate."

I narrowed my eyes. "Too risky for a Gifted, too. Perhaps you can't go on this operation either, sir."

His glare bore into my skin, but I held my ground. "All capable recruits are required to report, sir," I reminded him.

Mr. Harris clenched and unclenched his jaw. "You will be placed on standby with Mr. Walton then."

I jerked my hand out of his grasp. "My purpose is to protect Unfortunates. If civilian Unfortunates are in the crossfire, put me on medical relief."

"That doesn't guarantee your safety."

I scoffed. "Who cares about my safety? Your soldiers will be so focused on the hostile Gifteds. I'll be covered fine."

After several heartbeats, Mr. Harris shifted away from the door. We walked through together.

My body immediately pressed into the wall, shoved by other students. Their shadows danced in the dim red lighting, words deafened and blurred together in the tight space as they ran downward to the ground floor.

Mr. Harris drudged through the flood that would otherwise part for him.

Dazed in the chaos, I forced my way through to keep up with him.

As we made it to the ground level, Mr. Harris spoke through his walkie-talkie. I could only hear pieces of the conversation.

"Status on Sylvia... She's... what?"

Mr. Harris's teeth gritted as he cursed. He plowed toward the exit. I ran after him.

Cold sliced through my clothes, bitter enough to illuminate my breath as I spoke. "Mr. Harris?"

He didn't look at me, walking toward the fourth training field. I followed.

Ahead of us, an almost complete blackness enveloped the city. Galdor's eccentric nightlife was extinguished, dead. I shivered, noticing grey smoke in the near distance.

"Mr. Harris!" Prince Cassius ran alongside us.

"Your Highness," Mr. Harris forced himself to stop. "What are you doing here?"

"I saw the commotion. I'd like to join you."

Mr. Harris shook his head. "No. I can't risk royalty, sir. Keep yourself inside the castle and protect the princess."

The Makan narrowed his eyes. Had this excuse been used before when Prince Cassius volunteered?

He opened his mouth to say something when he noticed me in the darkness and stopped himself. "Princess Maya is already by the queen's bedside with several Royal Crest Knights. She will be fine. Is there anything else I can do?" he asked instead.

Mr. Harris begrudgingly nodded this time. "Actually, yes. Sylvia Douglas has breached containment. She shouldn't have gotten far in this mass mobilization. I need you to find her."

Prince Cassius nodded without question, running toward the palace.

I, however, couldn't help myself, thinking of what a radical Unfortunate could do loose in the castle.

"Sylvia has escaped?" I asked in alarm as Mr. Harris led me toward the training field. Military vehicles were already filling up with recruits and Royal Crest Knights alike.

He didn't respond again.

The rest of my classmates were already in a vehicle. I hesitated at the entrance of the caravan, but Fern reached out her hand to me, acknowledging me for the first time since Norburn. I crammed into the small space next to her.

The truck rocked back and forth violently, the hood of the vehicle darkening our features. We became silent statues, moving as the car did. Mr. Harris deafened any possible sound that could resonate inside the compartment with his authoritative voice.

"We're going into a dangerous zone with both Gifted and Unfortunate assailants. Our main objective is to detain any attackers and rescue any individuals who are injured or defenseless *regardless* of Gift or lack thereof. Is that clear?"

We called in agreement.

"No soldier is permitted to kill any civilian hostile individual regardless of Gift or lack thereof unless your own life or another's life is in jeopardy. Is that clear?"

We called in agreement.

"Assignments." Mr. Harris took out a clipboard, reading off its contents.

"Fern, Persephone, and Kai are to detain any attackers and hostile individuals."

I raised an eyebrow in confusion, speaking before I could realize what I was doing. "Um, sir?" I even raised my hand like a schoolgirl.

From the darkness, Mr. Harris stared me down, but I continued anyway. "With all due respect, Mr. Harris, Kai should be doing more. He knows more about medical aid than any other student here, so maybe also place him on medical relief."

Mr. Harris stared for a moment before responding. "We already have medics deployed to the riot, you included."

"Kai has a better time anticipating Gifted moves than anyone else—"

"Which makes him perfect for detaining assailants."

"Yes but—"

Mr. Harris extended his clipboard out. "Since your classmate is so confident that she can organize our front better than a Senior Royal Crest Knight, I'll let her assign what everyone is doing for this crisis."

I fell silent, any boldness disintegrating in my Unfortunate soul. Staring at the clipboard, I held my shoulder to stop a tremor. Skylar held a smirk, the first smile in a while.

Valerie, you liked to remind me that I always knew what Gifteds were thinking, what they wanted so they could be appeased. "One day, when we're out of here, I bet you'll be able to use that smart brain of yours to get us by."

Was I still capable of what you told me? Did I know these Gifteds well enough to still lead them? Did I deserve to? I wished you were here to tell me.

My fingers clasped the wooden bottom of the clipboard. I looked up to my Gifted classmates, "Kai, do you trust me?"

He silently weighed his options. "I trust Mr. Harris, and he's trusting you, so I shall do the same."

Nodding, I gingerly picked up the pen.

My voice started out quiet. "Kai, you will work under fire. You're skilled in both medical and combat skills, so use them. Help the injured you find and subdue any hostile suspects if possible. Recommend working with other RCs instead of attacking hostiles by yourself."

"Fern?" Her green eyes fluttered as if startled.

"I'm not mad at you," she said quickly, looking down. "I'm upset I couldn't do anything to stop..."

She glanced to Skylar and deviated, playing with her hair as a distraction.

"You're more capable than you know," I assured, remembering how she took down Kai in less than a minute during the combat exam. "You are responsible for subduing and arresting any hostile individuals. Focus on Gifteds."

"Persephone." We locked eyes. "You are also responsible for subduing and arresting any hostile individuals, but your main objective should be stopping these fires. The last thing we want is Galdor in flames."

The Mati sister nodded in the darkness. "Stopping fires won't be the difficult part."

"I don't doubt that, but you won't be alone."

A small silence filled the caravan. "What about Skylar?" Mr. Harris inquired.

I froze, glancing to the Aura who scowled at me.

"No, no, no, absolutely not." Skylar waved her arms in protest. "I refuse to take orders from her. Mr. Harris, this is ridiculous."

"Skylar, I—"

"No! Has everyone here just forgotten that the last time we listened to her, Cal *died!* And two others were *severely* injured," Skylar yelled furiously, huffing through gritted teeth. "Why isn't he here, Nora? Hm? Answer me!"

The other Gifteds shifted in their seats; I sharply inhaled.

"I'm sorry the mission didn't go as planned, but you can't keep blaming me for your involvement," I spoke in the sternest voice I could muster. "You almost killed me to go to Norburn. And you know who tried stopping you? *Your* fiancé."

"He wasn't supposed to die!"

I flinched, pulling the clipboard closer to myself. The warehouse stretched before me.

"That was never my intention," I managed to say. "You're not the only one who has to carry that weight."

Skylar's twisted anger shifted to an anguished surprise as we stared at each other.

I looked to my classmates shrouded in darkness. Fern's heartbeat thumbed against my side.

"I understand if you don't—"

"What is my assignment?" Skylar asked.

"—want to take orders from me."

I stared at her blankly for a few seconds.

She crossed her arms. "What is my assignment before I change my mind?"

My mouth hung open for another moment. I stuttered, "You can also detain hostiles with Fern and Persephone. Preferably Gifteds."

Skylar sank lower on the opposite side of the vehicle as a response, no longer looking at me.

"And what is your assignment?" Kai wondered.

I knew exactly what I was suited for in this situation. "I need to protect as many Unfortunates as I can."

The caravan slowed as we found our way through the city. A wave of warm air swept through, and yelling could be heard from outside. We had arrived to Galdor Square.

"This is your first official deployment as Iridion soldiers. Remember your assignments and serve the crown well. Go!" Mr. Harris ordered, and everyone flooded outward to the chaos.

"Nora, hold back," he added. My body stayed positioned there, one step in mid-air as an icy outside force held me there.

"Yes, sir?" I begrudgingly asked, regaining control to turn toward him.

"A leader is at their most difficult after failing their team." He spoke in an unnaturally somber voice. I remained still and silent as he continued. "I thought I failed you, Nora. When Isaac reported that you were in Norburn, I thought you had died by Gifted hands. I don't want that to become a reality here."

You clung to my mind, your limbs folded awkwardly to your sides.

"No," I shook my head at him. "I failed you, Mr. Harris."

His lips drew out in a line, looking away for a moment and then looking back at me with a soft smile. "Regardless of who is to blame, I'm glad you still picked up the clipboard."

My eyes widened in both shock and embarrassment. I tilted my head with narrowed eyes. "Did you give crappy orders *on purpose?*"

"Your mission is clear," Mr. Harris dodged my question. "Find Unfortunate injured and bring them to the medical relief. They'll be stationed here." He showed me the map of central Galdor underneath assignments, pointing five blocks East of Galdor Square. "A perimeter will be at the fourth block. They'll recognize your attire and let you through. If for some reason you bring an AGM member to the medic, for the love of the Divine, Nora, remove their armband first. Is that understood?"

"Yes, sir."

"Good luck."

I nodded, stepping out of the truck and into the open air.

Incoherent yelling deafened my ears. Gifteds and Unfortunates threw profanities at each other as both groups collided, trampling over face-down bodies to reach their opponents. Screams of brutality and agony blurred together.

The ground shook underneath my feet as an unknown Aura fought against Fern nearby. The Aura hovered in midair, dodging Fern's offensive as she churned the earth to her will. Fern's usual expression was that of serious determination I hardly recognized before.

The Aura said something cunning by the look of superiority on her face as she landed on top of a nearby building, but she was too far away to be heard through the immense chaos.

"Nora, watch out!"

A crashing sound erupted from behind me. I screamed, cupping my hands around my ears as the concrete split open. Turning around, I noticed *water* spill into the cracks, forming back together in an upward lift by Kai's hand.

"Sorry!" Kai called out apologetically as the water receded back toward him.

He forcefully spun to his right, launching water against an immense ball of fire. The two elements collided in the air, creating a massive grey spectacle. Small embers formed on the pavement. Kai split the remaining water apart to neutralize the new fires.

My eyes darted toward a small form pressed tightly into a crack in a nearby wall. I ran through the chaos, my heart leaping out of my chest as I jumped over crumbled rubble and fallen civilians—or was that the Iridion Crest upon that person's vest?

The little girl didn't see me at first, her head down and eyes firmly shut. Brushing chunks of rock away from the entrance, I spoke in a gentle voice. "Hey, hey. You're going to be okay."

I reached my hand out to the young girl, but she wailed, her eyes wide, and tried to move deeper into her hiding spot. Noticing her bloody knees and the tears that wetted her pretty pink dress, I frowned.

"No, no." I waved my hand passively to calm the girl down. "See this symbol?" I gestured to the Iridion Crest pin on my attire. "I'm a soldier. Okay? I'm not going to hurt you."

The girl noticed the pin, her cries turning to soft sobs. Fire collided with water again behind me. Pieces of brick fell to the ground like rain. I placed my arms over my head for protection, dust stinging my eyes. The little girl screamed.

I steadied my words. "Come on. We have to get you out of here."

From the corner of my eye, I could see Kai's head glance about in a nervous tic. He didn't have much time to resist his attacker. I reached my hand out to her desperately. The little girl twisted her body in an effort to push herself further back.

I bit my lip, trying the last resort I had. "From one Unfortunate to another."

She finally looked up, a soft gasp escaping her lips. Her fingers clasped mine. As I pulled her out, her weight reminded me of Melanie Montgomery, but Melanie would never be in this situation.

Four blocks away, I thought. *We'll make it.*

Kai held a small wall of water in front of him like a shield, dwindling with each blow taken by the Mati opponent and wincing with each blow.

"You see, that's the problem with you Mares," the opposing Mati said with a ravenous smile. "All out of water, and what do you do? Fire, though, don't have that problem myself." Heat ignited from his palms with ease, and Kai's shield vanished on contact. He huffed in exhaustion, his legs trembling.

"Kai!" I could feel my step tug toward him. The Mati glanced my way, igniting a flame in his palm. I wanted to draw his fire, but the little girl's face dug into my shoulder.

I sucked in a breath. "I thought all Gifteds respected the law."

The opposing Mati used his free hand to touch his chest as though offended. "I have done no wrong, officer," he stated with a sly smile. "You should be concerned with the Unfortunates."

"Yet you are attacking a soldier."

The Mati switched his free hand into an appeasing gesture. "You know as well as I that Unfortunates are the true evil in this world. I was simply defending myself when this Mare tried arresting me. Now hand that girl over so I don't burn you into a crisp too."

My blood boiled at the comment. My eyes flickered to Kai, who was still finding strength to stand. I looked back to the hostile Gifted, "You're as guilty as the Anti-Gifteds Movement. Stand down, or it'll only be worse for you."

The flame in his palm grew brighter. The Mati smiled, drawing back his arm to attack.

But the flame extinguished in his hand; he looked at the smoke in confusion.

"Here!" Persephone ran past Kai, throwing him a water bottle. She charged the other Mati. As he ignited a flame in his hand, she snapped it out of existence.

I took that as my getaway, heading east as fast as I could. My hand rested firmly on the little girl's neck, shielding her from the chaos. Screaming blurred in and out of focus. An Unfortunate in a red armband retracted a knife out of an unmoving Gifted. The residual wind from an Auran attack knocked me to the left, threatening to trip me. I forced my legs forward. If I fell now, we would surely die.

A thick perimeter of military vehicles quickened my speed. The little girl gasped, "Look out!"

I glanced behind myself in time to see a dagger propel toward my face. Turning to my side, I dodged the attack. The assailant moved forward with their original movement. I kicked below their closest knee. They buckled, and I kept running.

Closer.

Armored guards held the perimeter, watching me approach. I trusted Mr. Harris, but I still slowed my pace, worried they would mistake me for a hostile entity. Even as I recognized Mr. Walton in a glimmering command outfit, I ran up to him cautiously with one hand up in appeasement. He held his hand out to his men and hollered, "Hold your fire!"

They parted for me. I ran forward, past the barricade and toward the medical relief tent set up. A woman in a blue medical uniform from the infirmary stopped me. "Unfortunate civilian," I blurted, my adrenaline waning. "Help her."

The nurse nodded urgently. As I tried to hand the little girl over, she clung to my shirt. "It's okay," I forced her into the nurse's open arms. "They're not going to hurt you."

I looked back toward the remnants of Galdor Square, taking a deep breath before sprinting back.

As I passed where the girl had been hiding, Kai and Persephone were no longer in my sight, but Minister Gabriel's voice boomed from above. Conviction laced his every word. I could see a bright light, but I could not see the minister. High beams casted Minister Gabriel's dark shadow over the plaza.

Movement flickered in every nauseating glance. A piercing scream erupted from my immediate left. A man could be heard shrieking, and another, and another…

Minister Gabriel continued to reign over all, every hateful word invading my senses. As a civilian Lux, he shouldn't be here. But as the Head Minister to the Church of Iridion, he justified Gifted retaliation. I looked upward for his plump figure to no avail.

I ran north along the strip that usually held an endless stream of shops. Now most of the tents lay abandoned or damaged. When I first arrived at Galdor, I noticed how Gifteds displayed their abilities for entertainment. Now, those same Gifteds aided in the bazaar's destruction: broken merchandise, sliced and burned tents, and limp Gifteds and Unfortunates alike littered the ground.

A wheezing grunt floated through the air. I approached, navigating the cluttered terrain. Her plain dress suggested that she was an Unfortunate. She stood facing away from me at the base of a missing statue, tugging at something low to the ground.

Closer now, the statue wasn't missing. Instead, the heavy stone mold lay on its side, crushing the Unfortunate's hand. She strained fruitlessly.

"Careful," I warned. She screamed at my presence, her pull more forceful in hopes of escaping. I held my hand out cautiously. "Careful! You're going to hurt yourself that way."

I side-stepped so she could see me better. She whined, her breath irregular and panicked. From the side view, I could see now that her hand was not only stuck, but a chain cuffed her wedged wrist to the dead man underneath the sculpture. "Are you going to kill me?" she asked through sobs.

"No, no," I assured. "I'm going to get you out of there."

She sniffled, a hopeful look illuminating her face. I stepped closer to her, "Is that alright if I get closer?"

She nodded quickly. We stood side by side. The chain dug into her flesh; a dark purple color enveloped her wrist and blood trickled from an unseen wound. Against my best judgment, I pushed upward to test the statue's heaviness. She used her free hand to lift too. The statue didn't budge; she winced as the weight pressed against her hand again.

I searched frantically for anything useful. The earth trembled under our feet. Rock and dirt broke through the concrete, thrust upward and enclosing us. The Unfortunate screamed, crying as she waited for her demise. I picked up a lose piece of concrete, holding it outward as I looked upward to the only opening above.

Red hair caught my sight.

"It's okay," I assured the Unfortunate. "It's a friend."

"Need a lift?" Fern asked, hovering above on her own platform. Skylar floated next to her.

"The statue is crushing her hand," I called back. "I can't lift it on my own."

Skylar dropped down into the enclosure as Fern examined the perimeter. The Unfortunate winced as the Aura made landfall. Facing the statue, Skylar stepped one foot to the right and swayed her arms in the same direction, lifting her flat palm upward to the sky. As her hands shook violently, she inhaled sharply, crossing her left leg behind her right, her arms pulling above her head.

Wind centralized below the sculpture with Skylar's movements, lifting the stone slowly. The Unfortunate pulled her hand back as the wind ceased and the sculpture fell back into place, the pressure snapping the chain that held her to the dead Gifted underneath.

Skylar flew back into the sky; Fern receded the earth. I reached out to the Unfortunate's unscathed hand. "Let's go!"

I crisscrossed the barricade, leading the Unfortunate to safety, and reentering the remnants of Galdor Square.

As I passed one of the office buildings, a rough and uncontrollable cough echoed through the collapsed first floor. I stopped mid-stride. "Hello?" I called.

"Help!" a boy's voice rang out from the rubble.

I wedged myself carefully into the caved-in entrance, electricity hissing from the broken lights above. "Help!" he begged again. Darkness enveloped my sight as I forced my way further into the debris. A small open space allowed me to stand slightly hunched. In front of me, I could see the boy through thin slices of light.

His body was wedged uncomfortably between two pieces of fallen ceiling like he had tried to squeeze through and got stuck. I stopped in front of him, noticing the dirt and dust on his face and the red armband on his forearm.

"You're going to be fine," I said, holding my hands out as I tried to think the situation over. "You can't get out?"

The boy shook his head with a whimper. *Okay.* Examining the fallen pieces that held him together, I walked up to the right side where less debris resided on top of each other. Holding the ceiling panel with both hands, I deliberately pulled it toward me. I heaved as the boy tried pushing forward.

I fell backward as he fell forward in front of me. An eerie snapping sound vibrated through the small space as the loose infrastructure shifted. I stared upward for several heartbeats, waiting for the building to collapse inward.

It settled.

Slowly, I adjusted to face the boy, my body still close to the ground. He jumped up, taller now, and pressing a knife at the nape of my neck. My breath hitched as the boy's hair grew out to a crochet hairstyle and his complexion darkened. I recognized this new face from her prison photo.

Ebony Nique brushed the blade along my skin. My heart thumped loudly in my ears.

Her lips gleamed into a monstrous smile. "The Divine shines down on me," she breathed, tilting her head as her eyes scanned my face. Every fiber in my being wanted to look away from her and conceal my identity, but her grip forced my nose to touch hers. Her knife steadied my neck.

"For an Unfortunate, your eyes have an intensity to them," she commented as her obsidian eyes found mine. I huffed my disdain. "I've mastered the sad little look in Unfortunate eyes. You'll be a new challenge."

Her face shifted in front of me. I looked on in horror as Ebony Nique morphed into my reflection. "How did I do?" she asked with a playful smile.

I screamed; Ebony Nique screamed back, mimicking me. My eyes widened. I squirmed in an attempt to break free. She pressed the knife into my neck, hushing me in a soothed voice. "Say something, Nora," she ordered, her voice a mix of hers and mine.

I suppressed a scream as I kept my mouth clamped shut. "Oh, Nora." Ebony Nique used her free hand to reach out and push loose pieces of hair behind my ear. "When you resist me, you're resisting His will. Now say something nice."

There had to be reason why she didn't kill me here as I sat hunched over at knife point. I remained silent, stretching my right hand out and finding a rock as Ebony Nique pulled me closer.

"Now!" she demanded.

I bashed the rock into Ebony's forearm. She yelled; the knife clanked to the ground as I weaved out of her hold. I snatched the knife, backing up as far as I could within the confined space. The impact mark on her arm had shifted back into her original complexion. She held her forearm firmly as the skin evened out again.

"Skylar, here!" Fern's voice called out from outside. Unknown Gifteds collided outside; a rippling effect shook the unsteady foundation inside the building. My body stiffened as Ebony Nique smiled at me.

"What if we say hello to your friends?" she prompted, stepping toward where she had come from.

My eyes widened. "No!" I sprang forward.

"No!" my voice yelled back at me.

Startled, I gasped, clutching my mouth with my free hand like that would take back what was spoken. Ebony charged me. The knife fell out of my possession almost effortlessly, and she shoved me against one of the free-standing pillars. I strained as she pressed her knee into my chest. My hands shakily opposed the knife pointing straight at my heart.

"Nora?" Fern's voice was closer now.

"Say something, *Nora,*" Ebony hissed.

As I hesitated, the blade sliced along my collar bone. Grunting, I forced the words out. "I'm here!" I called back to Fern.

Ebony pressed me further into the pillar. "Not as loud!" she urged. The ceiling rattled as the earth shook. "Now say something *nice and quiet.*"

I spat in her face as my response. Ebony recoiled, gagging as she stepped back. Using the pillar for support, I rose. "Fine!" she howled as she wiped the gunk away. "They call us Mutes for a reason. The Divine has given me what I need."

Dust peppered the air as a large vine structure twisted its way into the first floor. Roots lined the ceiling as support and pushed the clutter back. Glancing about, I couldn't find Ebony Nique in the debris. I cursed underneath my breath, running out to the street. The building continued crumbling behind me.

Fern, hoisted in midair by plant life, dropped to the ground as she caught sight of me. "I thought I heard you!" She embraced me; I huffed, disarmed, and distracted. "I don't want to lose another if I can help it."

That made two of us.

"Hey!" Skylar snapped her fingers rapidly. "We still have work to do! You can hug her when we're back at the academy."

For once, I agreed with Skylar. Fern released me, her fingers grazing over the cut along my collarbone. I stepped back first. "I'll see you once this is over."

Unfortunates out there still needed someone to care about their lives. She nodded, following Skylar toward an unseen struggle. I turned, Minister Gabriel's voice violently forcing its way into my mind. My feet propelled me in his direction.

The streets here were almost completely black; the atmosphere thick in dead silence. All lights cowered in the shadows.

I halted at unlit stores, peering outward to the vacant night. Smoke emitted from a nearby fire as I jogged along the sidewalk, suffocating any observant stars above.

As Minister Gabriel's voice grew louder, I slowed my pace, dread twisting in my stomach as shadows danced around me. My heart dropped as his voice drowned out the Gifts, the screams, the crackling fire...

Minister Gabriel stood on top of a nearby building. His shadow loomed over the street I walked along, his form casting me in darkness. He towered above like the Divine, his movements jagged as the minister spoke for Him. "We mustn't let this terrorist organization take hold!"

Almost there, I rounded the corner.

My eyes bulged at the sight before me. I forced down a scream, my mouth dry and throat clenched. I stopped moving altogether, my feet glued to the concrete. The violent shake in my arms reminded me that I was alive.

Stiff bodies lay scattered like common trash, like Valerie, along the street parallel to where Minister Gabriel's shadow casted. For the first time, I could see the terrible struggle that happened here, see what was happening all across the square.

Minister Gabriel spoke above the dead Unfortunates and preached why they deserved to die.

"From the great words of the Divine, 'Thou whom cast hence mine own Gift shall be forever condemned to an Unfortunate soul!'"

The closest Unfortunate was to my right. His feet dangled only centimeters from the ground, his body hoisted upward by two shards of unnaturally formed rocks that pointed through his eyes. He wore a permanent face of horror as blood dripped slowly to the ground around his feet. Bile rose from my stomach as I imagined the scenario in which he had met his demise. A bright red armband was tied above his elbow.

My mind flickered back to the Montgomery summer mansion; the image of the intricate and beautiful garden as a gift from an Avlis family. Could the Avlis who made the delicate white flowers make this gruesome scene?

"He who insults mine own power shall learn to hast no power!"

I almost missed two petite Unfortunates, hunched together against the wall of a nearby building. Their bodies morphed into one blackened mass, holding one another for dear life and now completely unidentifiable. No doubt a Mati was at work here.

A woman in rags held her own neck, her mouth still open in search for air. One eye had fallen out of its socket, hanging on her wrinkled cheek.

Two AGM forms lay close to each other on the pavement. They faced each other, posed in their last moments reaching out for each other. They would never be close enough to touch.

"To be an Unfortunate is to be sinful! Corrupt in nature; they must be subdued at all costs!"

A woman died in an uncomfortable position near an inactive water fountain. Her well-dressed attire denoted her as a Gifted; jewels adorned her slit neck and blood stained her blue silk dress. A dulled knife had fallen out of an Unfortunate's hand while dying nearby. The AGM rebel had wet hair, giving reason to believe she had died from a ruthless Mare—*the same struggle you fell victim to.*

"We must rise against these criminals of God! Rise my Gifteds! *Rise!*"

Tears swelled and fell from my eyes. I caught movement in front of me.

He appeared the same as he did in the abandoned warehouse. Blood drenched his dark clothes and splattered against his white faceless mask. I gritted my teeth, my heart beating faster in my chest.

The Diviner.

My body fiercely shuddered, my feet threatening to buckle underneath the weight of the world.

"Did you do this?" I shrieked at him.

The Diviner slowly shook his head. His left hand extended upward to the sky, pointing straight at Minister Gabriel's shadow. And with his right hand, he pressed a detonator.

The plaza shone brightly behind me; an intense heat threatened to burn my skin as flames brought about screams that cut out and illuminated the night sky. I fell onto my hands from the impact, a constant ringing sound registering in my ears. I looked up, the Diviner's form blurred.

Get up! My hands pressed harder into the asphalt, but I couldn't lift myself. *Get up!*

After several blinks, the Diviner's shape disappeared in the ash. *No! Not again!*

Gritting my teeth, I planted my foot down, wobbling as I stood. People scrambled past me with their mouths open in a perpetual scream, too covered in blood and cuts and soot to be discernable as Gifteds or Unfortunates.

I blinked rapidly, my eyes stinging. The ringing in my ears became distant and faint. Minister Gabriel was no longer spitting hymns, his looming shadow no longer present. I caught glimpses of civilians running past me. My throat burned as the thick layer of smoke continued to impede my senses.

My legs hobbled forward in the direction the Diviner had been standing.

"She's here!" I couldn't pinpoint Persephone's location.

She held her hands out, the smoke deviating away from her body. Fern swooped in beside her, peering around. We made eye contact, more concern washing over her face. We collided; my entire body slumped in her arms.

Tears streamed down my face as Fern held me. *They're gone! They're all gone!* My thoughts only came out as incoherent wheezing and sobs. Kai's urgent voice registered as a whisper even though he was nearby. I winced as Fern lifted us into the air; I shivered as we gained speed.

My face looked upward to the night sky, twinkling with stars too far in the distance to shine down on us; apathetic witnesses to the burning blaze we set onto this earth, and I wondered if the Divine observed us from such a strenuous distance too, silently watching as we split His creation to pieces.

CHAPTER TWENTY

An Unwelcome Surprise

"Nora, you need to eat."

Fern and Kai stared at me, waiting, but I kept my eyes toward the dormitory ceiling, my arms outstretched wide on my bed. The other Gifteds had already left well into the day, but Fern and Kai came back during their lunch break to check on what was left of me.

We stayed frozen like that for several seconds? Minutes? Time was irrelevant to my stillness, irrelevant to Valerie, irrelevant to all Unfortunates. Time remained still for us. We'd been stuck in the same position since the Divine downcast the first Unfortunate soul. What made me any different from that fate?

"I'll bring you a cookie," Fern's voice was soft, distant. I couldn't bring myself to look at her. Any glance recalled the sight of the impaled Unfortunate man; unearthed spikes broke through his skull and out of his eyes.

The door clicked.

For the past two days, my mind sank further into the riot's brutality.

All those Unfortunates... I couldn't save them.

Burnt, unidentifiable corpses brought about by Mati like Leo and Persephone. Looking to Kai only served to rehash the crying little girl crushed in a fractured hiding place and the young AGM rebel who drowned next to an empty water fountain. The Unfortunates all lay limp, their bodies contorted, staring up at the sky with horrific, pleading looks. Valerie held the same fearful stare, an expression solemnly seen but now permanently etched on her face.

Faces. Ebony Nique transformed into me with ease. What could she possibly want with my identity?

And the Diviner. *Did you do this?* An accusing finger pointed straight at Minister Gabriel before a bright flash, black smoke, screaming...

An erratic knock interrupted my thoughts. I tried ignoring it, but the *knock, knock, knock* quickened. Groaning, I shot up from my bed and dragged my feet to the door.

"I don't want a cookie, Fern!" I yelled out.

Sylvia Douglas stood in the hallway.

My eyes bulged at the sight of the other Unfortunate, my body shifting into a defensive stance.

Sylvia crossed her arms. "You'd attack your own kind?"

I lost my stance, but my muscles remained tense. "I don't want to hurt Unfortunates," I confessed.

"I'm glad we can agree on something."

Startled by that response, I remained silent. "I'm sure we could find plenty more to agree on," Sylvia continued. "Nora, you belong with the Anti-Gifteds Movement. You *should* be with your own people. You *should*—"

"I shouldn't be talking to you."

Sylvia narrowed her eyes. "You should be helping your people."

"I am trying to help my people!"

"You think being an Iridion soldier is going to change how Gifteds feel about us? You'll never graduate from this school as one, and even if by some dumb luck you did, that won't benefit our people like you think it will."

"And fueling Minister Gabriel will benefit us?" I questioned. "Splintering the divide further only justifies their hatred. Gifteds will learn—"

"The Gifteds will learn exactly what it's like to be us!" Sylvia interjected with a vicious tongue. "We've been underneath their carefully polished feet for too long. It's more than time we do something about it, and you're hindering progress pretending to be one!"

My fists clenched. "I am *not* a Gifted."

"No?" Sylvia mocked surprise. "Then why do you act like one?"

I flinched, narrowing my eyes. "Why are you still here, Sylvia?" My voice was surprisingly stable. "You could have easily escaped back to whatever hell hole you crawled out of by now."

I thought Sylvia would snap at my comment, but she chuckled softly instead.

"What is so funny?" I demanded.

"This is exactly why I want you to come back with me," she said. "You're not afraid to speak your mind. Most of the servants I've tried to recruit are too fidgety to even talk to me when they see the armband."

I didn't know how to respond, knowing her words rang true. I would have never considered those words if I was back at the Montgomery manor.

"That's because the armband is an omen for their demise," I replied.

Unfortunates lay below Minister Gabriel's judgment.

"It is a symbol of hope!" Sylvia snapped. "*Your* badge is the symbol for death! How can you possibly defend those who *bought* you? Who think you're nothing?"

Scattered like trash. Like you.

"You could do really good with the Anti-Gifteds Movement."

I glared at her. "You mean with the Diviner?"

She wrapped her arms tighter around herself, glancing about the empty hallway. I kept my eyes trained on her. "Don't lecture me about siding with Giffeds."

"The Diviner is the key to our salvation," Sylvia defended. "With him, we actually have a chance to stand equal to Giffeds."

"They fear you."

"Is that so wrong? You—"

Sylvia cut herself off, straight faced. Her eyes shifted around again to the empty hallway as though someone was fast approaching. I found myself doing the same. The fine hairs on the back of my neck flared, but the hallway remained unchanged, silent.

"I have to go," Sylvia Douglas blurted.

"What? Wait!" I grabbed her arm. "How did you escape imprisonment?" A darker question came to mind. "How did you know which dorm was mine?"

Sylvia ripped her hand away. "It's clear I'm wasting my time. You will not fight for us, so I will take my leave before I'm spotted. I must get back because unlike you, Nora, I'm making a difference out there. Enjoy your freedom while you can. From one Unfortunate to another."

She sprinted down the hallway. "Sylvia! Wait!" I stepped out, my arm outstretched, but she disappeared through the exit stairwell. "Who let you out?" I whispered to myself.

"Talking to someone, Nora?"

I gasped, startled. "Your Highness!" I unintentionally screamed, awkwardly folding my arms and bowing my head. "To what do I owe the pleasure?"

Prince Cassius raised an eyebrow, suspiciously squinting at me for several heartbeats. He didn't press. "I was looking for you with the rest of your classmates in the cafeteria. You didn't join them."

"I wasn't hungry," I lied, my voice shakier than I cared for.

"I guess you weren't."

A prolonged silence formed between us.

Why wasn't I telling him about Sylvia Douglas? Would he think we were in cahoots if I told him? She was right outside the door. She knocked on *my* door like she knew exactly where I would be. Of all the chances, could it really be coincidental?

"What do you have there, sir?" I blurted, pointing to the wrapped object in his hands. Its shape reminded me of the bo staff. He held the object horizontally in his palms.

"Oh." Prince Cassius looked down as though he had forgotten. "I came by to give you something."

Give me something? A burning developed in my chest, but then I remembered what happened at Galdor Square. "I am undeserving of your kindness, sir."

"Nora, no one is here." Prince Cassius extended the object out to me. "Refrain from calling me sir, and open your present."

A present. I slowly reached out, taking the object from his hands. It wobbled, weighing heavier than I anticipated.

Unwrapping the cloth revealed a weapon, a sword that shone brightly under the florescent light. As I tilted the hem, the metal reflected back an engraving.

"It's the Iridion pledge," the prince clarified. "When you graduate, you'll swear this allegiance to the sovereign." He pointed to the words, telling me what they were.

"What is this for?" My thoughts spilled out. What kind of question was that? My mind really was frazzled.

"What do you think it's for?" Prince Cassius chuckled. "I think you're ready to upgrade from a bo staff to something more practical."

My fingers carefully grazed the sharp edges of the sword. "It's beautiful. Thank you."

I lowered into a kneel, the sword pointed downward by my side and my head bowed. I expressed my gratitude by treating him as heir: "I solemnly swear to uphold the integrity of the Third Auran Reign and all Reigns before and thereafter."

Prince Cassius's lips twitched as he tried and failed to remain neutral. "You may rise."

I did. Standing to my full posture, I cautiously fiddled with the handle, trying to get a familiar grip.

"Can we practice now?" I asked. This was the first time I held a sliver of hope since Galdor Square. I needed to practice. I needed to get better for the Unfortunates I hadn't lost yet.

But Prince Cassius waved his arms in a dismissive appeasement. "We can train later."

My face scrunched up in worry. "Is there something wrong?"

"No. It's just a flair up from—when Sylvia ambushed me," he assured me, gesturing to his side, though I couldn't see his injury over his shirt. "It's almost healed."

"She attacked you?" I couldn't tell him now.

"Embarrassing, I know. I'll be okay. And besides, I'm sure Sylvia Douglas is back to the others by now. If you'd like, I can still explain how you should hold your sword and—"

Princess Maya burst through the main entrance doorway down the hallway with a mix of urgency and excitement in her face. *"Cas!"* she called. "I have great news to share!"

Prince Cassius's smile immediately faltered as we watched her run toward us. She stopped, panting slightly. "I didn't want to send a servant. Here!"

The princess shoved an envelope in her brother's hands. Taken aback, he almost dropped it in the exchange.

He eyed the paper cautiously. I could read parts of his official title decorated on the cover. "May I ask what the news is, Your Highness?" Prince Cassius asked.

Princess Maya shook her head. "I cannot spoil the surprise! Open it!" She turned to me with a bright smile I couldn't match. "You get one too as the unofficial Unfortunate representative. Here. I came up with that title myself."

I glanced from one royal to the other before reaching out and accepting the envelope she handed me. A surprise? Two royal members granting presents to an Unfortunate sprouted an anxiety inside my soul. The last surprise was still drying blood at Galdor Square. How could Princess Maya be so cheerful right now?

"Thank you, Your Highness," I replied instead of speaking my thoughts, tilting my head in a bow.

"Open it," she half-whispered.

I waited for Prince Cassius to open his first before opening mine. A simple white sheet of paper showed an invitation, but most of the words were lost to me. I waited again for Prince Cassius's reaction, which was a mixture of confusion and alarm.

"Since when do we get a formal invitation to a Senior meeting?" he asked, showing his sister the paper to prove his point.

Princess Maya giggled like a child, rotating slightly from side to side. "It's later today. Don't be late! There is a special announcement!"

"I can see that," Prince Cassius retorted, looking back down at the paper.

"Okay, I'll see you both there." Princess Maya waved as she turned to leave, a pinch of anger festering within my heart at the purposeful secrecy. This wasn't a time for cheeky royal invitations and announcements. The meeting *needed* to discuss what happened at Galdor Square and possible actions against the Diviner.

"Hold on, ma'am," Prince Cassius stopped his sister from leaving.

"Yeah, Cas?"

The princess remained motionless in place as Prince Cassius gently pressed the invitation to her cheek. The paper's edges blackened on contact, breaking into dust. He let go; the paper flaked to the ground in pieces.

"This better not be a waste of our time, Your Highness."

***

At the time designated, I followed Prince Cassius to the coveted Senior Royal Crest Knight meeting room.

"You didn't bring your sword," the prince noted.

"I didn't think—" Looking from him to the two Royal Crest Knights standing guard on either side of the meeting room door, I lowered my voice. "The Gifteds in there are already looking for a way to label me as a threat. I mean no disrespect."

The prince's shoulders slouched. He put his hands along my crossed arms, helping me unfold them, and keeping our connection as he spoke. "You're ready for the next step in your training. Wield the sword with pride. Soon, you'll have nothing to fear from Gifteds like Minister Gabriel."

I hoped with all of my life that his words rang true.

As we approached the door, the Royal Crest Knights opened the entrance for us. Prince Cassius and I hesitated outside in the hallway as Princess Maya caught our eye, her laughter escaping the room.

Prince Cassius's eyes flickered with recognition. He squinted, halting outside the door with a ruffled brow. Fiddling with his wrist, he noticed my waiting gaze and cautiously walked inward.

In the once-empty seat residing next to King Daltus, a resting woman in a cascading maroon dress held a bundle of maroon cloth in her arms. All Gifteds present kept their attention onto her. All were distracted.

I recognized her from the somber expression she held on the five-batch note, the same paper note used among mila to compensate for Mr. Montgomery's property loss. I was in the presence of Queen Charlotte.

Mr. Harris stood among the other Senior members, their expressions more softened than his. He maintained a blank, on-guard look.

The sight of Minister Gabriel perfectly healthy and standing to the queen's immediate left burned a dark feeling in my chest. Days ago, he stood over fallen Unfortunates and regurgitated divine mantras explaining why we deserved to die.

Here, the minister's fingers held tightly together in a prayer. He spoke with his eyes closed, "Oh blessed Divine, extend Your blessings to this young prince. I already see a strong presence in the young sir. Continue to nurture that strength so he may walk in Your footsteps."

Prince Cassius's body bristled in a chill with a shocked expression.

"Cas! Allow me to formally introduce Prince Henry Iridion, Third Born of the Third Auran Reign. Our new baby brother!" Princess Maya encouraged her older brother forward.

Queen Charlotte and Minister Gabriel opened their eyes and turned toward us as we approached.

"Your Majesty," I extended into a bow.

"No, no," Queen Charlotte's jewelry moved as she shook her head. "There shall be no unnecessary visitors. Get this student out of my presence."

"Oh, Mom, there's no worry! Nora is our unofficial Unfortunate representative. She's invited."

"Did you declare that, Maya?" Queen Charlotte asked.

Princess Maya fiddled with her gloved fingers behind her back. "I did, ma'am. The suggestion makes sense given the circumstances we find ourselves in."

Queen Charlotte glanced from her daughter to me with a disapproving scowl. "Very well," she sighed. "You'll be making a lot of important decisions as heir assumptive. No need to waste anymore on frivolous titles."

My nerves spiked at the comment, but I kept my composure, even faking an appreciative smile and resting my hands in front of me. Old habits slipped back into my subconscious. "Thank you, Your Majesty."

Prince Cassius glanced from the child to Mr. Harris and then back to the child again with a seeping rage. A low growl formed in his throat as he spoke, "Your Majesty, I was under the impression you were ill. We were *all* under the impression you were ill."

"Yes, well," the queen looked down at Prince Henry in her arms, "we didn't find it imperative to inform you about my pregnancy in light of your... previous reaction."

Prince Cassius's eyes drifted toward Princess Maya, who, now with hesitation, returned her older brother's stare. I remembered when Princess Maya mentioned she didn't remember meeting her brother until she was fourteen. What did he do to her as children?

"And with this whole Diviner business taking powers away," Queen Charlotte threw her free hand into the air and rolled her eyes as if the Diviner and Anti-Gifteds Movement were a minor inconvenience. "It's best to keep Prince Henry to ourselves for the time being. So instead of a large celebration, we're sharing his birth with the Senior Circle. He'll get a proper one when he can."

Prince Cassius continued to stare. "Why are you revealing him to me now, ma'am?"

Princess Maya answered in a chirped voice. "I just couldn't keep the news away from you anymore!" She nodded to everyone present in the room, "And we all agree that you are well past that point in your life. Oh, Cas! Can you please hold him for me?"

"I will do no such thing."

"Ma'am," Queen Charlotte snapped her fingers. "Remember your manners, Cassius."

Prince Cassius and I bristled.

He forced the word out, "Ma'am."

Princess Maya frowned, even tilting her body lower to the ground in a pout, but she didn't let the rejection seep into her. She turned toward me with gleaming eyes. "Nora, will you hold him for me? Mother isn't describing it right."

Queen Charlotte chuckled alongside her daughter. "I don't know what you're looking for! He's a baby, not much else yet."

"But I'll never know what holding a baby *feels* like," Princess Maya protested.

"Oh please, darling. You just have to marry a nice Nox like you."

She pouted her lips again, turning in my direction again. Was this what we were discussing at a Senior Royal Crest Knight meeting? Baby announcements and future marriages? Unfortunates in torn red armbands reached out to each other, reached out to me... their deaths left little room for unnecessary thought.

"Did we forget that the Diviner and Anti-Gifteds Movement destroyed Galdor Square only two days ago?" Prince Cassius asked what I was thinking. "Or are Gifteds disposable if Unfortunates are killed too?"

A deathly silence filled the meeting room. I glanced his way, silently thankful he held enough status to voice reason.

Minister Gabriel grumbled, ready to go on the defensive when Queen Charlotte raised her hand.

Her words were stern and irrelevant. "You're not the heir assumptive. If you're going to address the king or queen, you say Your Majesty. If you're addressing the princess, you will say Your Highness. Where are your manners, Cassius?"

His jaw clenched again, swallowing hard. "Why are you all acting like nothing happened?" he demanded. "Do you really think you're all so powerful that nothing can affect you?"

I stepped in front of him, redirecting their sour faces toward me. Bowing my head slowly, I delicately explained our anger. "We still have little understanding about the Diviner, Your Majesty. It would be important to find that understanding, especially after the Galdor Square massacre before that danger comes any closer to the palace."

Queen Charlotte huffed. "See, Cassius? The Unfortunate has better manners than you do."

A familiar pain spread through my chest. *Who cared about manners?* I wanted to scream at her. *Unfortunates are dying!* Did these Gifteds not care about their own lives? No, either Gifteds truly couldn't fathom something capable of hurting them or Prince Henry was a distraction—a happy moment they could enjoy and stay ignorant to the looming threat above all of our heads.

But my lips remained sealed, choosing my next words carefully again. "Your Majesty, we need to figure out who the Diviner is. We'll have a chance once we have an identity match."

Queen Charlotte made a humming sound, tapping a polished finger to her painted lips. "I refuse to discuss any other topic today, but we can move onto the *other* topic tomorrow once you complete your princess's request."

Tomorrow? Why did we have to postpone this? I hated this deal as much as Prince Cassius and Mr. Harris who both stepped forward to express their opposition, but Minister Gabriel interjected first.

"Ma'am, if I may, I would advise that this Unfortunate girl is sent away immediately. We went to great lengths to keep your pregnancy a secret from outside view, and for all we know, Mr. Harris brought in an AGM spy right to the young prince!"

Spy? Mr. Harris interlocked his fingers in front of himself at the dig.

I struggled to keep my voice steady. "I can assure you, I am no spy, ma'am."

Princess Maya transformed back into her calm and kind posture, holding her hands out to Minister Gabriel. "Minister, if I or Mr. Harris were concerned about Nora's loyalty, she would not be here now."

The king and queen stared at me with the same apathetic stare.

"If my daughter desires this Unfortunate to hold the Third born of the Third Auran Reign, that is what will happen," stated Queen Charlotte.

I would have to wait until tomorrow to discuss the Diviner with the Senior members. That only served to give the Diviner and Anti-Gifteds Movement more time to mobilize and cause harm. Galdor Square meant the AGM were getting bolder. It was only a matter of time before this very room would be stained with blood. Who would survive out of those currently present?

But what choice did I have? I couldn't refuse a queen, and tomorrow was better than never.

"Yes, ma'am," I nodded.

Cautiously, I stepped closer to Queen Charlotte. Any misstep could warrant an attack.

The bundle of cloth wiggled as the queen handed Prince Henry over. He molded to the shape of my arms. I supported his neck with the crease of my elbow, the act natural to me. The baby prince reminded me of Melanie Montgomery when she was born. Small and wiry blonde hairs sat on his head like a tomato stem, and the bright pink coloring of his skin enveloped his entire body and flushed his cheeks. His eyes remained shut, softly asleep.

In all my time holding Melanie, I had never considered how something so small could be so potentially powerful; *I had never considered how something so fragile could later use their Gift to kill someone like you.*

"How does he feel?" Princess Maya leaned forward in anticipation.

I looked up at her, taking a moment to find the right words. "He's soft." I slowly pushed a strand of his hair back, fearful of the eyeing Gifteds around me. Their stares demanded more. "As soft as a feather and almost as light as one."

Princess Maya waited.

"His heartbeat is faintly tapping against my forearm, and his leg is kicking every so often right below my ribcage." I rocked him back and forth. *Focus. You've held babies plenty of times. This one is no different.*

I continued, "You can see his eyes move underneath his delicate eyelids. He's in a deep, comfortable slumber, ma'am."

I looked over to Prince Cassius who wasn't blinking. His blue eyes drilled straight through Prince Henry's form, his anger justified. The stillness in Prince Cassius's face analyzed his new fate. Was this another sibling destined to surpass him? Another powerful sibling who would unravel his grueling efforts toward respect?

"The young prince is warm too, ma'am," I continued. "The warmth spreads through you and puts a smile on your face." *Almost everyone's. Not mine. Not Cassius's.*

A noise between a whine and gurgle escaped Prince Henry's small lips. I tensed, waiting for a Gift to take its most chaotic form. But almost all Gifts revealed themselves at the ages of three to six years. Prince Henry had time for his Gift to blossom in his soul if the Diviner didn't somehow take it away first.

Will you use your Gift to harm Unfortunates or to protect them? I wondered but didn't dare ask that question out loud.

Slowly, I handed Prince Henry back to his mother, freeing myself from the distraction.

"Thank you, Nora," said Princess Maya. "Would you like me to accompany you back to your quarters?"

I held back my disdain for the word *quarters,* thinking of the Servant Quarters on campus. "No, thank you, ma'am." A resolve restored itself in my voice as I looked up to Prince Cassius. "I have to get back to my training."

CHAPTER TWENTY-ONE

Seventh Law of Servitude

Sylvia Douglas's body was found the next morning.

A crowd of Galdor students and faculty alike crowded the Iridion flag pole at the center of the academy grounds. The concentration of Gifteds could not be ignored. I walked over slowly at first, alongside Fern and Kai. But something tugged me forward that I couldn't quite explain. My feet propelled me into a run.

I pushed through Gifted students as they murmured and whispered to each other. Their voices rose and fell together—so loudly I couldn't comprehend what they were saying.

I needed to get closer.

Squished between unknown Gifteds, I craned my neck upward to see the Iridion flag in all its glory.

Except "DIVINER" was painted along the grass and another word hung around Sylvia Douglas's limp figure from the flagpole. *Traitor* floated in the air as the Gifteds gossiped around me.

Bile rose within my stomach and burned my throat. Unable to scream, I clenched my teeth and swallowed the stomach acid. I couldn't throw up here. Not in front of Gifteds. Her head tilted to the side like Valerie. No. Her lips parted, agape in a struggle for air like Valerie. *No.* Her limbs by her side, motionless, lifeless like Valerie.

No.

Like yours, Sylvia's death was a preventable one.

A burn swelled in my chest again. Bile? No. An insatiable emotion I couldn't choke down suffocated my body. I pushed out of the crowd, charging toward the Iridion castle.

I wasted no time forcing myself through the entrance of the Senior Royal Crest Knight Meeting Room. The Senior Circle was already there in full swing, discussing their new plans of action.

"What do you think you're doing here?" Minister Gabriel demanded.

"As the Unfortunate representative of Iridion, I have every need to be here as you do Minister." I walked with purpose toward Prince Cassius, wedging myself in between him and Mr. Harris. Princess Maya faced us next to Minister Gabriel. I didn't blink, glaring at the minister with an unwavering stare.

I refused to be silent again.

I tried to present myself in a more professional posture, straightening my back and putting my hand over my heart before continuing. "I have reason to believe that Sylvia Douglas escaped her cell by the Diviner's aid and then he killed her for becoming a liability."

Prince Cassius gave me a concerned look. "Are you alright?" he whispered.

I ignored his look.

"We have no reason to discuss theories on Sylvia Douglas's death," said Minister Gabriel. "Your Majesty—"

My eyebrows ruffled. "You mean her *murder?*" I blurted. "Her publicized body with the word 'DIVINER' isn't concerning to you, Minister? *To any of you?*"

I looked around the table of Gifted elite who glanced to each other.

"Nora," Princess Maya began. "I think what Minister Gabriel is trying to—"

"Are you *seriously* taking the minister's side at a time like this?" Prince Cassius cut in.

Princess Maya stopped talking, her mouth slightly open. Prince Cassius and I glared at her for several heartbeats. Tilting her head in an appeasing gesture, the princess stayed quiet.

Mr. Walton shot upward from his seat. "Mr. Harris, your Unfortunate is interrupting a Senior Member emergency meeting. With all due respect, King Daltus, this child has done nothing but disrupt the academy and our proceedings. She must be dismissed immediately."

I glanced over to the throne on my left. King Daltus's stare sliced through my Unfortunate soul, but I didn't look away. His gaze held absolute power, but my eyes remained slits.

"I have no part in the Anti-Gifteds Movement, Your Majesty." How many times did I need to convince them of the truth?

"Likely story," Minister Gabriel interjected, pointing an accusing finger toward Mr. Harris. "You should be fired, Peter! Your little pet project has been nothing but a disaster!"

Princess Maya stepped forward, "Minister Gabriel please—"

"So you're taking *Nora's* side now?" Prince Cassius demanded. "Do you ever pick a side, Maya? Or are you incapable?"

"Cas—"

The minister eyed me with those bulging authoritative eyes. "You truly represent your status, girlie! The Unfortunate Laws of Servitude clearly aren't effective enough. You should be hung up like the rest of those immoral rebels!"

The noose already clasped around my neck as my throat squeezed and my voice silenced. I could already hear Sylvia Douglas's taunting words echo at the edge of my mind. *Do you really think they would allow an Unfortunate to become a solider?*

Mr. Harris stepped forward, his words chilled and his face stoic. "You throw those *damn* laws at my student one more time Minister."

"We have our laws for a reason, Peter!" Minister Gabriel spat back. He turned to the king. "We must strike back against the Anti-Gifteds Movement and the Diviner before they can organize another attack! This is the second instance at Galdor! Right outside this castle!"

It was my turn to interject. "Which is exactly what I warned about!" Tears swelled and fell from my face as I screeched, throwing an accusing finger directly at Minister Gabriel.

"An Unfortunate dies today, and it's *your* head tomorrow!"

The Gifteds gasped at my threat. Nearing, swarming. My heart raced, but I didn't care. *I will be with you soon, Valerie.* At least I would die without fear. *At least I've spoken my mind the way you always wanted to.*

But Prince Cassius grabbed my wrist and brought me closer to him, his hand outward defensively. Mr. Harris stepped out in front of us too.

The other Senior Royal Crest Knights didn't cross their path.

Over the yelling chaos, the prince leaned to whisper. "Nora," he repeated my name in a quick voice. "No one wants to kill the minister more than me, but not here. Not here."

All nerves were completely shot. I *did* want to kill him!

"How can he speak such *garbage?*" I sobbed.

"Just not here, Nora. You'll have your chance to prove him wrong."

A powerful gust of wind cut the air around us, swirling and thrashing us like a violent storm. We all cowered, covering our faces and trying to remain standing.

King Daltus slammed a gavel downward, and the wind stopped. We looked to our king. The Gifteds around me bent into a bow like a child's apology. I forced my neck downward, too.

"If the Unfortunate speaks out of line again, she shall be dismissed," King Daltus decreed. Dismissed from the meeting or from Galdor Academy? I couldn't decipher.

King Daltus continued, "Now, Minister Gabriel, you have the floor, sir."

Minister Gabriel gave me a wide smile. He straightened his composure and stood taller. "This is the most opportune time to discuss my proposition that can aid us in putting Unfortunates back into their natural state."

King Daltus raised an eyebrow, the only action that hinted at interest. Minister Gabriel took this as his cue to continue.

With a snap of his fingers, a large burly man—a blacksmith—entered the meeting room. He held a long metal rod, the end piece bright orange.

"King Daltus, our main concern is telling the difference between a Gifted and Unfortunate since there is no physical diversity between us."

His intense gaze sliced through my form as though I would change into something more demonically fitting. *Did you do this?* The Diviner pointed toward Minister Gabriel.

The minister's lips curled into a smile. "I propose an additional law to the Unfortunate Laws of Servitude. One that will allow us to identify an Unfortunate on sight! And more importantly, find corrupt souls conspiring against the crown."

Mr. Harris shook his head quickly. "No!" He turned to King Daltus. "No! Your Majesty, silence the minister immediately!"

"Your seventh law?" King Daltus ignored Mr. Harris's plea.

"Precisely, Your Majesty," the minister nodded.

"The law is simple. All Unfortunates ten years or older would be required to have a brand of my own design on the back of their dominant hand. Before their Choosing Ceremony, Unfortunates who are younger than ten years of age would be required to wear a bright green cloth on their sleeve—the exact opposite of the red Anti-Gifteds Movement armband. No exceptions."

Dread seeped into my heart; my nerves splintered along my back. *Branded.*

Prince Cassius's lips stretched into a wide smile at the corner of my sight. His laugh cut through the silence. The growl in his throat rose as he chuckled, looking down in disbelief. He shook his head. "This will only rally the Unfortunates more. By the Divine, Minister Gabriel, you are an arrogant, *stupid* man."

"Cassius—"

"*Shut up, Maya!*" The prince slammed his fist into the table, its impact rippling through the meeting room. His smile twisted into a scowl. "Don't you *dare* try and defend his new law! You're *always* trying to play both sides and nothing good every gets passed because of it."

Princess Maya froze, staring at her older brother as if for the first time. She lowered her arms and placed them in front of herself, her head down like an Unfortunate.

Minister Gabriel's rage swelled in his face, but it didn't escape his lips.

"Cassius," King Daltus warned. "You will show the heir assumptive respect."

Prince Cassius crossed his arms.

Minister Gabriel placed a delicate, pompous hand on his chest, his voice on the line between respectful and treachery. "I am the Head Minister for the Church of Iridion because the Divine's light goes through me and me alone, sir. This new law is the only way to protect our people."

You sound like the Diviner, I thought. Mr. Harris noted how the Diviner was capable of downcasting Gifteds into Unfortunate souls, a power that solely belonged to the Divine for Gifteds who went against His will.

Did you do this? A blood-stained white mask pointed straight at Minister Gabriel.

"Branding is the only way to separate ourselves from our servants," the minister continued. "The Anti-Gifteds Movement will become more exposed that way and could be better prosecuted as traitors. Your Majesty, I implore you to pass this into law effective immediately..."

His curled smile faced me. "...starting with our first Unfortunate soldier."

An uproar lifted in the air as Prince Cassius and Mr. Harris voiced their objections while other Senior Knights voiced their own opinions. Princess Maya waved her arms and shouted, but her voice was drowned out.

Throwing her hands down, the princess took her brother's advice by walking across the table toward me.

Everyone's voices faltered as they watched Princess Maya stride. No one dared to move; even Prince Cassius and Mr. Harris stepped back as the princess stood guard in front of me. Heat radiated off her poisonous skin.

"You are *not* branding her."

"Ma'am," Minister Gabriel's voice tried to appease, "every Unfortunate must obey the laws, and voluntarily branding will prove her loyalty to us. If she is of the Anti-Gifteds Movement, she will resist."

Princess Maya turned sharply to her left. "Father—"

King Daltus raised his palm to silence his daughter. "These are dark times. I will exact the seventh law under the Unfortunate Laws of Servitude. We cannot be sure of our enemies without it. Perhaps, in more peaceful times, when the Anti-Gifteds Movement and Diviner are detained, we can remove this mandate."

I wanted to wipe that smile off the minister's face, but I'd pushed too far already.

"Excellent decision, Your Majesty," Minister Gabriel bowed. "I already have everything organized and ready to execute at your command, sir. The marking will be a U shape to denote their status as an Unfortunate."

My legs shook violently beneath me. *Don't fall,* I begged, clenching my muscles as best as I could in hopes of silencing my reaction.

"Your Majesty, I request that those downcast by the Diviner must be branded as an Unfortunate too," Prince Cassius shouted quickly before anyone could interrupt him.

The other Gifteds looked at their prince with apprehensive expressions, but he maintained a professional, stern look. I looked at the prince with a hesitantly hopeful glance. If any Gifteds survived their encounter with the Diviner, they would have to be subject to their own oppressive law. That could sway them against Minister Gabriel's proposal. But that also meant that the only Gifted survivor would be branded with the rest of Iridion's Unfortunates. Was it bad that I liked the idea of Molly lowered to my level?

Prince Cassius and I relished in Minister Gabriel's failed attempts to worm his way out of this one.

"Only the Divine can pass judgment and downcast," the minister tried.

"The Diviner is doing the same work," the prince replied. "There is no discernable difference other than your hypocrisy."

No one spoke for a long time.

Finally, King Daltus said, "I shall accept your request, Prince Cassius. It shall be enough motivation for the Iridion military to extinguish the Diviner and Anti-Gifteds Movement at all costs. But any Gifteds downcast by the Diviner shall not be subject to any other ULS."

"Thank you, Your Majesty," the prince dipped his head.

"As for the Unfortunate student at Galdor Academy," King Daltus continued, "I will permit her continued training if she proves her loyalty to the crown and the crown alone."

My shoulders tensed as I watched the orange and yellow glow of the metal rod. *No.* My heart raced, adrenaline pumping through my veins. *Run away!* My thoughts screeched. Every fiber in my body told me to run away. *Run away into your arms. But you aren't here, and I made a promise.*

I swallowed hard, "If branding proves my loyalty... I'll accept voluntarily."

Princess Maya turned toward me with a concerned expression, but I didn't meet her eyes. There was no assurance I could give her. The princess stepped back.

My heart sank lower as the blacksmith stepped closer. His course hands forcefully grabbed my right hand. My fingers flinched as he spread them apart, holding the back of my hand out flat.

The metal stamp hovered. "Your Majesty," I prompted softly, looking up to his throne, "your cabinet cannot ignore the Diviner. Sylvia Douglas's death is a warning against yours. The Diviner must be in our rankings to commit such an act. I implore you to take action, sir, as I pledge loyalty to you."

The metal rod pressed downward. An uncontrollable scream escaped my lips as the thin flesh broke apart and bubbled under my skin. Several hands twisted around my body and held me in place as I involuntarily squirmed; I focused on Prince Cassius's pained expression. Fire consumed my hand, spreading up my arm like poison. The metal rod released; I whimpered. The burnt nerves in my fingers shook violently. I stared at the dark, irritated red color of my hand.

"Dismissed," King Daltus ordered.

Wincing and straining, I slowly placed my hand over the left side of my chest, a large U symbol visibly imprinted on the exterior of my right hand.

CHAPTER TWENTY-TWO

The Challenge

———

King Daltus broadcast the mandated seventh Unfortunate Law of Servitude the very next morning as the Unfortunate population awoke for the busy workday. Every Unfortunate citizen was now required to be branded.

As promised, the only exceptions were children under ten years of age, but they could not be left undeclared. Those who could not be marked physically were now ordered to wear a visible green band on their upper arm.

Any Unfortunate caught without proper identification was punishable by death as inscribed in bold lettering.

Minister Gabriel boasted as he laid the entire plan out. Government buildings across the country tailored to his every desire, executing and documenting the new branded Unfortunates.

Wealthy Gifteds from every city swarmed the offices to get their Unfortunates marked accordingly. Our scar became a status symbol. Several Royal Crest Knights and students in passing bragged about being first in line as soon as they heard the news.

Rioting increased in Unfortunate cities, pulling us toward the Anti-Gifteds Movement.

My left hand rested over my right as I walked down through the castle corridors.

I grabbed the latch to the private training room in one quick motion.

"You're late."

I stopped as I turned toward Prince Cassius. "Forgive me, Your Highness."

He gestured me forward, his face twisted in an irritable demeanor. "Let's get started. We don't have a lot of time."

As I approached the prince, his face softened. "Let me see your hand."

Clenching my teeth, I begrudgingly lifted my right hand. It had been two weeks since I received my brand, but my fingers still twitched in uncontrollable movements. Scarring split my skin along the lines of the dark U symbol.

Our hands touched. I flinched as his fingers lightly brushed against my wound. "The swelling has gone down. That's good. Kai knows what he's doing. You should be fine today."

His hand left mine as he crossed his arms and took a step backward. "Get your sword out from your sheath," he ordered.

Inhaling slowly, I forced my hand to turn downward. I clung onto the sword's hilt; my splintering skin stretched further apart as my fingers formed a fist.

I pulled upward, and the sword followed gradually. I rotated my wrist toward Prince Cassius, the sword out in front of me. My right arm throbbed.

"That was too slow," he commented the obvious, his face scrunched again. "Do it again."

I inhaled deeply again as my hand turned. Reversing the process proved just as painful.

"Again."

My brand burned, the scar burrowing deeper into my skin.

"Again."

My nerves jolted.

"Again."

The sword shook in my unsteady grip.

"You need to get better at sheathing and unsheathing your sword," he finally said. "You'll be useless otherwise."

Grief swirled in my chest. Too many Unfortunates were useless against Gifted temperament. I needed to get better.

"I will practice more," I promised.

He stepped closer to me. "Let's work on your form then."

His hands wrapped around my shaking forearm. "Is this from your brand or is the sword too heavy?" he asked.

"My hand."

Prince Cassius made a humming sound close to my ear, moving his hand down to mine. Gently, he led my right arm toward the top of the grip. I winced as his thumb directed mine to the cross-guard. With another movement, he pushed my left hand downward until I was holding the pommel.

"How does that feel?" he asked, his hands warm over my own.

I concentrated on the sword's point in front of me. "I'm not used to it," I admitted.

Prince Cassius scoffed with a small smile, the rumble in this throat similar to his sly remarks at the Senior Circle meeting. "You'll get used to it. I promise," he assured, his fingers tracing over my wobbling flingers. "It just takes practice."

A twitch of my hand ignited a sudden pain. I gasped, my grip loosening.

The sword clattered on the ground.

Prince Cassius cursed, inhaling sharply, and his face reddening. "What was that?" he demanded.

"I'm sorry," I stuttered. "I didn't mean to."

His voice raised. "There isn't enough time for you to be dropping your weapon! Are you trying to get yourself killed?"

"I'm trying my best."

"Well, it's not enough, Nora!"

We stared at each other for several heartbeats; his expression softened to one of urgency. "I'm sorry," he said, touching my shoulders. "I just—the only way for change to happen is if we're both at our best."

I stared at him for a few more heartbeats. I could understand that sentiment. Everything seemed to cave around us all at once. My loyalty meant nothing if I couldn't do basic actions anymore, but with my hand the way that it was, I didn't know if it was possible. I didn't want to let him down.

"We need to topple the Senior Circle like Minister Gabriel and Princess Maya together, yeah?"

My eyebrows ruffled. I would do anything to destroy Minister Gabriel if I could, but, "Your sister?"

Prince Cassius winced at the use of "sister." "Yes," he replied. "You've seen her lack of action. Her pacifism allows the minister to get away with whatever he wants because she's trying to appease everyone. If I was heir assumptive, everything would be settled by now."

After belittling Princess Maya for her indecision and the consequential seventh Unfortunate Law of Servitude, the prince had been more and more aggressive toward her and others lately. I remembered his similar outburst when we were alone. Her lack of willpower irritated him too, and I could see why.

Even so, she did step in front of me once. And she pardoned me when I was so close to a life back into servitude. I couldn't hate her the way Prince Cassius did.

Still, the pressure grew worse every day. I couldn't blame him for the frustration. The Diviner and Anti-Gifteds Movement were latching on to the walls and closing in all around us.

Every person I passed—Gifted or Unfortunate, it didn't matter—I anticipated an attack.

We didn't have much time before they made their next move.

Looking down, I chose my words carefully. "Would you like to call it a day, sir? My hand is still not where it needs to be."

Prince Cassius looked toward my right. A small sigh escaped his lips, "Yes, you're dismissed. Good luck in Faywater today."

I forced the sword back into its sheath before exiting the training room.

My feet directed me toward the infirmary building before I could process where I was going. I walked inside, heading toward Leo's cot.

But his cot was empty, folded and organize and clean, as though no one had been there at all.

I grabbed a nurse nearby.

"Ma'am. Do you know where Leo is—the Mati boy from Mr. Harris's first-year class? He was in that bed right there." I pointed.

She glanced at the empty cart. "Oh, yes, he was released this morning."

She walked away before giving me any more information. *Okay.*

I ran back toward the castle, using my intuition and memory to find Leo's hiding spot. Which vent was it again? I crouched down to one that I thought I recognized.

The screws had been taken out of this one. Opening it easily, I crawled inside.

"Leo?" I called out.

There was no response. I trudged forward, leaning my weight onto my left side. I approached a large empty space where a network of vents connected to each other. Leo sat with his back facing me, hunched over in silence.

"I thought you'd be here," I said, sliding down into the makeshift hideout. I noticed his right arm. His dark skin healed in fragments, the inconsistency creating a jagged pattern up past his elbow.

"How's that healing?" I hesitated to ask.

"When I tried to use my Gift," he began, not looking at me, "my arm caught on fire."

My shoulders slouched, looking down. "I'm sorry to hear that, Leo."

"It's easy for you to say," he fired back, but his voice remained soft, despondent. "You've never had a Gift to lose."

"No, I guess I haven't."

"I just don't know what to do now!" he blurted. "We were supposed to earn a House name by becoming a Royal Crest Knight. And if I can't—" Leo stopped himself, thinking of all possibilities that shouldn't be said out loud.

"I hate being so useless," he confessed.

That word was floating around today.

"You're not useless," I said. "I will never be able to properly apologize for what I've caused you."

"You didn't cause this." Leo turned toward me, his eyebrows ruffled. "The Diviner did."

"Yes, but I—I led you there. You're only injured because I made you come with me for my own selfish gain."

"You think we all agreed to go after the Diviner just for your sake?" Leo's lips stretched into his usual sarcastic smile. "A chance to be on a task force so early in our Galdor careers would have been perfect for any of us. I'd be one step closer to getting a House name if we actually succeeded. What happened in Norburn isn't entirely on your shoulders. You can let them down a little bit."

"Just feels like everyone's letting me off the hook way too easily," I confessed.

"Maybe you're just not used to people treating you like a Gifted."

"I'm not a Gifted though!"

Why was that an insult?

"Fine. Perhaps for once, you're not alone."

I flinched at the thought of you no longer by my side.

Leo changed the subject, "What's happened since I've been out?"

"A lot of bad things," I started, explaining what happened to him since our first Diviner encounter.

"Oh, I learned about Sylvia Douglas. And what happened to her."

I frowned, failing to hide my brand. "The AGM are only getting more violent. Prince Cassius was right. This new law is only rallying the Unfortunates more. It seems like nothing can get done and everything's closing in around me and I'm supposed to be some sort of symbol for Unfortunates—"

I could feel myself slipping already. Could it all be a waste?

"Hey, hey, hey," Leo kept his hands tucked into his crossed thighs instead of reaching out. "What did I just say? You're not alone in this fight. You have us, and you even have the prince in your back pocket."

Leo gave me a suggestive look that I swatted away. I crossed my arms, looking down in thought. "Prince Cassius has been restless and irritable like the rest of us. We still don't know who the Diviner is, and we don't even know what they want! Only what they can *do*."

We sat in silence for several heartbeats.

I sighed. "Does Persephone at least know that you're out of the infirmary?"

"No," he admitted. "I was discharged while she was at practice. I can't face her just yet."

"I'm sure she'd be happy to see you."

"I'm sure Skylar would be too." Leo laughed.

I scoffed, reaching out and lightly punching his left arm. Standing up, I said, "We're going to Faywater for a patrol soon, so you'll have more time to yourself if you'd like. I won't tell her where you are."

Leo remained sitting. "Going to patrol an Unfortunate town, huh? Good luck with that one."

"Thanks," I breathed. "Don't burn the vents while I'm gone."

I climbed back through, opening the vent with a large shove and wiggling out. Pushing the vent door back into place, I made my way out of the castle and toward the dormitories.

"We need to figure out a name for ourselves!" Fern gestured openly to the rest of the classmates as I entered.

"Only *you* would think of such things." Skylar rolled her eyes.

Kai beelined for me. "There you are. Let's check on that wound." His hand clasped into mine, leading me toward his bedside.

Fern defended herself, mimicking Skylar's crossed arms. "What are we going to do? Keep calling ourselves the team that goes against the Diviner? That's too many words. L.A.M.E."

"You creating an acronym now?" Kai teased as he navigated his dresser with one hand. He retrieved bandage wrap and an antibiotic cream.

Fern rolled her eyes.

"What are you going on about today?" I asked.

Persephone leaned in my direction. "Fairaway is determined to give us a proper team name."

"It's pointless," Skylar interjected.

"It's important!" Fern defended.

"Pointless!" Skylar stomped her foot. Molly jolted in the corner of the room, looking away at the window and not participating.

"Important!"

Is this what we were discussing? My lungs exhaled into a deep sigh. I should be more ecstatic that my classmates were more like themselves after Norburn and Galdor Square. But the Diviner was out there—perhaps in this very castle—and no one seemed concerned.

"What is your idea then?" asked Persephone.

The Avlis sprung her long arms and legs out in an excited gesture, nearly hitting Skylar's face. "The Defenders!" she hollered.

"Absolutely not." Persephone shook her head.

"I'm going to press the cream in. It might hurt," Kai whispered to me. I nodded, gritting my teeth in anticipation. His fingers pressed into my open flesh.

"The *Annihilators,*" Fern spoke in a low, deep voice, slamming her fist into her palm.

Kai snorted. "The Annihilators? Really?" He watched my shoulders tense. "I'm sorry. We're almost done. You're doing great."

"Then what about…" Fern made a dazzling show with her hands, "…the Protectors!"

"Protectors?" I couldn't help but ask, needing a distraction. "Of what?"

The Avlis scoffed. "Don't give me that tone! The Protectors! We protect the world from the Diviner and any others who want to destroy it!"

Molly adjusted inward on her bed, condensing herself.

We have to actually protect the world first, I thought.

"We haven't protected anyone from the Diviner," Skylar said flatly. My eyes widened, not expecting to agree with her.

"Fine! Whatever!" Fern threw her arms up in defeat. Kai finished wrapping my hand in gauze.

Kai patted my palm. "Done," he assured. "It's healing well."

I couldn't match his smile. "I'm not where I need to be."

Kai's lips became a line. He stood up, placing his hands on his hips. "You can't force a recovery. In the meantime, let's get to Faywater. Our patrol is starting soon."

***

Fern's red ponytail swayed back and forth as she talked and hopped. She clapped her hands. "Oh, I'm so excited! Are you ready, Kai, Protector of Water and Medicine?"

He groaned at the sudden nickname. "What does that even *mean?*" he asked as they approached the gate.

The last time I was this close to the outside, I led my classmates to their demise. I glanced over to Molly who stared straight ahead, pulling on her long sleeves to hide her hand.

Mr. Harris walked at the front of our patrol, clearing us without incident. We walked away from the safety of Galdor Academy.

We couldn't bypass Galdor Square, but as I stepped toward the plaza, Gifteds moved stall to stall with stretched, smiling faces. They walked over the cracked pavement as though it was an intentional architectural decision. As though they didn't days earlier murder their servants and other civilians who reeked of the lower class. As though the Diviner and Anti-Gifteds Movement wasn't a threat.

We reached the train station and boarded in silence.

The towering skyscrapers dwindled and shrank as we approached Faywater. As the doors opened, less people collided at the train station, and the smell of fish and the buzzing market place reminded me of Thunder Bay. *A knot twists in my gut thinking about your resting place.*

The team all exited onto the platform, following Mr. Harris's lead. I stayed toward the center of our patrol formation, trying my best to obscure my bandage from view.

For most of the walk, there wasn't any trouble. I watched as citizens completely redirected their movements to pass us. Brands caught my every sight. I knew this was a predominant Unfortunate city, but it was Saturday. Unfortunate servants surely would be here in droves tomorrow.

"—take you and your Gifts and go back to the king!"

I turned my attention to the front of the patrol in time to see a rotten tomato fly through the air. It landed at Mr. Harris's feet.

A group of what appeared to be thirty people rallied in front of the patrol, all wearing the same brand on their hand and the same expression on their faces—pure hatred.

"What is the problem?" Mr. Harris's voice remained calm.

A man with a red, scrunched-up face similar to the tomato in his hands stood at the front of the protestors. "*You* are the problem! We want you out of here right now!"

The group made a harmonized sound of agreement.

I noticed a woman holding her baby against her body protectively and a brave young girl who couldn't have been eight years old using her bright green armband as a decorative headband.

My throat tightened as I rubbed my fingers against my own scar.

"I see," said Mr. Harris. "I'm sorry, but we are on patrol to keep this area safe. Surely, you must want that."

The leader of the group didn't miss a beat. "What we want is for you *Gifteds* to leave us alone! Haven't you already caused enough damage?"

Another agreement from the other protestors.

"I assure you, sir, the crown is doing everything to protect you. There is no need to rally against us. I—"

A rock hurled through the air.

"Hey!" Skylar yelled. She blocked the attack with a wave of her hand, the wind expanding around us.

"Stop! Do not engage!" Mr. Harris shot his hand out behind himself but kept his eyes locked onto the protestors. She begrudgingly did as she was told.

But more rocks bombarded us as the Unfortunates cursed.

Mr. Harris stepped back, his voice calmer than it should have been. "It's time to leave."

An ache grew within my heart. These citizens, these Unfortunates, saw me as a Gifted…

And they despised me.

"Wait!" I grabbed his arm before he could give me a contradictory order. I couldn't leave them like this. "They could have valuable information about the Anti-Gifteds Movement."

Mr. Harris clutched my bandaged hand. "We're falling back."

I shook my head. He squeezed; my skin pressed tighter. A stinging pain spread throughout my body, leaving me completely defenseless. "We're falling back *now*." He strained.

Mr. Harris's eyes caught mine—a dark brown abyss that iced my nerves and muted my disobedient thoughts. We fell back like cowards.

***

Reporting the protest to the local city guards, Mr. Harris and I arrived back to Galdor Academy in time for another Senior Circle meeting I wasn't invited to.

The sound of yelling festered in my ears. The meeting was already in full swing, but the Gifteds halted as the doors swung open. They stood at attention at the sight of their First Senior Royal Crest Knight, but their jaws twitched in forced silence.

I walked over to my unofficial spot next to Prince Cassius. His palms leaned against the wooden table, his back arched forward in Princess Maya's direction. He pushed his blond hair back and straightened his posture, but it was clear that the stress weighed on him.

Mr. Harris started. "Where were we?"

After several heartbeats and hesitant glances, Mr. Walton answered. "More Unfortunates are showing hostile intent."

Mr. Harris scoffed, "Yes. We ran into that ourselves in Faywater. Perhaps branding didn't have the effect you were all hoping for?" He looked over to the orchestrator.

Minister Gabriel grumbled and shook his head. "We must separate ourselves from Unfortunates as best as we can! The seventh Unfortunate Law does exactly that. So what if some Unfortunates are upset? They'll fall in line. They always have."

I narrowed my eyes at his comment. "And if they don't, Minister Gabriel?"

"Then they shall be dealt with."

"That's too vague, Minister." Prince Cassius rolled his eyes. "There's only one way to fix this situation."

He reached into his pocket and displayed a map of Iridion. His voice rose for everyone to hear as he laid the map out on the table. "As expected, this meeting isn't going anywhere," the prince sneered. "Lucky for all of us, I brought an actual plan of action for dismantling the Anti-Gifteds Movement."

"Sir—" Mr. Walton started.

Prince Cassius's finger glided across the paper. "We start by reinforcing the city guards in the small Unfortunate cities since they have the least resources."

"Sir—"

"and then position some Royal Crest Knights—"

"S—"

His finger pushed upward on the map. "Here, we can—"

"You're not the heir assumptive!" Mr. Walton's words finally broke through. "Princess Maya is the only one who has the authority to plan any of this. A Makan could never—"

"*Mr. Walton!*" warned Princess Maya.

Prince Cassius halted, his knuckles curling. "No."

He kept his gaze downward to the floor, his voice quiet but edged, cutting. "I know what you all think of me. Go ahead, Mr. Walton."

The prince looked up. "Finish your sentence."

The silence pierced as sharply as Prince Cassius's glare. Mr. Walton's mouth remained agape, glancing at his subordinates who offered no assistance. His words treaded on thin ice, on a knife's edge.

"Princess Maya oversees the Diviner and Anti-Gifteds Movement situation as her first crisis management. She is the heir assumptive, sir. That is all."

Prince Cassius's face twitched in an agitated smile. "Right." We watched his palms flatten on the wooden table. His shoulders raised; his posture straightened back to his full height. He inhaled slowly. "The heir assumptive."

Fixating on Princess Maya, Prince Cassius spoke in a frigid and methodical voice, his words slicing through our souls, "Princess Maya, Second born and the Third Auran Reign, House of Iridion, I challenge you to a Determination."

His sister flinched and gasped. The silence thickened. I stared, my eyebrows raised.

"What?" Princess Maya's voice was incredibly soft, cracked. On the verge of tears. On the verge of breaking. "No." She stepped back, her hands wrapping around her torso as she shook her head. "I might not be the heir anymore."

"I don't care." Prince Cassius didn't miss a beat. "You still are the heir assumptive, and you've done absolutely *nothing* to earn that title. I am challenging you to a Determination immediately. You cannot refuse me."

A stream of tears fell from the princess's face like rain. Her lips quivered as she struggled to speak.

The Senior Royal Crest Knights murmured to each other. "Have you gone mad, sir?" asked Minister Gabriel.

Prince Cassius turned to the Gifted, his voice stern. "Quite the contrary, sir. Iridion deserves an heir assumptive they can count on. Based on our current status and Princess Maya's failings, a Determination must be challenged. I'm mad for not declaring one sooner."

He turned back to his sister. "We're of qualified age. You cannot deny me."

Princess Maya whimpered. "Killing you will solve nothing."

An uncontrollable rage built in his throat. "You're already leading us toward death and disarray, ma'am. I refuse to hide my disdain any longer."

Princess Maya's face twisted as she wept. Prince Cassius continued to stare through his sister's anguish.

"A Determination has been challenged," King Daltus spoke in a monotone voice. "Princess Maya, you must accept this challenge."

The princess's breath hitched as she trembled, her response barely above a whisper. She stuttered, "I accept your Determination, Prince Cassius."

"And so the Determination has been accepted," King Daltus continued. "It shall be held at the Determination Arena."

Princess Maya tried covering her sobs with her hands.

King Daltus looked over to his son. They shared an apathetic glance. "When do you wish to complete this Determination, Prince Cassius?"

"It shall be held tomorrow, Your Majesty."

Tomorrow?

"Don't you think that's a little too soon, sir?" Mr. Harris interjected. "Please, I beg of you, Your Majesty—"

"So it shall be held at the Determination Arena tomorrow evening. Dismissed."

"Thank you, Your Majesty," Prince Cassius nodded.

As he turned to leave, Princess Maya carelessly grabbed the edge of the large circular table, slipping and slamming her chin onto the wood. "Princess!" Minister Gabriel called to her but didn't dare step forward.

The wood disintegrated as an unseen poison consumed its material around where the princess had touched. We watched as the black, charred pieces fell away into rot around her.

Prince Cassius calmly walked toward the exit.

I caught him, but he kept walking forward, forcing me to walk alongside him as we left the meeting room.

"What did you just do?" I demanded. "What is a Determination?"

I had never seen him walk with so much purpose before. "How is your hand feeling?" he asked.

"It's fine." I struggled to match his speed. "What—"

"That's good. You're the brightest Unfortunate I've ever seen."

"Cassius, what did you challenge your sister to?"

He stopped abruptly as we came to a bend, closing the space between us. My back pressed against the wall, his fingers holding my chin and forcing me to look at his face inches from mine.

Complete resolve swelled in his dark blue eyes.

"Nora, can I count on you at the Determination Arena tomorrow?"

My stare lingered. "What *is* the Determination, Cassius?"

He pushed loose strands away from my face. "I promise to tell you if you promise me now."

I've only seen such a certainty once before in your eyes when we made our own promise.

"You can count on me."

An almost child-like delight washed over his face. He leaned downward, his lips finding mine. A warmth I thought I'd lost blossomed in my chest; my heart beat faster.

We looked at each other, our faces close. "I knew I could," he beamed.

But the small smile on my face didn't stay there long.

"What did you challenge your sister to?" I whispered.

"A fight to determine who is the rightful heir to the throne—who has the most powerful Gift, who is more worthy of that title, who can survive against the other." He smiled, looking away for a moment in relish. "It's a public event, too, so all of Galdor will be watching. Isn't that exciting?"

My nose wrinkled, all of the terrible possibilities crossing my mind. "Cassius, she'll kill you! And the Diviner—the last time there was a large flux of Gifteds was when—"

His expression hardened as he shook his head, pressing closer. "Don't worry about any of that right now. We need a leader in power who takes sides, makes *actual* decisions, and is suited for this type of crisis. A Determination is the only way for progress to happen."

My hands held over his chest for dear life as if I was already mourning his heart stopping and his body decaying underneath his sister's touch. I couldn't lose another. Not again.

"Don't worry about me. I know what I'm doing," Prince Cassius assured me.

"But—"

"I know what I'm doing." His face softened. "I can count on you, right?"

Both at our best. I nodded in agreement, no longer trusting my voice.

"Then there's nothing to worry about tomorrow."

CHAPTER TWENTY-THREE

The Determination

Rain splattered against the Determination Arena walls. Each drop the same as the last, no different from when this all started.

I watched as the arena seats filled, rows of Gifteds from all over the kingdom, all coming to witness this great tragic event.

Black clung to my clothes. We were required to wear funeral attire—an all-black suit with a royal purple line on the shoulder like our very own Anti-Gifteds Movement armband. One royal member would die today in a test of who could survive against the other. How does one safe guard against a poisonous touch?

The Royal Crest Knights had a similar outfit, except they had a gold line underneath their purple one. Senior Royal Crest Knights like Mr. Harris and Mr. Walton wore two gold lines underneath their purple one, and their purple and gold pin shone brightly against the darkness of their chests.

As Gifteds walked past to get to their seats, I could hear them whispering their bets against Prince Cassius. My shoulders bristled at the treachery, trying to block out their voices. Dark clouds swirled above. Coins fell into Gifted palms as they exchanged wagers.

Focus. My eyes glanced about at the Gifteds packing into the stadium. The more they arrived, the more my heart pounded loudly in my chest. Any abnormal sound, my ear picked up. I turned my head sharply to its caster, expecting a ticking bomb, a blood-stained mask, a red armband...

But I found nothing.

King Daltus and Queen Charlotte's position at the center of the stadium caught my sight instead. They sat facing where their son would enter and sat behind where their daughter would enter. They sat in silence, surrounded by Royal Crest Knights adorned in black attire. Queen Charlotte wore the most color with her jewelry: gold and purple earrings, necklaces, and diamonds. The cameras were drawn to her every movement and strictly forbidden from highlighting Prince Henry who was obscured by his tending Unfortunate servant and other Royal Crest Knights bound to protect him.

Minister Gabriel sat in the designated Royal Spiritual Advisor seating in the same section next to the queen, leaning in her direction and sharing the limelight. Mr. Harris stood silently beside King Daltus.

But the arena's protection stopped there. Insecurities screamed at me from the arena's edges to the unattended entrances and exits, distracting me from the oncoming storm. I approached Mr. Walton speaking to several younger Royal Crest Knights, my hand securely over my sword's handle.

His wrinkles somehow sank deeper into his face as he saw me. I ignored his repulsion. "Mr. Walton, it would be in everyone's best interest to assign Royal Crest Knights there, there, and there." I pointed at the empty spaces.

Mr. Walton snorted, and the other RCs crossed their arms. I could feel their eyes on my hand, but I kept the scar open, my fingers unmoving from the sheath.

"You think I'm going to take orders from *you?*" Mr. Walton scoffed. "Understand your place."

I forced my gaze to remain on him. "My place means nothing here, sir. If the Diviner does make an appearance and you act careless, there will be dire consequences."

He stepped forward, an accusing finger pointed straight at me. "Are you threatening me, Unfortunate?"

"No, sir." My voice shook at first. "But you know what the Diviner is capable of doing if he gets his hands on you." I dared to step forward. "On the king…" I pointed straight at his chest. "And on the young Prince Henry. So this isn't a *pissing* contest. Place soldiers where they need to be."

Waiting, I enjoyed the embarrassed and nervous look Mr. Walton held. He began barking orders, and the Royal Crest Knights fell in line.

Invisible fingers brushed against mine. I flinched as my hands folded and intertwined with the thought of you. The clouds overhead continued to darken; the rain continued to dampen my clarity.

Prince Cassius's voice whispered in my ear. My nerves shot down my back like lightning. "Don't react. Follow me."

My lips couldn't help but twitch into a small smile as he led me inside the coliseum and into the room underneath meant to prepare for the Determination. He materialized in front of me, his hand still around mine. Glancing about, I noticed the lack of security here too. "There aren't any guards here."

"Oh, I asked for complete solitude. I don't need any Gifteds making bets against me to my face." He smiled like that truth didn't hurt him, pulling me forward into his arms. My body molded with his. "I much prefer your company."

His left arm wrapped around my waist; his right hand led mine upward. He glided, my scarred hand instinctively grabbing his left shoulder to keep up with his movements. This wasn't a time to dance. He shouldn't be smiling.

The world became his eyes staring into mine—a night sky with a twinkle of starlight. We danced for several more rotations, my muscles relaxing and my movement matching his. I wanted to stay in this comfort, in his dance.

But Prince Cassius slowed down and brought his left hand away from my waist to gently hold my scarred hand. "Do you feel better?" he asked.

"I should be asking you that."

"I guess so." Prince Cassius rolled his eyes playfully. "I'm content. Everything is finally coming together."

I stared at the outline of his face, hoping it would etch into my mind. When it rained again, would he dance with me? Or would he be a memory, another reminder of my failings?

A smooth surface rubbed against my fingertips. Looking down, I noticed a beaded bracelet on his wrist. One black bead resided among a collection of vibrant colors, gleaming even in the dim light. "When did you get this?" I asked.

Prince Cassius looked down with an unfazed smile, "I've had it on this entire time, Nora."

The entire time? Something so bright should have been noticeable. Why hadn't I noticed... I remembered when we stole Mr. Harris's ID; how the prince could hold the card one second and then seemingly not the next. How it became invisible. My fingers rubbed the smooth, delicate exterior. Small enough to fit in my palm.

Prince Cassius leaned down, his hair falling from his face and tickling my cheek. "A kiss for good luck?" he whispered.

I moved my hands away from his wrist and cupped his face, reaching upward and hovering there. "I thought you didn't need it."

He chuckled lightly, his arms wrapping around my frame and pulling me closer. He bit his lip, "How about one anyway?"

My arms wrapped around his neck as I kissed him hard. His hand moved upward and rested at the nape of my neck, keeping me steady as we continued to embrace. The bracelet grazed along my skin.

Gradually, our pace slowed and stopped. We looked at each other in silence.

"Stay with me," I begged.

Prince Cassius's forehead pressed against mine, his eyes never leaving mine. "I promise."

Slowly, I withdrew, stepping back before I broke down. *Hold your tears,* I urged. He's not dead. He's not dead yet.

As I walked back toward my original spot, breaches spotted my vision. The Royal Crest Knights positioned had seemingly vanished. Storming over to Mr. Walton, I crossed my arms. "Why are the guards moved from where I requested?" I demanded.

Mr. Walton let out an exasperated cry. "An Unfortunate of mine would never be such a thorn in my side! You keep coming back to *me* with these conflicting orders! Oh, we should put guards here. No, we need to put guards there. I only tolerate you because you have Mr. Harris's protection. We're keeping the guards as they are."

Conflicting orders? That didn't make—

But Mr. Walton stomped off before I could process that statement.

The flashing lights in the stands and in the sky flashed brighter. Thunder rolled overhead.

The Determination was about to begin.

I stood on the lowest end in the seating section, facing Prince Cassius's side so I could see him. Piece by piece, most of my classmates stood by me too. Leo was still off somewhere in the arena doing his rounds, and Molly was held back at the castle with Isaac Winters and other high-profile military Gifteds. She didn't have the physical strength back to be useful here, and the more she silently tucked herself into the background meant that she didn't have the mental strength either.

Thunder mixed with drums, reverberating through my entire being. All eyes and cameras trained onto the arena itself, waiting for their royal leaders to make their entrance.

Princess Maya walked out first. An uproar of applause, shouting, and excitement filled the air.

But Princess Maya could not bask in that glory. She wore the same outfit as Prince Cassius, a short-sleeve black body suit—her outfit ready for battle but her hesitant demeanor suggesting otherwise. Gloves still covered her fingers, but her pale arms were exposed. She was grasping at straws, and I couldn't blame her.

Prince Cassius entered the Determination Arena from the right side. An uproar followed, not quite as spectacular as Princess Maya's, but an uproar nonetheless. I couldn't decide if the Gifteds wanted to see him succeed or perish. I needed to check the perimeter, but I couldn't look away from Princess Maya's tears.

Prince Cassius didn't look at her. His eyes fixated toward the royal section directly in front of him; the king and queen, the First Senior Royal Crest Knight, and the Royal Spiritual Advisor all stared back.

"Begin." King Daltus's voice remained as monotone as ever as it rang out across the stadium and to the rest of the prying country. My blood boiled; how disconnected could a Gifted be from his son's death?

My breath hitched as Princess Maya brought her hands to her chest, expecting her to end his misery quickly. I pressed against the bar that separated me from the oncoming fight.

Princess Maya sobbed desperately. "Please, Cas. I don't want to do this."

Prince Cassius did not respond. He denied her that comfort, stepping forward.

The princess flinched, inhaling a sharp scream. "Why are you doing this?" she cried. "Can we just go back and talk things out? Why do we have to make this a Determination?"

Prince Cassius stepped forward, growing closer and closer to his demise. *No.*

"Because..."

Prince Cassius curled his right hand, breaking a bead off the bracelet and crushing it into his palm.

"...the world is watching."

A black light erupted from his fingertips, suffocating the arena in darkness. Blinded, I winced, shock and alarm rippling through my nerves. The light receded as quickly as it came.

Prince Cassius's hands cuffed his sister's shirt.

But he wasn't decaying.

He leaned close, pressing his forehead against hers, speaking a fury of words.

But he wasn't rotting.

The princess's face twisted and remained in horror, her arms securely on his shoulders, struggling helplessly against his hold.

Only a Nox could make physical contact with another Nox. But Prince Cassius wasn't a Nox. The only person who could change his Gift was—

He spun her around to face the country, her future subjects. His thumb pressed against her forehead, his hand forcing her head upward at an odd angle. To the eyes of the world, the Diviner yelled.

"Don't move, or I'll take her Gift away!"

Dread seeped into every pore of my being as my heart beat faster, thumping in my ear and swelling with the stadium's distress. No, no, no, no.

All Gifteds hesitated, afraid to place their future queen in jeopardy.

A red wave of Unfortunates flooded the stadium—the Anti-Gifteds Movement.

No.

Mr. Harris clasped his hands over his ears, shaking his head. The AGM swarmed the royal section in droves. The Unfortunate holding Prince Henry broke away from her barricade.

"Skylar!" The chaos drowned out my shriek, but the Aura was already in the sky. "We needed to get to Prince Henry!"

I unsheathed my sword as Unfortunates with red armbands ran toward me. Looking up, I could still see the Unfortunate holding a bundle of maroon cloth.

The earth churned and splintered along Avlis nerves; fires raged and extinguished between Mati fingers; rain swirled and splattered and sliced alongside Mares and Auras; Unfortunates lived and died in between these moments. But Unfortunates persisted, taking Gifted lives as theirs ceased.

"Kai!" I blocked an Unfortunate's attack with my blade as Kai's makeshift ice shield shattered. Swinging hard, I yelled, "Alert those at the castle *now!*"

I didn't watch him run off.

Pieces of cement flew through the air, grazing my skin as an unknown Avlis tried to protect themselves.

Fern grabbed my attention. "Go! I'll clear a path for you."

I nodded. "Persephone." I gestured the Mati upward alongside me.

Fern slammed her foot forward, encased it in rock, and threw her hands forward. The stone bleachers crumbled like an earthquake ripped through. She strained and grunted as she pulled her arms apart; the stone sluggishly pushed out to the sides, building a wall between us and the Anti-Gifteds Movement.

Fire swelled in Persephone's hands. Where was Leo in this chaos?

Skylar dropped down behind the Unfortunate holding the baby, spreading her arms apart and knocking down the oncoming Anti-Gifted rebels.

Persephone and I sped up at the opportunity. The Unfortunate crouched as the wind hurled rain against her body. She covered her face and held the baby close to her chest.

"Hand over the prince," Skylar ordered.

The Unfortunate laughed. A flash of teeth shined as lightning cracked the sky. As the Unfortunate turned, Skylar gasped, eyes widening. "Nora!"

Persephone and I halted at the sight of another me.

Nora lunged forward, narrowly missing Skylar's head. The Aura tried floating upward, but the rain slowed her down. Nora grabbed Skylar's foot, bringing her down and throwing her against the cement bleachers.

Skylar grunted, shock keeping her back pressed against the cement block, her neck laying awkwardly toward the sky.

Another Unfortunate neared; the sharp curve of their axe reached higher in the air. Gasping, Skylar pulsed enough wind out of her hand to push her to the left, colliding with more broken cement rather than her demise.

Nora stalked forward.

Rain pelted harder, blinding Skylar in a dark blue hue. The AGM rebel swung their axe again, right for the Aura's throat.

Skylar fumbled as the broken concrete bleachers separated beneath her weight. The axe drew closer.

Persephone and I finally caught up.

Clubbing the AGM's face, Persephone pressed her other hand against the axe and wedged it into the ground. The blade melted beneath Persephone's touch.

I reached Skylar, holding out my hand to her. To my surprise, she took it with little hesitation. Nora halted in front of us.

"Nora?" Persephone asked in disbelief, glancing from me to the imposter. "How?"

"A Mute," said Skylar in disgust.

Ebony Nique.

A recognition gleamed in Nora's eyes, *my* eyes. Her smile stretched across *my* face.

"It's a lovely form. I'd hate to part with it." She squinted, her smile fading before sprinting off with the child.

With a sharp flick of the wrist, a twisting wind knocked Nora to the side. She lost balance as her pace slowed enough for Persephone to catch up. The Mati tore Prince Henry from his captor, throwing the Unfortunate down in the process. But Nora sprang back up, ready to attack.

"Get to the castle!" I commanded. Nodding, Persephone sprinted away with Prince Henry in her arms.

Be safe.

My laugh echoed from the imposter's mouth, a twisted version of cheerfulness I could never match. "Oh, Divine, this should be fun," Nora said before charging straight at us.

Skylar placed her hand out in front of me. "Allow me."

"Are you—" I ducked and shifted out of the way before I could finish my question as a cleaver swung where my chest was. An Unfortunate woman swung again, yelling and thrashing as she did so. My hand clenched tighter around the hilt of my sword as I tried blocking her advances.

Skylar grabbed the edges of Nora's shirt, lifting her into the air. The Unfortunate dangled in Skylar's mercy as the Aura climbed higher and higher. Nora struggled in her hold. She sank her nails into Skylar's forearm, and I could hear Skylar scream from my position below. They became shrouded in the clouds.

Blood caked my hands as Unfortunates fell around me. Their faces were twisted in a desperate rage I could understand, but they didn't see the brand along my hand. They saw the crest residing over my heart.

A loud crashing noise followed as Skylar and Nora dove into the concrete nearby. Nora groaned, her body, *my* body, shaking involuntarily from the impact. How long had Skylar wanted to do that?

I ran over. Skylar ripped her hand free, sucker punching Nora's cheek. The Unfortunate's face splintered in a mismatch of different features as Ebony Nique's true form broke free from the façade.

"Oh no." Ebony Nique dragged out her fake concern, coughing as she fully transformed back into herself, bearing that monstrous smile. "You've ruined a perfectly functioning suit."

Another echo of pain reverberated violently in my ears. *Mr. Harris!* I turned sharply to the sound of my instructor. His entire body shifted up and down in a pant, on the defensive against the Diviner in the pit of the arena. Princess Maya lay face down. And Prince Cassius...

Ebony Nique's nails sank into Skylar's arms. The Aura winced, her muscles tensing as she tried to pull away. I turned sharply back to Skylar. Conflict swelled within my racing heart.

"I guess the only thing left to do is make sure you never tell," Ebony Nique rasped.

Wind swirled around Skylar's form, violently breaking herself away from Ebony. Blood trickled down Skylar's arms as her flesh ripped open. Falling backward, the Aura landed upright with her hands behind herself. She winced, struggling to stand as her arms shook without control.

My feet propelled me forward until I stood firmly in front of Skylar like I had in Norburn. The sword pointed squarely in front of me.

Ebony Nique grunted as she rose, observing Skylar's blood drip down her hand. Ebony's mouth opened, her tongue grazing her fingers as she giggled through whispers seemingly to herself. "Blessed be the Divine for giving me a treat today."

"Stanton!" Leo called as he arrived.

Ebony twisted behind herself. Leo stopped in his tracks several feet away, his face quickly changing from grave to bitter recognition.

Gasping, Ebony turned back to Skylar with a hungry grin. I gripped the sword tighter in my hand.

The Mute serial killer squealed. "A *Stanton?* I knew the Divine blessed this day with me in mind. I get to deliver a *real-life* Stanton to judgment!" She brought her bloodied hands close to her chest. "Thank you for using me for this purpose."

Mr. Harris's yell instinctively forced my head in his direction.

"Nora!" Skylar threw me to the side as Ebony lunged, the wind knocking me down from its suddenness.

Raising my head up, I could see that Mr. Harris was still alive...for now. I needed to reach him, but red danced along my vision. The world blurred and wobbled.

Wide-eyed, Skylar backflipped upright. She punched the air, wind following her aim. Ebony dodged, closing the distance between them. Leo fell backward as Skylar's attack hit him instead.

Skylar gasped, her hands clashing with Ebony's. The two Gifteds pushed on each other. Open wounds expanding and ripping, Skylar's feet dragged along the uneven concrete. She relented; her feet slowly pointed to their toes, the wind picking up around them.

Ebony laughed as Skylar struggled to keep her momentum. "You're supposed to be a Stanton? I thought all rich pompous Houses were excellent fighters. I expected more."

Leo cut through Ebony's hold. His left hand grabbed onto Ebony's, pulling her closer and punching her with a right hook.

The Mute's head tilted downward, but her body remained standing, unaffected.

Her head snapped back up, clamping down onto Leo's right arm. Her nails dug into his scars and dragged downward.

Leo's scream pierced through the thunder, falling to the ground as the pain consumed him.

Rain surrounded him in a violent splatter. His arm shuddered against his best efforts. Completely useless without his Gift; the threat of burning himself must have been at the forefront of his mind.

Skylar intervened, yelling against Ebony as they fought, both fiercely trying to defeat the other.

Thunder rumbled overhead. Leo held his burned arm, his pained grunts becoming more and more controlled.

"Nora." I didn't like the lingering dread in his expression.

The clouds swirled and collided above as Skylar and Ebony did below.

Leo slowly raised his scarred arm to the sky. Water slid down his arm in rapid movements; his fingers twitched along his bruised skin.

"Go help Mr. Harris and save the princess," he ordered. "I got this."

Leo kept his hand raised, his arm stretching higher and higher. He waited for something I couldn't see, watching as Skylar and Ebony fought in front of him.

I opened my mouth to protest when his face twisted in a serious outcry. "Go! Now! No time to argue!"

Mr. Harris groaned behind me. No time indeed.

I turned and ran downward as lightning cracked the sky.

Rock hovered around Fern's body, her open palms out to the side defensively. Unfortunates slinked forward. With a pulse of her fingers, the rocks shot out from all sides.

Her eyes caught me approaching. "Fern." I swallowed hard. "Follow me."

She followed without hesitation. We jumped down into the arena.

Princess Maya lay unmoving on the ground in an odd posture like she was thrown there. Like trash. *Like you.* Her white gloves were missing and adorned the Diviner's fingers instead.

"Get the princess and get out of here as fast as you can," I urged. My eyes locked onto the Diviner as he fought Mr. Harris.

"What about—"

"*Now!*"

Fern flinched. Her left hand held tensely in front of her, her other hand curving into a half-crescent shape. The earth swirled around Princess Maya's form. Steam emitted from her skin touching soil; Fern's hands shook violently as she tried to combat the princess's Gift.

Through gritted teeth, she shot herself upward into the air on an uprooted platform with the princess in her care. Thunder rumbled with the earth as Fern and Princess Maya escaped.

The Diviner scoffed, giving Mr. Harris a sly smile. "You swore an oath to the crown, Mr. Harris. Or have you forgotten my title?" he asked, faking sincerity.

Tears lined Mr. Harris's eyes.

They lunged at each other again.

Weaving out of the way of his instructor's clutches, the Diviner purposefully flicked his gloved hand against Mr. Harris's body, effectively pushing him aside.

"Not using your Gift against me, huh?" the Diviner taunted.

Mr. Harris didn't respond through clenched teeth. "Don't worry," the Diviner laughed, "I've gotten used to your tricks. It wouldn't work on me anymore if you dared!"

They collided, both aiming with concentrated precision. If Mr. Harris miscalculated, he would meet a poisonous demise.

My feet propelled forward. I couldn't stand and watch those I cared about die all over again.

But joining the fray wasn't an option. Mr. Harris contorted his body with the sole purpose of casting me aside, which left him vulnerable.

Don't come close! Mr. Harris's words echoed in my ears, but he didn't open his mouth.

Before I could comprehend, the Diviner kicked Mr. Harris's feet from underneath him. Mr. Harris stumbled, reaching out to attack, but the Diviner grabbed the instructor's sleeve. Their wrists lightly touched.

Mr. Harris's skin along his hand instantly swelled and bubbled in bright red blisters.

The Diviner cursed irritably, yanking Mr. Harris forward and pressing a gloved hand along the instructor's temple. The instructor's hand throbbed upward without any power emitting from his fingertips. A dark purple color illuminated

Mr. Harris's body, extending to the Diviner's unwavering latch on the man's forehead until Mr. Harris's light dimmed, transferring completely to the Diviner's will.

Crushing the purple bead in his hand, the wind picked up from the epicenter as it had before, the light drowning the arena in a dark purple hue that could have been mistaken for black. As the light receded, the Diviner ripped off the white gloves and flexed his fingers in awe.

Mr. Harris slumped over. *No!*

I ran over to Mr. Harris's fallen body, yelling his name. Shaking him did nothing; his eyes remained closed, but his shallow breaths granted me hope.

Looking over at his hand, his fingertips were already blackened, his nails cracking and rotting away. I gasped, hovering over his wound. *What do I do?* My thoughts screamed.

The sword's cool handle brushed against my touch. The idea jolted my body. But what else was there? No time to think. No time to pause.

I secured Mr. Harris's forearm to the ground, withdrawing my sword from its sheath.

An agonizing scream escaped Mr. Harris's lungs as I sliced his skin, pushing past the bone's resistance. I was thankful for the clean cut, a phrase Kai had expressed before with gratitude.

Using the sword to cut his extra fabric, I hastily wrapped his wound, my hands soaking in his blood. The metallic smell suffocated my senses. Mr. Harris groaned through gritted teeth, applying pressure with his other hand while the amputated one disintegrated into a black dust nearby.

"You're going to be okay," I half-whispered, my voice high-pitched from sobbing. Mr. Harris's eyes grew heavier in front of me.

"I finally have it."

I turned toward the Diviner.

He stared at his hands with relish before tilting his sight toward the cameras, "The Animus Gift is where it belongs, back within the true royal bloodline. *Within me.*"

Animus? No. That would mean…Mr. Harris wasn't a Fera all this time.

The Diviner gasped in disbelief before looking upward to the sky in childish wonder and spinning with his arms out to the heavens as the Anti-Gifteds Movement slaughtered all those who defied him. Rain darkened his hair and drenched his clothes.

Slowly, I stood. "Cassius."

He turned to my direction, giving me a familiar smile and reaching out his hand.

The same hand that took away Molly's Gift.

The same hand that now took away Mr. Harris's Gift.

The same hand that threatened to take Skylar's.

The same hand that killed Cal.

The same hand that scarred Leo.

The same hand that killed Sylvia Douglas

…and the same hand that held mine.

"Would you dance with me, Nora?"

I searched for any semblance of the prince I laughed with, aligned with. His kiss still marked my lips as I drew out his name. "Cassius." Lightning crackled overhead, flashing his face in a white hue. "You're scaring me."

The Diviner recoiled and grunted in disgust. "Don't talk like my pathetic sister. It's unfitting for someone so much brighter than her. You understand more than anyone else why the world doesn't need leaders like her."

A Determination is the only way for progress to happen. But this wasn't the progress we could agree on.

My legs treaded forward. "In replace of what? Leaders who do *this?*" I pointed up to the stands of piling bodies. Flames from fearful Mati burned away their sliced corpses. Gifteds and Unfortunates fought, screamed, and died all around us.

I swallowed hard. "Come back to me," I begged. "You're acting no different from Minister Gabriel."

The Diviner pushed his hair back. He spat through gritted teeth. "You'd compare me to that stupid, lying *worm?*" He scoffed, shaking his head. "Where's the Divine light he claims to have? Who does the Divine favor now? It was always me. He is *nothing.*"

His face unnaturally softened, a flash of his previous mask coming to life. He stepped closer to me, glancing at my scarred hand. "And he used that falsehood to hurt you."

I reached out my scarred hand. "And he'll pay. But not like this, Cassius."

His face hardened back into the Diviner. "He hurt *your* people. When he dies today, the Divine will declare his judgment, and we won't have to worry about Gifteds like him ever again. I can set you free!"

We can be free.

Valerie's hands grasped mine, pulling me forward, her face gleaming in a smile.

We can be free.

We can be free.

No. This wasn't the promise we made. I winced, closing my eyes. As I open them, you no longer stood in front of me. Only the Diviner remained.

Mr. Harris winced; I turned sharply behind myself. I watched the shallow rise and fall of Mr. Harris's chest and hoping for a miracle.

"Leave him, Nora. Come here."

His desire was absolute, and a sharp pain wormed its way through my mind. Before I could scream, my lips were glued shut. My body turned away from Mr. Harris, my feet stepping forward toward the Diviner—a complete disconnect from my urged thoughts to repel.

The Diviner wrapped his arms around my smaller frame, forcing my eyes toward the bright chaos. King Daltus and Queen Charlotte slumped over, their bodies obscured by red. Mr. Walton was hardly recognizable by the large gash in his face. Thousands of more Gifteds met the same fate, swarmed by the one threat they could never fathom.

Red armbands exacted justice upon the stadium.

"They're finally out of our way." The Diviner pressed me closer to him; my nerves spiked but my skin remained unflinching, calm.

Movement caught my attention toward the right. Skylar struggled against Ebony Nique. Leo still held his hand up in the air, his eyes closed and concentrated.

"Finally." I sighed in relief though my mind dwelled in apprehension. I couldn't fight back. Couldn't resist.

Resting his head along my exposed neck, his fingers found my chin. I concentrated my attention in front of me to see what he was seeing. "I thought you would think so. We can finally make the progress we want."

Several Royal Crest Knights broke through the chaos, charging toward us. Would I act as a shield if he commanded it?

The Diviner stared straight at the oncoming attack with an intense stare. Before they could even step foot into the arena, their heads stretched and popped off their necks. Projectile droplets splattered against my cheek and flung into my hair.

My throat hitched, a small whimper escaping through my pursed lips—the only terror I could manage against the Diviner's hold. So *this* was the power of an Animus Gift.

Rain washed away their existence, but the iron smell lingered. The Diviner scoffed. "Mr. Harris was really holding back all these years."

He pressed into me again, my body bending to his will. *Stop!* My hand pushed him away, but my palm lightly touched his shoulder with little resistance.

Rain threatened to drown me here. Maybe it should. The clouds swirled darker above my head, the Diviner's heart beating faster against mine. Lightning illuminated the battlefield.

All the bodies in front of me shared your likeness. No, they *were* you. Thousands of dead Valeries laid before me, thousands of your glassy stares piercing through me. Everything I had wanted to prevent—right in front of me.

A fire ignited every fiber of my being. I screamed, the sound breaking through. "Get off me! Make it stop!" All of my thoughts spilled out in a shriek, violently trying to free myself from the Diviner's grasp.

My fingers dug into his healing wound—the same wound I inflicted in Norburn during our first confrontation. He winced, the distraction enough to allow me to claw my way out of his hold. I fell forward to the muddied ground. Just as the pain had begun, it ended. I panted in puffy breathes, my throat clenching and contracting between sobbing and screaming.

His calming voice clung along the edges of my subconscious. "Oh, I'm sorry. That must have been painful." He crouched above me. "I need to get used to the Animus Gift, especially since I plan to take Prince Henry's too. Will you forgive me?" His hands methodically moved up and down my arms.

Ice crawled up my veins like a spider web, entangling me to him. "No!" I spun around. My hand reached for my sheath, drawing the sword in a slicing motion.

But my body trembled, forced in a mid-attack position. The sword's blade hovered inches from the Diviner's cheek. He looked at the weapon with disappointed eyes before training onto me. Unable to look away, I watched wide-eyed as the Diviner searched my face for something I couldn't understand.

"There's no need to be frightened, Nora. I promise."

Don't make promises you can't keep!

Breaking through the invisible restraints, I swung the sword with all my might. The Diviner's eyes widened, dodging and stepping away in one fluid motion. I sliced the air.

Like Valerie, Sylvia Douglas died needlessly by Gifted hands. No longer useful to the Diviner. Murdered. Abandoned. A public warning. He couldn't possibly care about his Unfortunate followers. He only wanted power. He always wanted power.

My brand burned as I held the sword shakingly in front of me. "You kill and maim for your own benefit, pretending to care about Unfortunates because they fell right into your hands. Because they can serve *your* justice."

I shook my head. "I will never stand with you."

"Justice for *us*, Nora!" His voice raised in distraught, waving his arms about erratically. "I thought you understood. Your people stand by my side because they know it to be true."

He caught up to me before I could step back, grabbing my wrists. I forced my body to remain steady; he could kill me with any sudden movement.

I forced my gaze toward him. He held the same expression when we spoke freely to each other for the first time in the training center—vulnerable.

"I want *you* by my side."

I saw the pain in his eyes and knew he was sincere. But I also saw the warehouse illuminated in flames, the buildings crumbled under his name, Sylvia Douglas killed by his command—all the pain he caused fell from my eyes like rain.

I upturned my wrist, crossed my arms, and drove my hands downward. His grip released, and I broke away from him.

His jaw tightened as the shock twisted to betrayal, his eyes cast downward. "You choose Princess Maya then?"

I couldn't answer that question. My silence filled the distance between us.

The Diviner looked up, his eyes a stormy grey color. "Then you shall unravel all the same."

Bright light fractured the sky above, crashing downward in a white hue behind the Diviner—up in the stands where I had last seen Skylar and Leo. Red, orange, and yellow ignited a fire, so bright my body instinctively coiled, my arms blocking my face. The Diviner turned toward the high-pitched screech that followed. Ebony's scream mixed with the loud clash of thunder.

I snapped my attention forward as the dark color of the world took over once again, the Diviner's voice echoing in my mind but his form no longer in front of me.

Until we dance again, my Unfortunate.

Epilogue

I sat bedside to Princess Maya. She rested upright, eyes closed, and an IV bag dripped from tubes to her veins.

Fern sat next to me in silence.

Purple and black bruises lined our bodies. And we were the lucky ones.

A darkness sank deeper into my Unfortunate soul as Isaac Winters continued to run down the list of all we had lost, all the sorrow the Diviner had costed us. As one of the few who witnessed the Determination and lived an encounter with the Diviner, I became a default point of contact.

King Daltus: dead.

Queen Charlotte: dead.

Mr. Walton alongside countless other Royal Crest Knights, Senior level included: dead, dead, dead.

And those who hadn't met the Divine were nearing His grace.

Mr. Harris was hooked up to intensive medical equipment too, though I wasn't allowed to enter that room.

Skylar anticipated a faster recovery compared to Leo, but both lay dormant in the academy infirmary where Persephone watched and waited as we did here.

Separate, intentional fires covered Galdor in smoke. "Our military force is spread thin, but the ERS are making the most progress," said Isaac.

My voice remained low. "Can we request other cities to give us their ERS?"

Isaac sighed. "We would need either royal or cabinet approval."

My head tilted his way, frustration swirling in my stare. "Make the request without approval. There isn't a cabinet or royal member capable of doing it for us."

The Ice Mare paused but nodded after several seconds. I looked away as he continued down the seemingly never-ending list.

"There hasn't been any more sightings of the Anti-Gifteds Movement, Ebony Nique, or the Diviner."

My shoulders tensed, an icy jolt running through my nerves at the mention of his title. His greedy hands brushed along my back.

Fern reached out, but I swatted her away. She sank lower in her seat, but I couldn't find it in me to apologize.

Isaac watched this exchange but didn't comment. "Ebony couldn't have gotten far after Leo struck her with lightning, so we should find her soon. The palace and academy are still intact. Kai's early warning helped us fortify the defenses, but we didn't encounter any Anti-Gifted hostiles."

That fact hung in the air like a curtain. If only I could peel back its unspoken secrets. Why would the Diviner conduct a large-scale attack without ever attacking the castle itself?

The world is watching...

I closed my eyes, desperately fighting back tears as my mind flashed to happier moments I longed for. My lips quivered, remaining silent.

Prince Henry was safe, I tried to reassure myself. Persephone was safe. Kai was safe. Fern was safe.

I stared at Princess Maya's unmoving body. *Please be safe.* I didn't know what I would do if someone else slipped through the cracks.

A small movement—a jolt of the princess's ring finger—piqued our attention. Isaac stopped talking. We leaned forward.

More fingers twitched, slowly curling along the bedsheets. Blue eyes fluttered open, training on my frame.

"Nora..." Princess Maya's voice barely registered over a whisper as she recognized me.

"Your Highness," I acknowledged. We all bowed to her, Isaac and Fern echoing their respect.

"...you're..."

Her head tilted, sinking into the pillow as she fluctuated between sleep and consciousness. "Where's," her eyes throbbed as she glanced around the room, sitting up with a concerned look, "Cas."

My heart squeezed into a tight pain at the mention of his name. Princess Maya placed a delicate hand to her chest, "Did he take my Gift?"

She searched around the room again for something organic to potentially poison. "I need flowers."

Fern hesitated but gave in to Princess Maya's urgency. The Avlis fiddled with her fingers into a circular motion, closing her hands into loose fists, pulling them apart for the flower's stem to expand into a long line. She delicately handed the princess a bundle of pink petals.

The moment Princess Maya's fingertips touched the stem, the flowers wilted and lost their star-like shape. Tears lined her eyes as she watched the plant erode in her delicate hold. She glanced to the IV and noticed how the synthetic needle pricked her skin and didn't dissolve.

The Nox lay back in her cot, her shoulders slouching in a pained sigh. "I still cannot reach my subjects," the princess whimpered to herself.

We sat in her agony.

Princess Maya slowly turned her head to me. "Nora," she inhaled slowly, "I would like you to be my personal royal guard effective immediately."

My eyebrows ruffled, giving her a confused look. I didn't deserve any important titles. "I am inexperienced for such a role," I told her. She needed a Gifted to protect her.

"Well, I imagine we're understaffed," Princess Maya huffed. "If you three are here instead of..." She trailed off, not wanting to bring her thoughts into reality.

She sighed, straining as she forced her body to sit upright. Her face hardened into a serious expression, a semblance of her usual professional demeanor breaking through her anguish. "You'll be able to continue at Galdor, and you'll be able to contribute at Senior Circle meetings against the Diviner moving forward."

I bristled, a thousand versions of you bruised, bloodied, and matted flashing in my mind. It wasn't enough to be Iridion's first Unfortunate soldier anymore.

I nodded, placing my scarred hand over my heart. "Understood, ma'am."

A soft smile formed on Princess Maya's lips.

"Isaac Winters." She slowly turned her head toward him. "Is the king or queen alive?"

His lips formed a line, his hesitation speaking for itself. Princess Maya glanced downward, swallowing hard.

"Prince Henry?" she hesitated.

"Yes, ma'am. Prince Henry is unharmed and in custody now."

She sighed deeply again, relief and grief both trying to take control over her expression. She glanced back up to Isaac with an unbothered façade. "Without knowing his Gift, that means I'm still the heir assumptive. How would you like to be the Second Senior Royal Crest Knight if Mr. Harris is alive?"

The Ice Mare jumped, startled at the proposal. He straightened his posture, placing his hand over his heart. "I would be honored, ma'am."

A knock rattled the door.

My hand quickly rested on my sword's handle in anticipation, my muscles still tense as Minister Gabriel entered. Of all those who lived... he had to be one of them.

"Oh, praise the Divine!" he cheered as he noticed Princess Maya. He clapped his hands together, the sudden sound shuttering through my body. "You are still a Nox, yes?"

The princess's composure faltered. "Yes, Minister."

He clapped his hands again, hollering his praises to the ceiling. "Then we have prevailed!" He glided closer. "Princess Maya, we must get you up to speed and begin our plan of action against the Diviner and Anti-Gifteds Movement. I propose—"

The princess waved her hand out in an effort to stop him. He silenced himself. "At ease, Minister. Our first priority is to stabilize Galdor and assure the country that we are stronger than ever."

"*Are* we stronger than ever?" My thoughts spilled out from my lips.

Minister Gabriel squinted his eyes in my direction.

Princess Maya bit her lip, correcting herself. "Assure the country that we *will* prevail from this situation. They need to know that I am alive, so sovereignty still rules over chaos."

"As for the Diviner, Minister," she looked directly at him, "we cannot deny his impact, but we cannot hunt him down blindly right now. When we have enough willpower, units shall start sweeping Norburn day in and day out. But we must first protect our citizens. I will not forfeit my people like my parents did."

The princess visibly shook, taking a deep breath to relax herself, her face reverting back to a stern glare toward Isaac.

"What is our current infirmary count?"

As they exchanged knowledge, their words drifted into the background as a searing, ringing noise—a flat line—overtook my thoughts.

"Nora, can I count on you at the Determination Arena tomorrow?" Prince Cassius's blue eyes twinkled brightly under the sun at the training field. Our first meeting cut abruptly to our one-on-one training session. He handed me a bo staff. "I much prefer you as an Unfortunate. You're more valuable that

*way.” He leaned downward. “Nora, you don’t have to do this,”
he assured me at the emergency meeting. After the first AGM
attack. After his first public slaughter. His lips brushed against
mine. “You’re the brightest Unfortunate I’ve ever seen.” The
Diviner smiled at me to the backdrop of the bleeding stadium.
“Come here.” His hand reached out to mine. “Would you dance
with me, Nora?”*

I winced, the memories flourishing from its dark corner,
flashing in fragments. But the sun illuminated the room in
a yellow glow; the sky remained clear.

I can reach you. His relieved voice lingered in my ear like
a whisper, like he was in this very room with me. My shoulders coiled inward, glancing around frantically but seeing
nothing. You can hear me. Can’t you, Nora?

“Nora?”

I snapped my attention to Princess Maya. The Gifteds
looked at me expectantly. “Are you alright?”

The fog receded from my subconscious but didn’t lift.

“I’m fine,” I assured them, constructing a fake smile. “It’s
only a headache.”

The Diviner’s unearthly chuckle mixed with Prince Cassius’s lighthearted laughter. *Tell them whatever lie you feel
necessary. You cannot deny me.*

Acknowledgments

Publishing means nothing without readership. I want to acknowledge and appreciate each and every one of you with all the love I can give. You bring my dreams toward reality.

Thank you for pledging loyalty to Iridion:

Katelynn Schmidt, Angelina Vita, Delly Haseldine, Brooke Tipton, Chaz Giles, Carrie Irick, Molly and Izzy Rich, Michaela Clancy, Mei Scott, Tyler Yancey, Carl Tompkins, Lexi Sterling, Dakota Allen, Edward Haynes, Anna Connelly, Carol Yee, Heidi Haynes, Darya Maysam, Michel Way, Isaac Cook, Elisha Caudill, Daysie Weihert, Sandra Mackiewicz, Riley Jones, Lauren Hughes, Darian Ray, Jose Rosas Canseco, Mikayla Kennedy, Vani Lozano Enriquez, Alexis Johnston, Emily Craig, Gracie Centracchio, paperclypse, Macy Gault, Paul Wilcox, James Poston, Alyssa Zamora, Bradley Camacho, Emilia Ferreyra, Jordan White, Makoto Booth, Joey Plyer, Catie McKee, Marcus Green, Elliott Dodge, Caitlin Littlejohn, Karen Russo, Michelle Weeks, Ronald E Hermann II, Connie Yun, Maddie McGready, Kelly Garrity, Donovan James Dixon, Rita Rose, Wendy Calcutt, Lauren Talley, Dr. Fahra Ali, Dr. Franklin Rausch, Joyce Cavignac, Lauren Krechel, Eliza Moore, David Rolon, Lydia O'Neal, Morgan Ferqueron, Loraine Cipriani, Elizabeth Hanan Taylor, Emma Colvin, Jacob Bellows, Brady Neff, Cassandra Fouse, Mr. Kenneth Bedwell, Grace Kerby, and Kimmy Weaver.

Thank you for joining the Anti-Gifteds Movement:

Aimee Robinson, Neil Myers, Stephen Walters, Jeremy Pugh, Robert Siebens, Ridwana Rahman, Josiah Cornelius, Neranjan Kuppuswamy, Ryan Thompson, Cristin Rigney, Justin Lipson, Alba Olveros, Noel Siebern, Ethan Yamashita, Ki James, Christian Johnson, Rebekah Smith, Keara Walsh, Hannah Enriquez, Elizabeth Caroline Thornell, and Annette D. Daniel.

Special thank you to Joel Seymour, William and Brenda Wilder, Tristan Hilbert, Seth and Josh from Mellow Mushroom, and Kamy Threatt for donating.

Congratulations to Bethany McKie, April Reynolds, Hanan Taylor's Library, Hannah Enriquez's niece, the Anderson Public Library, Rebekah Smith, Lauryn Young-Fenwick, the Abbeville County Library, Kimmy Weaver's Library, Inlet Lee's Apothecary, and St. James High School for earning a free copy of *UNFORTUNATE!*

Appendix

GIFTS

Animus: Ability to manipulate objects, read minds, and influence human actions. Only granted within the royal bloodline.

No current living examples

Aura: Ability to manipulate and control air.

Examples: King Daltus Iridion, Skylar Stanton, Cal Hilfrey

Avlis (Ah-v-ILL-ss): Ability to manipulate and control nature.

Examples: Fern Fairaway

Fera (F-AIR-a): Ability to read emotions and speak to a specific animal.

Example: Mr. Peter Harris

Imitation: Ability to gain features, behaviors, and attributes of a specific animal.

Examples: Mr. Montgomery, Molly Montgomery

Lux: Ability to see in the dark. Night vision.

Examples: Minister Gabriel, Mrs. Martha Montgomery, Melanie Montgomery

Makan (M-ah-kin): Ability to transition between the visible and invisible plane.

Examples: Prince Cassius (Ka-see-uhs) Iridion

Mare: Ability to manipulate and control water.

Examples: Isaac Winters, Kai Lancer

Mati (M-ah-t-ee): Ability to manipulate and control fire.

Examples: Leo, Persephone

Mute: Ability to shape-shift into any seen humanoid.

Examples: Ebony Nique

Nox: Poisonous to the touch.

Examples: Princess Maya Iridion

www.ingramcontent.com/pod-product-compliance
Lightning Source LLC
Chambersburg PA
CBHW051753050726
47598CB00006B/2272